Still Rolling

Still Rolling
Inside the Hollywood Dream Factory

DWIGHT LITTLE

McFarland & Company, Inc., Publishers
Jefferson, North Carolina

All photographs are from the author's collection.

LIBRARY OF CONGRESS CATALOGUING-IN-PUBLICATION DATA

Names: Little, Dwight H., author.
Title: Still rolling : inside the Hollywood dream factory / Dwight Little.
Description: Jefferson, North Carolina : McFarland & Company, Inc., Publishers, 2023. | Includes index.
Identifiers: LCCN 2023029918 | ISBN 9781476691299 (paperback : acid free paper) | ISBN 9781476649566 (ebook) ∞
Subjects: LCSH: Little, Dwight H. | Motion picture producers and directors—United States—Biography. | Television producers and directors—United States—Biography.
Classification: LCC PN1998.3.L56 A3 2023 | DDC 791.4302/33092 [B]—dc23/eng/20230711
LC record available at https://lccn.loc.gov/2023029918

BRITISH LIBRARY CATALOGUING DATA ARE AVAILABLE

ISBN (print) 978-1-4766-9129-9
ISBN (ebook) 978-1-4766-4956-6

© 2023 Dwight Little. All rights reserved

No part of this book may be reproduced or transmitted in any form or by any means, electronic or mechanical, including photocopying or recording, or by any information storage and retrieval system, without permission in writing from the publisher.

Front cover: Director Dwight Little on location in Fiji (author collection)

Printed in the United States of America

*McFarland & Company, Inc., Publishers
Box 611, Jefferson, North Carolina 28640
www.mcfarlandpub.com*

For my beautiful wife Sandy,
who saved me and makes it all possible.
And for Jackson, Graeme and Jason,
who make it all worthwhile.

Acknowledgments

    To my editor Cliff Carle, who guided me every step of the way.
    And to all the producers, writers, agents, executives, managers, actors, musicians, teachers and talented crew who always gave it their all.

Table of Contents

Acknowledgments	vi
Preface	1
PART 1. MOVIES	3
ONE. Welcome to the Hotel California	5
TWO. Follow the Money	26
THREE. Into the Great Wide Open	47
FOUR. It's Not Your Fault But It Is Your Problem	71
FIVE. A Game of Thrones	90
SIX. Three Strikes and You're Out	115
PART 2. TELEVISION	141
SEVEN. The Writer's Revenge	143
EIGHT. Too Many Cooks in the Kitchen	163
NINE. It's Always Personal	183
TEN. The Long and Winding Road	194
Epilogue	212
Index	221

Preface

I have loved the movies since I was a kid. Movies transported me from my little corner of the Midwest into exciting new worlds, exposed me to characters and cultures unknown to me, and educated me about the human condition in ways that school never could. I loved movies so much that I decided I wanted to make them someday, even though Hollywood seemed a million geographical and cultural miles away.

But the truth is they haven't always loved me back. On the one hand, being the director of feature movies has given me a daily purpose, allowed me to travel the world, and put food on my family's table. But the movies have also disappointed me, cheated on me, and left me bloody and bruised. Some projects that were deemed "sure things" flopped. Some that were dismissed by critics and tastemakers became hits.

Still, I happily forgive this dysfunctional relationship, because in spite of all its failings … the magic, the creative fulfillment, the praise and the money that has come my way because of this love affair with movies has been worth it.

I wrote this book for enthusiastic movie lovers and aspiring filmmakers alike. It is a deep immersion into the life of a film and TV director, and the demanding work that he or she does.

So, whether you just love movies like I do, or are a beginner with a dream, I'm certain you will find *Still Rolling* to be an interesting trip down the Hollywood rabbit hole.

Cheers and "break a leg" to you all.

Part 1
Movies

ONE

Welcome to the Hotel California

The producer's voice carried down the hall of the old Sam Goldwyn studios like a tuba. Deep and insistent, Sandy Howard was barking out ideas. Like Roger Corman at New World and Sam Arkoff at AIP, Sandy was the poster child for the self-made independent producer in the pre-digital world. Charming, brash and full of enthusiasm, Sandy was always fighting off bankruptcy while selling his next hit.

I heard his commanding voice as I walked down a hallway for an unexpected job interview. Sandy's office was in a white, Georgian-style building in Culver City, famously seen in the logo "The Selznick Studio" that precedes the start of *Gone with the Wind*. The building was dripping with film history. I was a recent film school grad, young and hungry, dressed in boots and jeans. I had the beard and longish hair of the time and I moved quickly past black-and-white photos of famous movie stars.

In the reception area, I marveled at the colorful movie posters lining the walls. *Deadly Force, Vice Squad, The Neptune Factor, Meteor, Man in the Wilderness, The Island of Dr. Moreau*. These were movies for second-run theaters, drive-ins and foreign markets … but they were nevertheless theatrical movies and I was excited.

Sandy's latest picture was the second sequel to his one real hit, *A Man Called Horse*, starring Richard Harris ("English Bob" from *Unforgiven*). The sequel, *Return of a Man Called Horse*, had done well enough that Sandy was now editing a third film, *Triumphs of a Man Called Horse*. This movie had turned out so badly that Sandy had to throw out many ineptly filmed scenes, and the picture now ran only 82 minutes. The problem was, the foreign buyers who had guaranteed the money would, per contract, require 90 minutes of "color, 35mm film, with synchronous sound." He was eight minutes short. No delivery meant no money and Sandy always needed money.

My USC student film *Americano* had won an award and was written up in *The Hollywood Reporter*. The article had caught Sandy's attention and the idea of cheap talent prompted a phone call from his office.

"Can you come in and meet Sandy Howard?" asked the assistant. "He's got a job for you." A job? No one ever called about a job. I had been invited to pitch meetings, lunches, breakfasts, coffees, drinks, etc., but no one had ever called me about an actual job.

I was working as an office clerk in a brokerage house in the mornings, and as an unlicensed real estate salesman on the weekends, so a film job of any kind sounded like Heaven to me.

Sandy had cobbled together a few thousand dollars for some second unit shooting to "enhance" the troubled *Triumphs of a Man Called Horse*. He had the wardrobe of the lead character Koda stored in a cardboard box behind his desk. Michael Beck, who had played Koda, was not available, and all that Sandy had was his hat, chaps, vest and boots. Sandy also had the rights to "He's Coming Back," a Rita Coolidge song that he had inherited from another picture. (Rita Coolidge had recorded a few pop hits, including "Higher and Higher," and was famously married to Kris Kristofferson.)

The idea was to have an opening title sequence where the hero would ride from Boston to Wyoming, generally right to left for exactly four minutes. Then, at the end of the picture, the character would ride back to Boston, left to right, for another four minutes of end titles. With this new footage, Sandy would magically have his "90-minute picture" and he'd be able to finally deliver to the foreign buyers.

One big problem was that Sandy didn't have the actor or the horse!

"You figure it out, kid," he said. "You get me eight minutes of film I can use and we can talk shop."

"Talk shop." Did that mean a movie of my own to direct? A possible movie? It didn't matter. This was going to be my big break after three years of underemployment since leaving film school.

"Yes sir," I said with confidence, "I'm the right guy, I can do this no problem … but, I'll need my partner, he's a DP [director of photography]."

Sandy smiled the salesman's smile. "As long as it costs me the same."

He shook my hand. No contracts, no agents, no lawyers, no deal memos. Just a man in a plaid sport coat and gold cufflinks giving me $5000 in cash hoping that he could escape disaster one more time.

* * *

Peter Collister was a high school friend and we had both come out to USC from Cleveland with the same mad idea of making some kind of life in the movie business. Growing up, my friends and neighbors were manufacturing people and other "folks" who made things. Industrial products, drafting machines, boating supplies, ball bearings and tackle boxes.

One. Welcome to the Hotel California

There were insurance men, salesmen and bankers. The world of writers, actors, composers and directors was, for all practical purposes, on another planet. As Hemingway said about Oak Park, Illinois, "It was a land of broad lawns and narrow minds."

But now Peter and I were in a Volvo station wagon, heading east towards Flagstaff, Arizona, to shoot a title sequence for a feature film!

We had packed an Arriflex 35mm camera, three lenses, several 400-foot rolls of film and a wooden tripod. As we drove through the vast empty southwest, what we didn't have was a producer, a crew or a plan. Not to mention an actor and his horse. Hailing from the leafy Midwest, the desert always seemed dangerous and unforgiving to me. It was beautiful to look at but deadly to be out in. Pretty much like Hollywood.

Peter and I knew we had to deliver Sandy his eight minutes of film, no matter what. It was do or die. Four years at USC and three years knocking around Hollywood had come down to this one assignment.

By this time, I had worked as a grip, shot a music video, worked at a TV station, written unsold scripts, shadowed directors, directed a half-hour TV drama, produced a documentary, and suffered through many "general" meetings with countless executives and agents. As Pauline Kael famously said, "Hollywood is the only town where you can die of encouragement."

In Sidney Lumet's *The Verdict,* there is a scene where star Paul Newman, playing a lawyer, is at the end of his rope both personally and professionally. He holds a drink, looks down at his legal files and repeats many times, "This is the case, there is no other case … this is the case, there is no other case…."

The Verdict had resonated with me when it came out and now I was chanting to myself, "This is the film, there is no other film … this is the film, there is no other film…."

Flagstaff was a disappointment. The landscapes and scenery were okay, but they were not going to make for dailies that would impress my one boss back in L.A. I just didn't see a magical title sequence I could get excited about.

A trip to a local convenience store for drinks turned out to be an inspirational break. The postcard rack by the door had photos of the area taken by local stringers. On those cards I saw a wealth of beauty. Rock formations, canyons, rivers, gorges and birch trees. These locations would be perfect for our shoot and, I noted, they were all from Sedona, Arizona—not much farther up the road.

Now that we had some locations we could work with, we just needed a horse and a cowboy who was a dead ringer for Michael Beck. We hit the phones at the motel and found a nearby stable that was more than happy to help us.

"A movie?" the guy practically shouted. "Sure, I'll help you with a movie. Who's in it?" Here's a truth that will never change: *Everyone* is interested in the movies, and *everyone* is starstruck.

"Richard Harris?" the owner repeated after me. "I've heard of *Richard Harris*! What do you guys need?"

For 500 bucks we rented a chestnut horse with a white stripe down the nose (close enough to the picture horse), and selected a cowboy about 5'10" who could fit the wardrobe and hat and be a passable double for Michael Beck. A pick-up truck with a horse trailer got us moving and it turned out the stable guide knew where each of the pretty postcard pictures had been taken. So off we went, our little production now in business.

There are a few simple tricks I'd learned over the years for shooting landscapes and exteriors. It's best to wait for the sun to be low in the sky and shoot into the backlight (easy on the lens flare). It's good to wait for clouds if you can. A bald blue sky is boring. Try and get three levels of depth: foreground, subject and background. The more three-dimensional the shot, the better. Create movement.

The great independent producer-director Roger Corman said about directing, "There are three kinds of movement: camera movement, actor movement and editorial movement. Make sure you have at least one kind in every scene."

Design the shot. Think first and then shoot.

Today's digital cinema has taken the pressure off wasting film but knowing what you want and going after it is always better than just rolling and praying something good will happen.

After Arizona, we flew up to Montana and repeated our now bullet-proof plan. Find the best locations (postcards), hire the best people (local guides and stable hands), and shoot the best material (wait for the light). We knew what we were getting was excellent, and it was all cheap and under budget!

When we had used up all the film, we went home.

* * *

It was a rude awakening to be back at work sorting mail for stockbrokers in Century City during the week and selling condos in Playa Del Rey on weekends. But these two meager checks were all I had to keep gas in the car and fish sticks on the table. You find out quickly, after graduation, that the gas company, grocery store, landlord and phone company do not care about your career, your artistic instincts or your favorite films. They want payment every month or you're out on the street. You don't hear much about this while studying the *mise en scène* of the French New Wave in a large USC lecture hall.

One. Welcome to the Hotel California

But good news comes quickly, and a few days after our return to L.A., there was a message on my answering machine. Sandy Howard's assistant had called!

"Sandy loved the footage! Great job! He wants you to come in and take a meeting."

My heart raced. What could this mean? Something real? Or maybe another set-up for the next series of disappointments.

* * *

A year earlier, Henry Winkler had liked a short dramatic film I made and called me into a meeting. This was "The Fonz" from *Happy Days*, a legitimate celebrity. I was nervous to meet him but thrilled when he told me he was interested in having me direct an *ABC Afterschool Special*. Everyone at his production company was on board.

All I had to do was fly to New York and meet with the network executive. Winkler's company wouldn't be able to pay for the travel, of course, but they encouraged me to find a way to get there.

Fortunately, I had a high school friend living in Manhattan, working for an advertising agency, and he had a couch. I got a ride to the airport so that I wouldn't have to pay the crazy parking fees, and the redeye flight was cheap.

I had been to New York once before, working on a "behind-the-scenes" documentary about the making of Allan Carr's *Can't Stop the Music*. Allan was a flamboyant producer who had struck gold with *Grease* a few years earlier. As a glorified production assistant, I had watched Garrett Brown (the inventor of the Steadicam), roller-skate backwards down 42nd Street while filming Bruce Jenner, the Olympic Gold Medal champion. Jenner was a huge name at that time and many years away from becoming Caitlin.

The producers invited me to see dailies at the lab, and I was in complete awe when the images were projected onto the extra-wide anamorphic screen. There was 42nd Street and Bruce Jenner as I had seen them shot the day before, but completely transformed. Larger than life.

The dailies were stunning and seemed to turn an ordinary day into a kind of mythic reality. Bruce Jenner was 12 feet tall, bronze, and looked every bit the star. New York was alive with color and sound. Even the pedestrians looked important.

Movies have the power to take the ordinary and turn it into something timeless. This is the sensation that all of us feel when we go to the movies. The curtain pulls back, the screen stretches wide, and something extraordinary happens. A movie is about to start!

Turning on the television is just not the same thing.

As Alfred Hitchcock said, "It's like life, but with the boring bits cut out."

* * *

Now, two years later, I was looking up and down the Avenue of the Americas in midtown Manhattan trying to find the ABC Building, when a pigeon quite literally shat on my head. A bad omen if there ever was one.

I did not do well in the meeting. Tired, confused and shat on, I was underwhelming and never did get the job. Besides, I later figured out that the whole set-up had been a political effort to appease Henry Winkler. ABC was never going to give a 23-year-old film school graduate with zero credits a network directing job.

Winkler was nice enough to send me a card saying he was sorry, but I was quite let down, and that is what I mean by a disappointment.

* * *

Once again, I heard Sandy Howard's voice before I saw him. He was coming down the stairs of his bachelor pad above Tower Records in Hollywood. "Come on in, kid, you saved my ass," he bellowed.

The apartment was frozen in time, as if it was a 1962 Dean Martin pad. There were cut glass containers holding bouquets of Kent cigarettes. Even though Sandy himself had quit years before, it was considered impolite not to offer your guests a cigarette. Times do change.

Dusty late afternoon light filtered ominously into the living room, making me feel a bit like the William Holden character in *Sunset Blvd.*, the Ohio writer who ends up floating face down in Norma Desmond's pool, telling his own story from beyond the grave.

But Sandy was all infectious enthusiasm. He was first and foremost a salesman.

"The business is changing," he said. (Turns out the business is *always* changing.) His last two movies, *Vice Squad* and *Savage Harvest,* had been commercial flops and now he needed to make films even cheaper for a new home video market.

VHS machines had sprung up everywhere (driven largely by the sudden availability of porn), and new companies were appearing every day. Vestron, Cannon, Atlantic, New World, Trimark, New Line, Cinergi, Carolco and others were all looking for fresh product. At that time, *product* was the word you'd often hear to describe your passion and film school dreams. Today it is called "content."

Sandy needed a low-budget movie to sell and he didn't have anything coming up soon in his pipeline. He knew I was cheap and, thanks to my audition with the cowboy and the horse, he knew I could do it.

One. Welcome to the Hotel California

"What do you have that we can shoot for $300,000?" Sandy wanted to know. I didn't realize I was taking a meeting to pitch him ideas, so I was not quite prepared. (A director should always be prepared.) I scrambled my brain for an idea.

Up popped a cheap paperback I had once read called *The Grave*. I started to pitch Sandy the premise as I remembered it. I was vamping.

Sandy shook his head. "No books!" Books meant money and agents and complicated rights. He was done with all that. Sandy wanted an original idea that I could write (for free of course) working with his development executive. While he was talking, I suddenly realized that I had exactly the right idea....

* * *

A year or so earlier, a USC classmate brought me over to KABC-TV to field-produce an evening magazine show called *Eye on LA*. The show aired at seven, after the news. The producers wanted bikini-wearing roller-blading girls on Venice Beach, and cute panda cubs born at the zoo. I gave them stories about headstrong teachers in South Los Angeles schools. "Viewers have just seen the news!" the producers complained. "We need something fun."

I was sent over to the public affairs department where they thought I'd be a better fit. I took an idea they were considering about foreign espionage in Los Angeles and developed it into a 22-minute documentary script. KABC gave me $30,000 and I was to deliver a final print of the film to them in ten weeks! I hired a cameraman and we dove in. "Let's go find us some spies!"

The Soviet consulate was up in San Francisco, so off we went.

My cameraman and I were planning to photograph Soviet diplomats as they went in and out of the building. Then we were going to have recently retired FBI agents identify and "out" them as known spies. The agricultural attaché, the minister of culture, etc.—we assumed these were all cover jobs.

The Soviets' security cameras spotted our camera right away and they weren't too happy. They called the FBI.

Our arrest was so well done that I used the experience later in an action film: We had finished our day and were heading away from the consulate when four government cars squealed into position around our little Volvo. They were in front of us, behind us and on each side in seconds. We had never even noticed them. It was a precision operation. The FBI agent closest to me rolled down his window and badged me, and we followed them back to some plain wrap building.

Both KABC and the FBI in Los Angeles verified our story and we were

Sandy Howard and Dwight Little filming *KGB: The Secret War*.

allowed to leave with a warning. Though it was a free country and we had a free press, they "highly recommended" that we pursue our documentary in another manner and leave the Soviets alone. We got the message and, besides, we already had the film! That hardscrabble TV documentary ended up winning an Emmy.

* * *

All of this was filed away in my head and I just sort of pitched it to Sandy on the fly, making it up as I went along: "What if a Soviet spy is working undercover in a hi-tech California defense facility, and steals a valuable microchip only to realize he can't leave his American wife and child? Caught between two worlds, the spy is hunted down in the streets of L.A. by the CIA and the KGB."

Sandy was up and out of his chair. "That's gold! I can sell that! We'll call it *KGB—The Secret War*! We'll get Michael York. When can I have the script?"

"T-t-there is no script," I stammered.

"Well, get me one, I'm starting on the poster now," the producer announced.

So, this was it? I could be directing a feature film with Michael York, the well-known English actor from *Cabaret* and *Logan's Run*? I told Sandy it might take a while because I couldn't afford to quit my two part-time jobs.

He smiled and told me to do just that. "If you have something to fall back on, that's what you'll do ... fall back."

I left Sandy's B-movie producer apartment walking on air. I called Peter and told him he'd soon be shooting a feature film. It would take all the nerve I had to quit my two jobs but somehow, I mustered up the courage.

My boss at the real estate job was an 80-year-old ex-vaudevillian. He liked to show me old press clippings of him doing his act in the 1930s. He told me about the strippers, magic acts, comedians and singers ... but there was one act that brought the house down week after week and put "asses in the seats." It was a guy with a trained seal that could balance a beach ball on the tip of his nose: "The audiences loved that! Went crazy for it." When I told him I was quitting my job to make a movie, he said, "Remember to find a trained seal who can do a fucking trick!"

Good advice and something you probably won't hear in film school.

Now 27 years old, I was still living on macaroni and cheese. Old friends were getting married, settling into proper jobs and moving up in life. But right at this moment, I had reason to hope. Making my spy documentary had given me an idea for my first feature film.

A few years earlier, a different real-life experience had arrived uninvited on my doorstep and ended up giving me an edge in the highly competitive world of USC film school. One night in Madrid, Spain (I was on a semester abroad program), I joined a group of fellow students and we went barhopping in the city center. Drifting down some timeless cobblestone streets, we were drinking and smoking Fortunas and having a fine time. By now, I had picked up some Spanish and the local girls spoke broken English so we were all having fun.

In one of the small plazas near the Puerta del Sol, we broke off into smaller groups. Around two a.m., we were startled by the loud wailing sounds of police sirens. The Spanish police (Guardia Seville) flooded the plaza, some wielding night sticks or machine guns.

This was only a few years after the fall of dictator Francisco Franco, and the sight of these storm troopers sent the Spanish kids scattering in panic. But the Guardia had cut off all the exits to the plaza so there was really nowhere to go. Next thing we knew, we were all corralled and shoved into police vans. I lost track of familiar faces and became disoriented. I tried to insist that I was an American student, but these Gestapo types did not care in the least.

Not far from the Puerta del Sol was an underground warren of ancient hallways, tunnels and jail cells. It seemed as if every stone and iron bar was ages old. God knows what torture went on down there over the centuries.

We were herded into holding cells, and there were as many as 15 of us crammed into an extremely small, suffocating space. Concrete benches and a toilet hole in the corner. Meals were cold, two-day-old rice served in cracked wooden bowls. It was such a cliché … and yet it was happening.

Over the next 72 hours, I frequently heard the beating of students by the guards. The cops wanted information on drug dealers, and to extract a confession from radical dissenters. The technique was to hold the prisoner's bare feet out and whack the soles with a wooden baton. By the sound of their screams, the pain was excruciating. This type of beating had an advantage: The swelling and cuts could be easily explained away by bad shoes and bare feet. Some of the unlucky kids were shoved back into our cell where they just curled up and cried.

I found out later that all kinds of drugs had recently flowed into Madrid and the bars where we had been drinking were the ones distributing the dope to students. The crackdown was both a general sweep and a move by the government to clamp down on student protests.

On the third day, a guard came to the cell and called out my name. He could not begin to pronounce it but I knew who he meant. The thought of a beating sent a wave of panic through my body, but I was tired and a bit pissed-off at this point, and think I carried myself pretty well as they led me out.

I was taken up to a street-level office, given my passport, then a hard shove out a side door into an alley. No explanation or apology. In post–Franco Spain, anyone could be held for 72 hours without being charged. I was let out at hour 71. The feeling of standing in that squalid little alley free and unhurt was profound. I had dodged a bullet because while I did like to drink, I didn't like hash or pot. They both gave me a headache. I was one of the lucky few who didn't have anything on me when I was arrested. Drug crimes in Spain at that time were punished in draconian ways, and other prisoners were not so fortunate.

* * *

My harrowing overseas adventure became helpful in several unexpected ways. While other film students were writing about break-ups with their girlfriends or boyfriends, their parents' divorces or routine teenage longing, I was writing about an American student, studying abroad, caught up in a political demonstration (true story) and thrown in jail until he gives up information about the student resistance movement (I made this up).

There was, of course, no way to shoot this as a student film … or was there? The most important thing was that *it was a story*! At the end of the day, the question remains about nearly every script and film: "Is it a good story?" It may be a good character piece, a tone poem, an art film, a fascinating think piece, but ask yourself first and always, "Is it a fucking good story?"

The student film I eventually wrote and directed from my experiences, *Americano*, won the gold at the Chicago Film Festival and the Focus Film Festival, and it was written up in *The Hollywood Reporter* which was how Sandy Howard heard about me in the first place.

But getting it made was nearly impossible; and this was just school!

The senior thesis film at USC was called "The 480," and in order to direct a project at this level, your script had to be one of seven or eight approved out of over 50 submitted. It was also required that the director have also written the script *and* worked as a crew member on another student's "480" in prior semesters. I had been the sound recordist on a 480 documentary about aspiring models in L.A. the semester before.

I put together my two experiences in Spain (caught up in a student protest, thrown in jail) and combined them into one story about an innocent abroad and his sobering "coming of age." I worked through draft after draft of the script until I had a coherent 15 pages. I submitted my script to the committee along with everyone else … and waited.

I felt fairly confident that the reaction to the script was going to be good. After all, it was different from all the rest and it checked the "good story" box. On the other hand, I suspected (rightly) that the professors would assume that there was no way this film could be produced by a student crew with very limited resources.

Anticipating their concerns, I went to work on weekends trying to figure it out. My first stroke of luck was the discovery of a little-known agreement between the USC film school and Universal Studios. It turned out that Universal had conditionally offered film students limited access to their backlots on Sundays. The conditions: There'd be no electric power used, no vehicles, and no firearms or explosives of any kind. The university had insurance to cover the general liability.

When I learned about this (by chance), I couldn't believe it. No one had ever taken advantage of this offer, but it existed on the books. Now I had access to an outdoor street café and a prison exterior on European streets! We'd bring our own set dressing and reflectors for lighting.

At one point or another, every aspiring filmmaker who has ever come to L.A. has "scouted" the Universal backlot because they've been on the tour. Steven Spielberg famously just got off the tram bus and never got back on.

Second stroke of luck, my DP friend Peter's mother was a docent at the San Diego Fine Arts Museum and knew the management quite well. If we were able to come in at an off hour, we could shoot in front of a genuine Rubens painting. It was the same as if we'd traveled to the Prado museum in Madrid!

I found alleys, food markets and dirt roads within a five-mile radius of USC that would pass for Spain. The one thing that every film student will need to know in their academic career is how to *produce*. Whatever your talents as a writer-director, at the end of the day you are going to have to put your projects together *yourself*. I have essentially "produced" every project I've ever done, not for credit (that can go to somebody else) but for the opportunity to direct.

In high school, I had "produced" a Super 8 movie about two Civil War soldiers who try to make peace with each other until "reality" hits and they're forced to become enemies again. I won second place in a student film festival sponsored by *The Cleveland Plain Dealer*. First place went to a film about an alien invasion. I should have seen the writing on the wall right then. An alien fantasy will win the day every time over a period drama. But, more importantly, I realized that what I had done was not *produce* my little short; what I had done was *direct* it. "Oh," I thought to myself, "what I really want to do is *direct*."

When I was called in for my project review, the meeting with the senior professors went about how I had expected. They thought the script was intriguing, ambitious and fresh, but unfortunately beyond the grasp of a USC student film. College dorms, high school hallways and suburban living rooms were common, but a location shoot meant to reproduce Europe within a short distance of the USC campus was a bit of a reach.

Point by point, I showed them my locations and letters of permission from the San Diego Fine Arts Museum, Universal, the L.A. City Permit Office and others. I explained how passionate I was about the script, and that I had actually *lived* the story. I could build the jail cell itself from existing flats available on the USC sound stage.

I sweated it out for the next 48 hours before I heard back: The faculty green-lit my film. This was very much a big deal with the heavy competition for each 480 film. James Foley (*50 Shades of Grey*) and Albert Magnoli (*Purple Rain*) were just ahead of me, and Josh Donen (*Gone Girl*) ended up being my editor so that he could get his 480 credit and later do his own film.

USC had recently become a real hot spot because several alumni had really "blown up" and were making a mark in the business. George Lucas, John Milius, John Carpenter, Randal Kleiser, Robert Zemeckis and others were bringing a ton of attention to the film school, and to the very idea that film school itself could be a gateway to the motion picture business.

One. Welcome to the Hotel California

It is commonly understood that medicine, law, architecture, etc., are insanely competitive fields, but anyone who says out loud "I want to be a film director" has just stepped into the most competitive footrace in the world. And it is quite literally *the world*. Huge talents from England, Germany, France, Italy—and, more recently, Mexico, Chile and much of Asia—not to mention Australia and Canada—all come to Hollywood to build their name and a career. Christopher Nolan, Danny Boyle, Guy Ritchie, Alfonso Cuarón, Guillermo del Toro, Luc Besson, Alejandro G. Iñárritu, Roland Emmerich, Denis Villeneuve, John Woo, Baz Luhrmann and many others from around the world have each inspired whole new generations to come here from afar and take their shot at fame and fortune. Hollywood is the big time. It attracts every dreamer and schemer as it always has, and always will.

Bottom line, you won't be just competing with your classmates. You are competing with the whole world.

There are sons and daughters of directors and movie stars and moguls; children of politicians and rich families (Trump was interested in USC film school); plus all the just plain talented filmmakers like Quentin Tarantino who worked in a video store and wrote scripts.

Plus *hungry* kids like Robert Rodriguez, who sold his own blood to raise money for a short film that would become *El Mariachi*. I was an unconnected, Midwestern Gentile, but I believed enough in my own talent and competitive spirit that I felt I could win the fight for a spot in the Hollywood food chain.

I knew something about competition, strangely enough from high school football. I remember standing on a frozen field one November afternoon, watching an opposing team get off their travel bus. The players looked huge and I was scared to death. At our first kickoff, I ran down the field and made brutal contact with one of their return team blockers.

The sound of the hit and the ringing in my head jolted me as I was flattened to the ground and could barely breathe. But somehow, I bounced right up off the turf in perfect position to tackle the return man with the ball.

That's pretty much it. The opposing team in filmmaking is intimidating and you are going to get hit hard. Steamrolled even. But if you get back up, you might find yourself in the right place at the right time.

The filming of *Americano* was an avalanche of hard work, sleepless nights and sheer will. One day, at the equipment locker, I begged the professor to let me check out the quiet sync sound camera instead of the noisy one. I told him, "I signed up for it and it isn't fair that one of the other 480s has already checked the good camera out."

The professor looked at me with the most matter-of-fact expression and replied, "Who said anything about *fair*?"

Remember that, because it is true from morning to night in the film business.

The final part of the story was some good luck with casting. Through the USC film school, Peter knew Randal Kleiser, the director of the smash musical *Grease*. One of the supporting actors, Kelly Ward, had expressed interest in doing a student film. Peter told him about our film and at the last minute he stepped in to play the lead. Kelly had an honest face and genuine innocence, which was right for the character, and most important, he was also a very real actor and the camera believed him.

If story is *everything*, then casting is *everything else*.

Americano ended up having the right script and the right actor. All the elements came together, and it worked as a short film. I won a new car in a student film festival, which was probably the best thing that could have happened. I drove that Datsun hatchback all over L.A. for many years.

Because of *Americano,* I was invited to be a guest on a late-night TV talk show hosted by Tom Snyder. I showed up at the NBC studios and waited nervously for my five minutes as the last guest on the show. I don't know if I did very well but my parents saw the broadcast and were excited for my "five minutes of notoriety." Here I was barely 23 years old and on *The Tomorrow Show* at NBC … how hard could this movie thing be?

The deadline was coming up for Sandy Howard to sell my spy idea to foreign markets and raise a few hundred thousand to make *KGB—The Secret War.*

I was under the gun, and though I never really thought of myself as a writer, I had to deliver a good script—and fast.

Where to start? Dramatic conflict, three-act structure, second act twist, hero's journey, ticking clock, etc. Maybe those dramatic writing classes at USC weren't a waste of time after all. The basics work.

Who is your hero? Mine was Peter, a Russian spy so completely undercover that he has a normal wife and job in Los Angeles. Even his family doesn't know his true identity.

The spy is ordered by his KGB bosses to steal a top-secret microchip that the Soviets will be able to use to improve their own nuclear forces. Second act twist: As soon as he completes this assignment, he will be returned to the Soviet Union, a country he barely knows, forced to leave his wife and child behind.

Taking advantage of his wife's security position with the defense contractor, Peter does what is asked of him. He reports to a private pool party where the big boss will be waiting for him to deliver the chip. At the party, Peter realizes that his own people are going to kidnap and possibly kill him, or his wife and child, and he bolts. The CIA is on to him; they're tracking this whole operation and our hero is on the run.

- **What does he want?** Peter (the spy) wants his freedom and his family.
- **Who is trying to stop him?** The KGB and the CIA are *both* trying to stop him and get the microchip.
- **Who is his ally?** His American wife ... once he tells her the truth.

Keep the pace moving, elevate the stakes to life and death, come up with a legitimate twist at the end of the second act and get in some small or large part of the following for the trailer: fight action, nudity, a car chase, something blowing up (even *Thelma and Louise* had a truck blow up) and some gunfire. The rest is negotiable.

Although this may seem a bit formulaic, it is true of most Hollywood movies, from *Jason Bourne* to *Die Hard*, *Lethal Weapon*, *Baby Driver*, *James Bond*—not to mention nearly every tentpole Marvel–DC CGI spectacle ever made.

* * *

Sandy Howard had arranged for me to meet with an important actor to play the *KGB* lead for $75,000. He was the distinguished British actor Timothy Dalton, who later played James Bond twice. I met him at a swank bar in West Hollywood. I tried to wear something that was entirely black. You can never go wrong wearing black to a Hollywood event. Mr. Dalton seemed quite interested in playing the part and was taken by my real-world stories of spying, ex–KGB officers I had interviewed, etc.

Unfortunately, some part of the money fell out at the last minute (it always does) and suddenly we needed a lead actor to play the part for $15k, not $75k. There was another English actor, Michael Billington, who had auditioned for Bond several times. His girlfriend was Barbara Broccoli, daughter of the legendary Bond producer "Cubby" Broccoli. Michael had very little experience, but he would have to do, and we could get him for the $15K.

This would be the first of many lessons I'd have to learn about moving forward with what you have and making the best of it: Most actors in most movies were not the first choice. Sharon Stone, not first choice for *Basic Instinct*. Hugh Jackman, not first choice for *Wolverine*. Anthony Hopkins, not first choice for Hannibal Lecter. Humphrey Bogart, not first choice for *Casablanca*. Tom Selleck was the first choice for Indiana Jones, not Harrison Ford.

One of my first shots on *KGB* involved our hero in a phone booth receiving instructions from his handler. I had set up a dolly track so that during the phone call, I could slowly push into a big close-up as the drama unfolded. We rehearsed the shot with the stand-in, then called in "first team." I explained the shot, what had come before and what the next scene would be. I was ready to see a rehearsal. I walked along next to the camera with headphones on. There was no video village. (Video village is the area on set where the director, writer, DP and script supervisor can look at small monitors and see exactly what the camera is seeing.)

Michael started saying his lines. It was horrible. It was loud, cringeworthy, and not believable. My stomach was in knots. *How can I make a 90-minute movie with a performance like this?* I didn't want to show my panic to the crew or the actor. I told the camera operator to make an adjustment and then I approached Michael. I told him, "Your character is possibly being watched and recorded. He's in danger and should make as little sound as possible ... *just whisper.*"

He seemed to understand the "note" and we rolled on "take one." As the camera pushed in, Michael did the same scene as a whisper and it completely worked. He was no longer acting ... just saying the words simply and believably.

Never tell the actor the result you want ("angrier," "funnier," "more emotional," etc.). They are the ones who have to "get there," not you. If you do give this kind of note, they will resist and be offended. Instead tell them particulars about the scene and that this leads them to the layered performance that you want. It is all a manipulation. The main goal is to

Filming *KGB: The Secret War.*

communicate so that the *actor* makes the acting choice you want on their own, and so the note becomes *their* idea, not yours.

For example, the director could say, "I think you woke up today feeling the loss of your father and have been in that emotional place all day. It's been hard to hold these feelings in at work and pretend everything is fine. By the time you get home, you just feel like the dam could burst and you somehow have to release all that emotion in this scene." This, instead of "I need you to cry."

Sometimes an actor just wants a second opinion, and some support and encouragement. On the first day of *KGB*, Michael Ansara (well into his sixties, he'd been a significant TV star for decades) approached me from the base camp trailer. I was 28 and looked even younger. He placed his hand on the top of his head and pulled off his hairpiece. "Do you want it on or off?" he asked.

I looked uncomfortably at the top of his bald head and said "on." I don't know if this really was the right decision, but it was a decision. Sometimes that is the best that you can do as a director: make a decision.

There are cranes, Steadicams, unusual lenses, remote heads and all kinds of great toys available to a director. But it is the very carefully chosen words that you can say to an actor that will change everything in a scene. If they are the right words.

This is the job: telling the story with the *actors*. Remember, the first instinct of an actor may not be right. They may not be making the same film you are. As a director, you have to engage. Argue if need be, but also be open to the fact that you might be wrong and the actor may be right. It is a tricky dance. I've had huge stars with storied careers come on set and do a first rehearsal that is off-base. Don't be afraid of your own point of view. If you've got enough of an ego to say "I want to be a movie director," then you should be strong enough to fight for what you want. It is hard when stars try to embarrass you in front of the crew or put you down for your ideas, but don't be afraid. They are just insecure, like everyone else. And big stars can be the most insecure people on the planet.

Sally Kellerman was rehearsing a scene on the docks at Long Beach where she was supposed to leap out of a panel van and approach a CIA co-worker with her machine gun. She was being unusually cranky, difficult, challenging everyone and everything. This was not characteristic for her. She was most often lovely to work with.

I had a sense that she didn't know what to do with the gun since this was not her area of expertise. I had the weapons prop man come over. "Please go over and help Sally handle her gun, I think she's struggling," I said. The prop man showed her how to sling the gun in such a way that it looked professional but was completely out of her way so that she could focus on her lines.

After that she was perfect and back to her charming self. She was just afraid she would look stupid and forget her lines.

For my first feature, I tried to do too much. I spent too much time on clever shots and fancy transitions, trying to show off to some imaginary audience of cineastes who were never going to see this movie.

Sandy Howard called me out on my tricks in the editing room. "They're going to kill you on 42nd Street with this shit," he said. Sandy had come of age in soda-stained, gum-covered, sticky-floored New York theaters, while I had been in comfy college classrooms studying Buñuel, Truffaut and the French New Wave.

I thought I could make *Three Days of the Condor,* but without Hollywood-level writing and casting (Redford, Dunaway); it was a fool's errand. A decent grade B spy thriller was the best I could hope for with a flawed script and second-tier actors.

The first shot of the film though was stunning. A slo-mo shot on a 600mm lens of a jumbo jet flying over the head of our hero. He is running for his life and then gets shot in the back. As he falls, we reveal the bad guy with the gun. It was a dream and a premonition of the hero's death, shot in real time at LAX. Perfectly executed. There is no way anyone could get permission to do a shot like that in today's heightened security state.

The score was also a plus. Sandy flew composer Misha Segal and me to London to record with a full symphony orchestra. To hear professional musicians play beautiful music to your movie as it rolls up on the big screen is an unforgettable experience. And not just the first time. Every time.

In an odd pairing, I was seated with Andy Gibb of the Bee Gees for most of the session because he was consulting for the music company that did the deal with Sandy. The disco craze had come to an end so he was just trying to reinvent himself, as everyone eventually must.

KGB—The Secret War turned out pretty and stylish, but it was a bit dull. The happy accident was again the instinct of Sandy, the old pro and showman, who took the film and cut an eight-minute promo reel for his foreign buyers. And it was *hot*. Sandy pre-sold each territory based on the reel. He always said he was selling the "sizzle," not the "steak." By the time each territory had acquired the film, the money would already be in his pocket.

Some agents and biz people around town had seen the promo reel and there was interest in me for a split second. After the film was actually screened, the buzz died down when it did not live up to the snazzy reel.

Our star's girlfriend, Barbara Broccoli, invited us all up to Cubby Broccoli's house in Beverly Hills for a private screening of *KGB*. The Broccoli house was so large it felt like a public building. Household help greeted

One. Welcome to the Hotel California

Dwight Little and Sally Kellerman filming *KGB: The Secret War*.

me at the door and drove my economy car away (as far out of sight as possible). I was ushered down a marble hallway to be introduced to Mr. Broccoli in a relatively normal and modest room. There he was, now quite frail, sitting in a Barcalounger watching *television* (*Wheel of Fortune*) with a TV dinner tray beside him. This was a sobering sight. All the money in the world provided not much more than a comfortable chair in front of a rather average-looking TV.

* * *

I couldn't help but think of another encounter I had experienced during my student days which was also a cause for reflection. I had been invited by some mutual friends up to a house in the Hollywood Hills for lunch. Over in the corner of a dark living room, an old man sat alone in a wheelchair breathing slowly from an oxygen tank. A plaid blanket rested over his arms and legs. I quietly looked at the bookshelves nearby and saw a shelf full of professionally bound scripts. There was a title embossed in gold on the spine of each one: *The World of Henry Orient*, *The Three Faces of Eve*, *The Dirty Dozen*, *Moulin Rouge*, *The Grapes of Wrath*, *Mr. Hobbs Takes a Vacation* and many, many more. That old man in the corner was Nunnally Johnson, the Oscar-nominated writer-producer-director. I had no idea who he was, and he had no idea where he was.

On that same day, in the driveway, some older lady was introduced to me simply as "Betty" and I also had no idea who she was. It turned out to be Lauren Bacall. I was clueless.

* * *

After dinner, we screened *KGB* in the private screening room by the pool. Cubby Broccoli was sound asleep by the end of the first reel. This was not to be my greatest audition.

Dwight Little and Peter Collister filming *KGB: The Secret War*.

I should have listened to the advice of my USC writing professor: "Don't cut the movie you *wanted* to make, or thought you were making. Cut the movie you *did* make." They are two very different things. I think there was a better version of my first movie in the dailies of *KGB—The Secret War*, but I will never really know. I think my older self could cut a really cool version of that movie.

But, five years after film school, and many false starts later, I was now for better or for worse a film director. I had directed a feature film with Hollywood actors. If I ever got the chance again, I vowed not to make the same mistakes I'd made on *KGB*. Although I had gotten a lot of things right, I still had much to learn.

Make the scene work with the actors—then worry about the camera. The scene should be lively or funny or suspenseful first. And then a great camera move can enhance. Work on the script. Make sure you think it works on paper, because if it doesn't, you probably won't be able to fix it on the set. And, as Orson Welles famously said, "Preside over the accidents." Things will happen that you didn't anticipate and they will often be the best moments in your movie. How many classic movie lines were improvised? "We're gonna need a bigger boat," "Here's Johnny!," "You talkin' to me?," "Here's lookin' at you, kid," all improvised.

I had many compliments on a movie I made much later, *Last Rampage*. Actor Chris Browning was crossing a trailer park and said to his young protégé, "You can have anything you want in life, as long as you know how to steal it." It's a great line and he just said it on the fly. It was not scripted and I just about fell out of my director's chair. Preside over the accidents.

The path to the first film is different for every director. Ron Howard became a young star first and leveraged that success into a Roger Corman film, *Eat My Dust*. The Coen Brothers raised money from dentists in Minnesota for *Blood Simple*. Billy Bob Thornton became a known character actor and then wrote his own script and raised his own money for *Sling Blade*. Robert Rodriguez made a movie for $7000 and called it *El Mariachi*. But as the common wisdom goes: Any idiot can make his first film. The question is: Can he make a second or third?

I wasn't sure ... but there was no turning back now.

Two

Follow the Money

Peter sat on sandbags in the back of a Ford pickup truck, hand-holding an Arriflex camera. I was trying to hold him in place as we sped along a Dallas runway at 90 miles an hour. It was 110 degrees at five in the afternoon and we had a Bell helicopter chasing us.

I had told the pilot to stay as close as he could because I didn't want to use a long lens. All the movement would have made the shot unusable. Also, shooting up at the helicopter helped us hide the fact that none of the cast was actually on board. The pilot and co-pilot were dressed as doubles for the actors, but they were not very convincing.

I was 29 years old, and the risk and stupidity of this shot eluded me. We were shooting a B action movie called *Getting Even* in Texas and it was a blast! (No first assistant director or stunt coordinator would ever allow this today, but we were largely unsupervised back then.) When you're young, you are invincible and play to win. When you're older, you play not to lose. We were playing to win big.

Some Texas oil men had come to Los Angeles with a couple million dollars looking to make an action movie. They were tycoons connected to the Hunt family silver and oil fortune. Their idea was to use their private helicopters and jets, plus ranches and office towers, in a movie, and essentially double the production value by showing off their toys.

They hired Al Belkin, an experienced indie producer. Al had seen my eight-minute "sizzle" reel. They needed a non-union director with some experience and had sent me the script. It was terrible. Plus, the girlfriend of the main investor was an actress from the television show *Dallas* and she was going to be the female lead. The idea of an oil heir making a movie for his girlfriend to star in is too cliched to actually be believed, but clichés become clichés for a reason.

The first problem to solve was the script. I knew the money was real and I needed the job, but if I shot what was on the page, my career would be over. I knew it had to be funny and tongue-in-cheek because the plot was so preposterous. My roommate, Jeff Rothberg, was a clever writer and he was between gigs. I offered him $2000 to do a new draft. I paid this money myself, and it was all I had. A huge gamble but necessary.

I told the producers, "I'll direct your movie if I can do a draft of the script." They agreed. Jeff only agreed if he could use a pseudonym which he insisted would be "Eddie Desmond." "Eddie" for Eddie Haskell in *Leave It to Beaver*, and "Desmond" from Norma Desmond in *Sunset Blvd*. It just popped into his head and he thought it was funny.

In the original story, these crazy Texas businessmen fly into Afghanistan to steal a lethal chemical weapon so that they can create an antidote and sell it to the American government for millions. Somehow the CIA and a deranged Texas rancher get involved. Chases happen, bullets fly, things blow up, romance rekindles.

Jeff did a brilliant job of turning absolute shit into a somewhat amusing action caper. It was a lifesaver. The producers agreed to this new script and I felt like I had a chance.

I needed money badly, so motivation was easy. Al Belkin really helped with the casting and we landed Edward Albert and Joe Don Baker. Now we had some names for the poster. I called Peter and off we went to Dallas.

It all started out well enough. I got along with Al and the Texans. We were all happy about the cast, the girlfriend was a sweetheart and so was Edward. Even Joe Don Baker was okay. He was cranky and hung over most mornings but not mean or vindictive. (Joe Don was famous for the original *Walking Tall* as Buford T. Pusser, and every Texas local kept wanting to fight him!)

Edward had started out fast. The son of Hollywood legend Eddie Albert, he'd been nominated for a Golden Globe for *Butterflies Are Free* with Goldie Hawn, and co-starred in some big Hollywood movies: *The Greek Tycoon, When Time Ran Out, Midway*. By this time, though, his career arc was headed downhill. He wasn't bitter about it, just a likable guy happy to be working.

Then a problem popped up from an odd and unexpected place. The first AD was the boyfriend of the line producer. The line producer knew Al and apparently the boyfriend was led to believe that he might direct the movie. This was all information I didn't have when I was presented with him as my first AD as a done deal. A few days into production, things took a bad turn. The AD was second-guessing all my decisions and trash-talking me to the producers behind my back. I quickly figured out that he wanted to get me fired so that he could take over. (This was not a DGA film, but the Guild specifically prohibits a first AD from replacing a first unit director for this very reason.)

I wasn't really sure what to do or how to survive this mutiny, so I called my old mentor Sandy Howard and asked for his advice.

Dwight Little (right) and Edward Albert filming *Getting Even*.

Sandy listened closely and then said, "There is only one choice for you. Go to the airlines and buy a one-way ticket back to L.A." It was very important that I actually had the physical ticket, he said. Then go to the producers and say, "Look, either I stay and direct the movie, and the AD is replaced, or I will go back to L.A. [show them the ticket] and you can have *him* direct your movie."

Sandy said anything short of this would be a disaster and I would lose a war of attrition and be fired eventually anyway.

I don't know why I listened to Sandy since I really needed the job, but I did exactly as he said. There was an American Airlines counter in the hotel, and I bought my ticket. I called for a meeting and made my demand: either him or me. They must choose and choose *right now*. It was another crazy gamble, but it went my way and the AD was fired the next day. I got lucky this time. A new guy was brought in and the rest of the show went along without any trouble.

This kind of power struggle will be a part of the career of any director in one way or another on almost every project. Struggle for control with the producers, the stars, the studio, the writers. Sometimes even a pushy DP.

It's important to have your point of view and stick to it. It is better to fail because of your own ideas rather than trying to appease someone and failing anyway.

I was also lucky that Al knew a famous second unit director and stunt coordinator, Paul Baxley. He was a lifesaver, helping me through helicopter and aerial sequences that I didn't have the experience to pull off. He never tried to do my job or take over the movie. He just made me look good.

For a movie buff like me, one of the great pleasures of working with old pros is that you get to hear their stories and feel like you are really part of Hollywood. Paul had been a stunt double for Marlon Brando and James Dean, and he'd stunt coordinated *Charlie Varrick*, *The Parallax View*, *Mr. Majestic* and a million more movies and television shows. He had stories!

On each movie project, you often meet key collaborators that you may work with on multiple projects. Christopher Young was just getting started when he did the incredible score for *Getting Even*. I worked with him again on *Murder at 1600* and *Rapid Fire*, and he has gone on to have an illustrious career scoring studio movies. Chris was so poor when he was scoring for us that he very carefully stubbed out his cigarettes and put the butts in a little metal candy container so that he could re-light them at some future time. His work area was a card table set up in a studio apartment under the 10 Freeway. But even then, you could tell that Chris was dripping with talent and would rocket to the top in no time. Chris went on to write the scores for *Wonder Boys*, *The Shipping News*, *Spider-Man 3*, *Entrapment* and many more.

Getting Even came out well enough but suffered badly from the one piece of casting that I had no control over: the girlfriend. The actress was pleasant and tried hard, but the posing, posturing and bad line readings just dragged the film down. There is a price to pay for casting anyone who is not the best actor for the part.

We went out to some multiplex in the Valley and screened an unfinished cut to a recruited audience. At that time, there was a guru who planned these screenings; the producers and studios listened to him like an oracle. His name was Joe Farrell and for a while he held the studios and filmmakers captive with his market research screenings.

Screening a rough cut with temp music to a theater full of young know-it-alls with nothing else to do on a Wednesday night is one of the most horrifying experiences a director had to endure. The ill-timed laugh during a key emotional scene, the restless coughing noises while the movie builds suspense, the getting up to go to the bathroom in the middle of an action scene. It is all a nightmare. The director is there alone, maybe with his editor, but all the other collaborators from the set are long gone. It is just you, no one is there to help you.

After the screening, cards were passed out and some organizer explained to the assembled how to fill them out and rate the movie. Once the cards were completed, they were handed in to the marketing people and a number was tabulated. "How many votes are in the top two boxes?" was all that anyone really cared about. That would be "very good," or "excellent." Anything below 80 percent would mean your movie was in trouble. Recuts, reshoots, etc., would be needed. This was the moment when a director often lost control of the movie because the producers could point to the cards. "You are under 80 percent. They hated it." This was how Orson Welles' *The Magnificent Ambersons* was recut and chopped to pieces by the studio.

Ambersons previewed in Pomona, California, to an audience that thought they had come to see a musical comedy. Walkouts, general restlessness and laughter in the wrong places followed. Of the 130 filled-out cards, 52 were positive, 17 mixed, and 61 negative. With that, RKO cut 40 minutes and reshot the ending. And this was done to Orson Welles right after *Citizen Kane*! Tough business.

There were also the comments that made you fear for the country when you saw the level of education achieved by these guardians of culture: "I wanted to see her tits." "The lead guy is a pussy." "Not enough shit blew up." Very depressing. We did manage to test in the low 80s and avoided complete disaster, but this would not be the last time a film of mine was at the mercy of the ticket-buying masses.

The film never really got any traction in distribution, although it played in 50 or so theaters. Later it was released on VHS and rented well. We had a couple of nice reviews but also some pans. It was fun and breezy to some, hackneyed and cheesy to others.

It's a strange feeling the first time you find yourself attacked in the press. Seeing your name in print being ripped to shreds can really make you cringe. The critics are vicious, but they go after everyone. Many of your favorite films and directors have been slammed by the critics. Once you get used to this, it's not so bad; then the good reviews become very satisfying.

I was frustrated that no one in the business seemed to have heard of the movie, good or bad. Nothing else was happening and I was running out of money. I took $2000 that I couldn't spare and bought a full-page ad in *Daily Variety* with my name highlighted. It included several critics' reviews (I had some good ones) and "congratulations" from the producers on our "big success" in New York and Los Angeles. I wanted it to *look* like the distribution company had taken out the ad to congratulate themselves. This whole idea was another crazy gamble but, guess what ... the phone rang!

* * *

Two. Follow the Money

I was called in for a meeting with the legendary B movie producer Sam Arkoff and his son Louis. Sam had forged a successful career in the '50s, '60s and '70s. Everyone had started with him. Scorsese (*Boxcar Bertha*). Coppola (*Dementia 13*). John Milius (*Dillinger*). Woody Allen (*What's Up Tiger Lily?*). David Cronenberg (*Rabid*). He had made 400+ movies. Beach movies, motorcycle movies, women's prison movies, hot rod movies. He made the original *The Fast and the Furious* and cleaned up on *The Amityville Horror*.

I was ushered into his office and stared out over Sunset Blvd. from the ninth-floor suite of American International Pictures, which had now become Arkoff International Pictures. There were billboards up and down Sunset for movies and pop stars as far as the eye could see. Movies like *Three Amigos!*, *Labyrinth*, *Flight of the Navigator*. Pop stars Wham!, Huey Lewis, Michael McDonald, all but forgotten now. As Paul Simon sang, "Every generation throws a hero up the pop charts."

I heard the toilet flush and then the private bathroom door opened. A billowing cloud of cigar smoke preceded Sam as he made his entrance. Another showman, he wore a classic '70s leisure suit and lit up the room. Sam was funny and knew exactly where he fit in the Hollywood firmament.

He had a script called *Nightcrawler* that he wanted to do for cheap. His son Louis had seen a good review of *Getting Even* in the *Herald Examiner* (L.A. once had two newspapers), and he'd seen my ad in *Daily Variety*.

Nightcrawler was basically a Jekyll and Hyde story about a schoolteacher who finds an abandoned motorcycle and takes it as his own. The previous owner was a Hell's Angels gang banger. His demon spirit transfers into the mild-mannered schoolteacher whenever he rides the Harley. As a possession story, it had possibilities. I was thrilled to be part of it and Lou suggested we go scouting for locations even though all the money hadn't been raised yet. I wasn't doing anything else, so I said I'd be happy to do some prep for free. Develop the script, scout locations, create storyboards.

I figured Sam Arkoff of all people was good for some money and certainly knew how to get a movie made. In a way, he was much like Sandy Howard. In fact, they knew each other, and Sandy had probably put in a good word for me.

After a disappointing look around Lake Havasu, Arizona (boring), we went on to Moab, Utah, and to Monument Valley, the signature location for many of the classic John Wayne–John Ford movies. Red buttes and staggering red rock formations. You could just see Wayne and Ford out there with the massive wide shots of cattle drives and wagon trains: *Stagecoach*, *She Wore a Yellow Ribbon*, *The Searchers*.

Again, it was a thrill to experience that connection to classic Hollywood and the feeling that you were somehow part of it too. We found motels, trailer parks and diners; all locations we would be able to use. On the flight from Moab to Las Vegas, our fragile single-engine Cessna was tossed about by violent up and down wind drafts, the unstable air created by the jagged buttes and canyons below.

Something every filmmaker can tell you about is harrowing plane trips on location scouts. It happens to everyone. I was on one flight in the San Juan Islands where the prop plane dropped hundreds of feet in seconds and only pulled off the water at the last possible instant.

Back in L.A., there was another kind of turbulence. Financing.

For *Nightcrawler*, the money was in, then the money was out. More budgets, more cast lists, more hopeful signs, then silence. I needed something to happen fast; I was now running on fumes.

I had spent the *Getting Even* money some time ago. I do believe Sam was quite sure he'd get *Nightcrawler* made, but he was at the end of his career and he just didn't matter any more to the new, slick corporate CAA crowd. Sam was a dinosaur, and no one had the heart to tell him it was over. He limped on to do a few TV movies after that, but his heyday was long gone. And I was long gone with it. I finally saw the writing on the wall and set about looking for something else. Anything else.

Unless you are on the "floor" actually shooting your movie, it is not really a "go" movie. They all tend to fall apart at the last minute for one reason or another. Even studio movies; *especially* studio movies.

* * *

I was feeling low, so I did what I always did when the tide was out, I worked on scripts. I met with writers and developed a Vietnam action movie, a period gangster–Western mash-up and an old-people, *On Golden Pond*-style screenplay based on a book I'd always liked. But none of these efforts paid the bills. What they did do was keep me busy and occupied and hopeful about some kind of future. Then, out of the blue, I received a phone call from an independent producer who knew me as "that non-union guy" who you could get for cheap. That was my hook: non-union + cheap.

It's good to be mindful of what you want your first movie to be. If it is any kind of success, then you will be known as "that guy" for a long time. The comedy guy, the action guy, the sensitive drama guy, the horror guy. You'll just get asked to do something like it again. This is fine as long as you like the genre you've landed in. I was okay with B genre movies for now. I liked them. Eventually, I thought, they would lead to something more.

* * *

My first meeting with producer Nico Mastorakis was at his "pad" in the Hollywood Hills. There was a bar-lounge area in the living room that looked out through a clear glass window into the deep end of the pool. Two girls were swimming in string bikinis and they were putting on a show for Nico. This was another cliched but true Hollywood moment: bathing beauties relaxing in the pool in the middle of the afternoon on a weekday! All viewed through a window. "At night," Nico said, "the bathing suits come off!"

Nico had been an important figure in Greece, a radio and TV personality, a concert promoter, filmmaker and writer. He once snuck onto Aristotle Onassis' yacht while Jackie Kennedy was there and wrote a movie about it, *The Greek Tycoon*. But now Nico was making B movies for the international market: *Sky High, Terminal Exposure, Hired to Kill*. He used Oliver Reed, George Kennedy, Ernest Borgnine and other character actors to boost his foreign sales.

Dwight Little filming *Bloodstone*.

At the moment, he had found some production money stuck in India and through Ashok Amritraj, an Indian producer and former tennis star, he had a commitment from a huge South India movie star by the name of Rajnikanth. Nico needed a non-union director to go to India and shoot this movie because he couldn't do it himself, and he didn't want to lose the deal. He wasn't offering much money, but I was broke and not in a position to negotiate. Plus, it sounded kind of fun.

* * *

Like all business negotiations, a director's fee is agreed upon according to the amount of leverage he or she has. If you're coming off a hit movie, then of course you can push for a big fee. You didn't make much money on the movie that became a hit, because when you made that deal, there was no leverage. The money is made not on the hit movie but on the *next* movie. After a flop, it is better to take what you can and hope you live to fight another day. I have watched many filmmakers lose opportunities by overplaying their hand with producers. Agents want to look strong and tough, but it doesn't really matter how tough they look if they lose the deal. Remember there is always somebody else who will be happy to do the job. Use your own judgment, and don't listen to posturing agents.

* * *

Nico's script *Bloodstone* was a kind of *Romancing the Stone* knockoff. The production was so cheap that we couldn't even use SAG actors. I had no idea that there *were* non–SAG actors, but it turns out there are, thousands of them who haven't gotten their SAG card yet. We rustled up some eager young actors and set off for India.

This is a line that I heard many times over, and it pretty much sums up the Indian worldview: "Do not worry, Mr. Dwight, the destiny of your movie is already decided!"

None of us is really "here" and nothing is in anyone's control. We are just passing through this current life on the way to the next one. In this life, you may be a cameraman and in the next a tiger or a moth. It's an interesting way to live but a difficult way to make movies. We had a 38-day shooting schedule and wrapped on day 75, with many second unit shots still not done.

India is a mirror world where up is down and down is up. For any Westerner, the shock of India can be considerable. Just riding in from the airport, the traveler passes by and through slums as far as the eye can see. The crush of desperate humanity and the smell of abject poverty is sometimes overwhelming. If one is there long enough, it is possible to acclimate to this new mind-blowing reality. Very few activists or protesters in the West have any idea what much of the world is actually like. The United States is Heaven on Earth when viewed from this perspective. But even though the environment was rough, the people were wonderful.

In my first production meeting, all the producers and staff members were shaking their heads at me in such a way that the answer to any question I had seemed to be "no." But I found out soon enough that the head movement really meant "yes," although "yes" really meant "maybe." Call times were ballpark, equipment would arrive sometimes and sometimes not. I had a DP and script supervisor from the U.S. who helped enormously, and a sound team that Nico sent from Greece.

One night I was invited to observe an Indian production to get the lay of the land. On the sound stage, the director called "Action" and everyone

Dwight Little (with camera) and Eric Anderson filming *Bloodstone*.

just kept talking and going about their business. It turns out that all the dialogue is added later so there is no need to stay quiet while the camera is rolling.

When all your creative comforts are stripped away, the instinct for survival kicks in. I just decided to power through even though I was sick with fever and dysentery half the time and could barely communicate with key department heads. This was an *away* game.

One afternoon, we were shooting on a sandbar in a muddy river. The hero of the story had been captured and would now escape by shooting his way out. The sandbar had been deemed safe to set off some squibs (small explosives). Everyone was exhausted because the rooms that were rented for us the night before had been overrun with feral monkeys. They flooded in through open windows! We all slept in the rented charter bus. It was the only place to avoid the terrifyingly aggressive primates.

Halfway through the day, rain started to pour down on us. We kept shooting as long as we could, trying to complete the sequence, but the river rapidly became swollen and the water rose very quickly.

Everyone pitched in to try and get the equipment and crew off the sandbar to shore. We'd been using so-called "boats" that were woven from palms and branches to ferry equipment out to the sandbar. These boats were really more like rafts. Some of the grips threw ropes across the water to create a lifeline in case the rushing water knocked down any of our cast or crew members.

I was helping to load the Panaflex camera and Nagra recorder onto one of our "boats." We wrapped the precious cargo in furniture pads, then started the evacuation that would get us to shore. The water was now nearly chest-high and the bottom of the river slippery with mossy rocks. There were three of us, the AD, DP and myself, stumbling and falling and half-swimming as the monsoon rains pounded us mercilessly.

Like a hammer and nail, these two beautiful pieces of technology were all we really needed to make a film. A camera and recorder were the tools that made films possible in the first place, and I felt like guarding them with my life. We didn't have any backups so a loss of either piece of equipment would shut us down for weeks. Eventually, we struggled to shore, keeping things as dry as possible, and then hurried the camera and recorder into the bus as if evacuating injured soldiers to safety.

The day's shooting was lost, and we hadn't finished the sequence. I paced around with the first AD trying to come up with a plan to shoot our way out, just like the hero in the story. I asked the AD for ten minutes in a quiet place with no distractions or interference. I knew that after this quiet time, I would have an answer.

I sat alone in one of the rooms (now cleared of monkeys), took a breath and then closed my eyes.

I have always had this ability to "see" the cut sequence of any scene I'm shooting. It's like a projector playing on the inside of my forehead. I imagined the action scene as I intended to shoot it. Put in the shots I knew I had, *seeing* them cut with the ones I knew I didn't have.

Filming *Bloodstone*.

I played and replayed the scene for about five minutes in my head, then I wrote down a shot list with image size, screen direction, actor action.

I stepped outside, sat down with the AD and went over the list with him. We found a nearby area that had a similar feel to the sandbar but on dry land. We had a production meeting with the art department, special effects, props, wardrobe, and made our plan for the next day's shoot.

The rain calmed down and by the end of the next day we had the coverage that I knew we needed to cut together an exciting sequence.

The only person on the set (among hundreds) who has the movie in his head is the director. Others can contribute and collaborate but, without the director's "vision," no one knows what to do. A crew in the morning is useless until the director arrives and communicates the first shot.

Every filmmaker should try to nourish this "vision" as it is vital to the success of the movie. Close your eyes and play the movie. Cut for cut. The rest is details.

* * *

The production of *Bloodstone* set the bar for my ability to cope with adversity. Our star was so famous in South India that wherever we were shooting, throngs of people would come for miles just to see him. As much as we tried to keep our movements secret, somehow word would get out and we'd arrive on location to find massive crowds already there, clamoring to get a glimpse of him.

One afternoon, a building collapsed from the weight of "looky-loos." Police smacked people with wooden batons to drive them back. Production sound was impossible because of the crowd roar whenever Rajnikanth appeared on the sets.

Trains were late or stalled. Chicken sacrifices delayed production, and astrology dictated our schedule. Water was poured into the gas tanks of the generators to sabotage and shut down our power (local political problem with the rebel Tamils).

The stuntmen had few pads and would break bones. The water used for making tea was contaminated. The food was sketchy, and the heat was brutal. Cars would not start and fireworks that were part of the big finale would not ignite. If a cow died on the highway, traffic was delayed to allow time for its soul to safely pass on to the next life.

But beyond the hardships, there was beauty. I rode bareback, alongside a stuntman, through the grounds of a prince's palace at sunset. The light was reflected on the stone faces of 12-foot-tall elephant gods (Ganesh). The echoes of the British Empire still reverberated in the forest.

In one Raj polo club, there were many black and white photographs hanging on the walls of the dining rooms and parlor rooms. Generations of esteemed members from centuries gone by stared out into the abyss of time. I studied the faces of the men and woman who had lived lives of exile and privilege for 200 years in the searing heat of India. They were all long gone now, and they looked a lot like me.

Finally, after months of shooting, we completed a feature film in 35mm color with good production values. Some of the acting was not so great and the story was all over the place, but there were gunfights, car chases, nudity, comedy, explosions, exotic locations and high falls, a good recipe for success.

The real second act twist, however, was how it got me a meeting on the next one.

* * *

My manager had heard that independent film producer Moustapha Akkad was looking for a director to help reboot the *Halloween* franchise. The new project was to be called *Halloween 4: The Return of Michael Myers*.

Halloween III had moved away from homicidal madman Michael Myers, and the fans were not happy. The movie failed, and that seemed to kill the franchise. But Moustapha had his own money and his own distribution company and wanted to try again, this time with Michael, even though "The Shape" had been blown up at the end of *Halloween II*. Moustapha had bought back all the rights, and was now ready to hurry into production. The film would have to be ready for October and it was already January. Time was short, and there was no script!

Moustapha's development VP had seen my *KGB—The Secret War* promo reel and was impressed enough to be interested. My reel was one of hundreds pouring in from all over town as word had gotten out that there was an open directing assignment at Moustapha's company, Trancas International Films. Agents and managers had started pushing their clients. Short films, student films, independent features, TV movies, commercial reels, episodic directors, everyone wanted a bite of a franchise sequel.

It was only when Moustapha was told that I had just returned from filming in India that his attention was piqued. That is how I jumped the line and got a meeting: because of India!

Moustapha Akkad was an accomplished director himself. He'd made a huge international success with an Anthony Quinn picture called *Lion of the Desert*. A religious spectacle with thousands of extras, epic battles, swordfights, massive armies—the works. He was very curious to hear about shooting in India. I think he may have been considering shooting there himself. Moustapha was born in Syria but studied and graduated from UCLA film school. He knew his stuff. I was getting a chance to get in to see him, and I didn't want to blow it.

The company sent me a treatment for the proposed film, and I was to pitch them my take on it. Like the first *Getting Even* script, it was terrible. There were a bunch of horny teenagers running around being stalked by a crazed killer who would attack them before, during or right after sex. After the first *Halloween*'s success, an avalanche of teen slasher movies had been unloaded onto the market all through the '80s: *Prom Night*, *Terror Train*, *Friday the 13th*, *Silent Night Deadly Night*, *April Fool's Day* and many others had come and gone. I had no interest in doing just another slasher movie.

I did think Halloween itself was a very interesting holiday, and the Midwest in autumn offered a moody landscape. I imagined a thriller with an evil escaped convict, and a town with real kids having real problems. Also, there was of course the lead detective, Dr. Loomis, hunting down the relentless killer. Loomis would be played again by the great Donald Pleasence. I'd been working on a spec script with Alan McElroy and I told him about my upcoming meeting. He turned out to be a huge fan of *Halloween* and together we worked out the bones of a story.

When I got to the meeting, I was asked how I'd shape the material if I was chosen as director. I replied, "While I appreciate all the work that has gone into the treatment, I don't see any part of it as a way forward for me. I don't want to use any of it."

The room of course went painfully silent. The development VP who had liked my reel cleared his throat and asked, "What would you do?"

I pitched them *Halloween 4*, very much as it exists today. I took them through all three acts, from Michael Myers' escape to the final showdown with Rachel and Jamie. (I included the twist ending.) When I was done, there was deathly quiet.

The VP eventually thanked me for coming in and told me, "We'll get back to you by the end of the week."

I thought that I had blown the meeting. As I left, I tried to shrug it off. At least I had "left it all on the field."

There were many people in my world who didn't want me to do this anyway. Friends, family, agent, colleagues. "*Halloween 4?*" they'd say. "That's not even a VHS movie." A knockoff of a John Carpenter classic? I'd be drawn and quartered if I made this "piece of shit," and: "You will never be heard from again."

But I knew things they didn't. This was to be a Directors Guild of America movie, so I would finally get into the guild, get a decent payday and health benefits. I'd do almost anything to get into the DGA and get my name off the "cheap, non-union" list once and for all. Also, as always, I was broke and needed the job.

Choosing a project is not always just an artistic decision. Be careful about taking the advice of other people. Listen to the pros, but in the end, it's your life and career on the line, not theirs.

Interviewing directors for film assignments is often called a "beauty contest." The producers work with agents to bring in candidates who interest them. To win one of these affairs, you have to have a competitive advantage of some kind.

Are you funny and entertaining in the room? Do you have family money you can invest in the movie? Is your last name Kasdan (son Jake), Winkler (son Max), Reitman (son Jason), Eisner (son Breck), or Bochco (son Jesse)? Are you a great writer who will pen a next draft for them for free? Are you an established actor who is willing to take a pay cut to direct? Have you won some major festivals, and are now a critical darling? Did you have a surprise box office hit? Does your gender or ethnicity match the current zeitgeist?

As Sean Connery said in *The Untouchables*, "You can't bring a knife to a gunfight." Just being passionate and having some ambition is not likely to get you very far.

In my case, I think the one advantage I've had is that I've always been good with story and able to articulate my ideas in a room with confidence, so the producers and executives are left thinking, "What if he's right?" Because they know that *they* don't really have a clue.

Development comes easily to me and I am able to "fix" broken scripts with structural changes and useful ideas. I think this "talent" has helped me win some directing assignments that may not have otherwise come my way. Whatever the director's advantage is … it's important to have one.

The manager finally called. The producers had decided, after much deliberation, that my pitch was the right way to go. But they'd be starting from scratch and were terrified about the time left to make a movie that needed to be on screens in eight or nine months. To make things even more complicated, there was a big writers' strike coming up at the end of March and all scripting would have to stop on April 1. I went back in to see Moustapha with Alan and we assured him that we could finish a script in four weeks and go right into prep. We could start scouting locations *now*.

The amazing thing is that, of all the writers I've worked with, Alan is the only one I know who could have pulled this off. He is so fast and so good that even his first draft pages are very readable, and even shootable. We worked hand in hand on story, but Alan did the writing. The script was turned in days before the strike began and off we went to Salt Lake City to shoot a movie.

It is hard to describe how much easier it is to make a movie when you completely "get" the material. The houses, schools, parks and bars of

Salt Lake City were right out of my Midwestern childhood and would be a great match for Haddonfield, Illinois, the town in the movie. I had lived the scenes that Alan wrote, and I knew how to shoot them.

When I got up to Utah, I kept asking myself one question: "What is Halloween—what is it really?" It's not just a previous John Carpenter movie. It is a pagan agricultural holiday meant to celebrate the harvesting of the last crops and a preparation for the long dark days of winter ahead. Empty husks of corn in barren fields, old farm equipment laying fallow in a barn. Scarecrows without purpose. Heavy clouds and dark skies. I had looked at pictures of Halloween from the turn of the century and was incredibly moved. How unbearably hard life must have been in New England in the 1890s. I asked the location manager to help me find locations that could recreate these images.

We drove around the open lands outside of Salt Lake City and even though it was April, I found the evocative landscapes I was looking for. I took Peter out to the fields with just his camera and a tripod and we shot the title sequence for *Halloween 4*.

The script was working. The structure was solid, and Alan had crafted a shocking ending where Michael Myers' evil spirit is transferred to his niece, making her, in the clown outfit, the same as the young Michael in the original film. It played perfectly, even on paper. It was haunting. Now my job was to not screw it up. I needed a cast.

In Los Angeles, we read and read actors for the two sisters who were the heart and soul of the film. We'd be spending 90 minutes on screen with these two leads and the casting had to be perfect. The actresses who came in for the older teenage sister, Rachel, were too glam. They all had this "Valley–L.A. knowingness" that was a million miles away from the sensible Midwest values of Haddonfield.

There were the New York actresses (now based in L.A.) who were worldly beyond their years and tough, but not really empathetic. All the agents were sending sexy and hot, but no one seemed real.

I expressed my frustration to Moustapha and he suggested I go to New York and look there. Here was a producer who wanted me to be happy and was willing to spend a little extra money! It was so empowering to have someone really behind you, rather than trying to second-guess and sabotage you. My esteem for him grew.

In New York we set up a session with a casting director after I explained what I was looking for. In addition to Rachel, we needed a young girl to play six or seven years old and be completely believable for Jamie (the younger sister). At that age, most child actors have done a commercial or two if they've done anything at all. They've been coached by agents and moms to be peppy and perky and winning. But it was all fake.

But then, about the tenth person to come in was a young actress named Danielle Harris. Danielle was older than the character but looked young enough. I knew when she walked in the room, before she even spoke, that she was the one.

It's hard to say what that feeling is or where it comes from when you just "know" that an actor is right. Danielle was smart and sweet and had these great big movie eyes that the camera would just love. She was natural and pretty, and there was nothing forced or fake about her. I finished the session out of courtesy to the other actors, but I put Danielle on tape and told Moustapha that we had found our Jamie Lloyd.

Back in L.A., we had come down to two choices for Rachel Carruthers, the older foster sister. Moustapha and his team liked one L.A. actress, and I liked the East Coast actress, Ellie Cornell. We were at a bit of a stalemate. Moustapha had been so supportive of me with Danielle that I didn't want to force him into something he was not 100 percent on board with.

I suggested a screen test. A proper 35mm screen test on a stage with lighting and hair-and-makeup, which I would direct with scenes from the script. Then we would project both actresses up onto a big screen and see if we could come to a joint decision. This would also cost money, but again Moustapha agreed.

I had Peter light the two actresses on a Hollywood stage and I gave them both my full attention. I didn't want to be right or wrong. I just wanted what was best for the movie. The dailies were processed and put in sync and we screened them in a fairly large screening room at Raleigh Studios. There was really no question after that. Ellie was natural and beautiful and you just cared about her. She was pretty but not "like a model." Her eyes just drew you in. The other actress also did well but I knew Ellie would work better with Danielle. Moustapha agreed.

Casting, as all directors will tell you, is the life and death of your movie. I pride myself in my ability to direct actors, but who you cast will be 80 percent of your directing. Many people will want to tell you who to cast. There will be money people and studio people and producers. They will all have their opinions but fight for your choices.

Many years after *Getting Even*, Martin Scorsese cast Joe Don Baker in his *Cape Fear*. I was very interested to see what the master Scorsese would do with Joe Don as an actor. It was pretty much the same performance that I had gotten from Joe Don in *Getting Even,* but without the humor. Scorsese had cast Joe Don for what he knew he would bring to the part by being who he was. He directed him by casting him.

Today, much of casting is done with auditions recorded on phones and sent out to be viewed on computer screens. There is really no way to evaluate a film actor this way. It goes back to the age-old question about what makes a star. Steve McQueen, Kevin Costner, Bradley Cooper, Emma Stone, Meryl Streep, Denzel Washington; what is it, really, about them that's different than a thousand other actors who get off the plane and arrive in Hollywood? No one really knows.

The camera sees things that sometimes even the best-trained people cannot see. A screen test, with the actor projected up on a screen, will tell you almost every time whether they've got "it" or not. It's almost painfully unfair. An actor with four years at Juilliard and years of theater can come in and be blown out of the water by a grocery clerk who just flew in from God knows where. It's this cruel thing called talent. Salieri in *Amadeus* is driven mad by Mozart's talent because it is wrapped up in the mind and body of an annoying, immature, uneducated man-child.

Halloween 4 was the first film where I really was able to bring a part of myself to the material. Even though it was a sequel and already well-known as branded entertainment, I knew what it was like to walk those Midwestern streets on Halloween night. Older brothers, crazy friends, teenage love affairs, meddling parents; I had traveled down all these roads many times. Most directors bring more than shots, edits and techniques to their films. They bring themselves. For a film director, it's always personal.

Scorsese brings his feel for the Italian-American New York neighborhoods that he grew up in, to his classics *Taxi Driver* and *Goodfellas*. Spielberg understood the loss and loneliness of divorce when he made *E.T.* De Palma brought his conflicted relationship with his surgeon father to *Obsession* and *Dressed to Kill*. John Singleton brought the street life of South Central L.A. to *Boyz n the Hood*. Each camera set-up, each edit, each sound effect is the director's choice, and your own vision and personality will find its way into the material.

Before *Halloween*, I had taken up the habit of writing down creative ideas for camerawork, when I'd take notice of something in other movies. A style of lighting, a camera move, a special piece of equipment, etc. I'd jot these ideas down in a simple spiral notebook and those notes often became a lifesaver. My idea bank.

When Dr. Loomis (Donald Pleasence) sees Michael Myers in a diner for the first time in ten years, it is a huge moment in the movie and in the franchise. I knew I couldn't just shoot a normal POV (point of view) of Michael. It wouldn't do justice to the moment. Flipping through my notebook, I found an old entry that just said, "*Jaws* shot." This was a reference to the well-known reaction shot where Police Chief Brody first realizes that the shark is out in the water with the swimmers in Spielberg's *Jaws*. The camera pulls back and zooms in at the same time, creating a distortion in the background. For the audience, it creates a strange feeling of unease and dislocation that you can't really put your finger on. Of

Dwight Little and Donald Pleasence filming *Halloween 4*.

course, this is not really the *Jaws* shot. Spielberg "borrowed" it from Hitchcock, who used it to great effect in *Vertigo*. I have no idea if Hitchcock borrowed it from some even earlier director, but I wouldn't doubt it. All these great filmmakers are avid students of movies and apply what they've seen to their own work.

In this case, I thought this shot would be the perfect way to see Michael for the first time. We set up the dolly track and placed Michael in a kitchen area just off the dining room. The assistants carefully measured each foot of track and each distance of focus so that the pull-back and zoom-in would match perfectly. We accomplished the shot in only five takes and it stands out as a great moment in the film. It also helped that the shot was one of the main character's POVs, because in a POV you can comfortably do something that is subjective.

In another scene, a police cruiser pulls up a neighborhood driveway and the officer gets out and goes into the house. Very simple. The interesting part is that we know Michael is hidden in the back seat of the cruiser because this was shown to the audience in the previous scene. This is a faithful following of the first Hitchcock rule of suspense: Showing the bomb under the table is more entertaining than just having it blow up unexpectedly. In our case, we were showing the audience where Michael was but not letting the characters know.

I also felt that I should do something more to distinguish the shot. I had jotted a reference in my notebook that said something like "French Cars." I had seen a French thriller where all the police cars had yellow headlights instead of white ones, and I thought it was visually interesting. I told Peter to put soft yellow gels into the headlights of the police cruiser. As the police car comes up the driveway, the headlights are yellow and there is suddenly a very eerie feeling to the scene that wasn't there before, and you can't put your finger on why. Something is just a little "off."

It's always good to push yourself to think of some way to make each scene a bit more interesting.

Halloween went on for 35 days and it was mostly night shooting. There is a strange separation that happens when you shoot many weeks in a row of nights. You arrive on set at five o'clock in the afternoon, get something to eat, and know that you are going to be there until six in the morning. The only people you really see are the cast and crew members that you are working with. The rest of the world is made up of "day people" and you don't have much to do with them.

After six hours, it's time for dinner which is now in the middle of the night. At first light, you can feel the new day coming and you know you are out of time. The birds start chirping and there is always more work to do, so you switch to closer shots to mask the fact that it is getting light out.

By 6:30, it's pretty much over. The producers and ADs "pull the plug"; the shooting is done. Now it's seven in the morning as you drag your tired body back to the hotel. The blinds are drawn and while the rest of the world starts its day, you try and sleep until two or 2:30, and then get up to talk to the lab in L.A. or whoever else you owe a call to.

Shooting nights for weeks is a surreal experience, and when you come out of it, there is a strange period of "re-entry" that has to happen in order to rejoin the rest of the world.

The first *Halloween 4* test screening was held in the basement of the Thalberg Building on the Sony (then MGM) lot in Culver City. It was a smaller theater and (thank God) the screening was not being run by marketing people. The audience was recruited from a publicist's list of people who might like a horror movie. Moustapha just wanted to see for himself how the film would play. In this screening, there was no coughing or bathroom breaks. The audience sat completely absorbed through the whole movie. They laughed at the occasional joke and *screamed* several times, which is all you can ever hope for in a horror movie.

We were very excited. Moustapha asked for a few additional shots to increase the gore and shock when Michael escapes from the van. These were shots we weren't able to get in Salt Lake because we ran out of time. An additional day or two of shooting after the film is cut is always useful. Inserts and detail shots that you may not have had time to get can greatly enhance a scene.

We worked around the clock to finish the mix, looping, sound effects and music. Then there was the lab work and the color timing and the making of the prints. TV spots and movie trailers had to be cut, and the end of October was coming up fast. As hectic as post-production is, it's an extremely rewarding process for the director. As each new piece is added to the whole, your movie just keeps getting better and better.

A bunch of us drove into Westwood on the Friday night of opening weekend. *The Accused* with Jodie Foster was opening along with a James Caan sci-fi movie called *Alien Nation*. As we drove up Gayley Avenue, we saw a line that came out the door of the Regent Theater and continued down the sidewalk. We assumed that we had written down the wrong theater and drove around the block to see where our movie was really playing.

Coming around a second time, we checked the address and realized that the long line was for *Halloween 4*. We couldn't believe it!

Moustapha was right, there was an appetite for another *Halloween* movie. Michael Myers was a seal who could do a fucking trick! He put "asses in the seats" then, and still does today.

Ten years after shooting my USC student film, I had a theatrical hit. *Halloween 4* was #1 at the box office two weeks in a row and the reviews were mixed to positive. Now I had an identity. No more taking out my own ads in the trades. I was "the *Halloween 4* guy" and I could smell more opportunities coming my way.

But navigating at the next level would require a knowledge of the business that I really didn't have. I would have to learn on my feet, the hard way.

Three

Into the Great Wide Open

A lot of people saw *Halloween 4*, or at least heard of it. And one of the people who saw it at a private screening at Warner Brothers was the emerging action star Steven Seagal. Steven's résumé is now pretty well known, but at that time he had starred in just one film, *Above the Law*, which was well-received but didn't do a lot of business. There was considerable mystery surrounding him as a person, much more than most actors. Aikido master from Japan, former CIA mercenary, client and martial arts instructor to Michael Ovitz at CAA. Warner Brothers decided they could groom him for their action stable, which already included Gibson, Eastwood, Costner, Kurt Russell and Stallone.

The phone call came in soon after the movie opened. "Steven Seagal wants to meet with you."

Time to clear the calendar!

This was a real meeting with a real star on a studio lot. I drove to the Warner Brothers guard gate and stared at the water tower. Can anyone not be at least a little humbled and excited to drive onto a studio lot?

Steven's office was in a bungalow just off a courtyard. Joel Silver, Richard Donner and Mel Gibson all had offices there and I was suitably impressed.

Warner Brothers wanted Steven to do a picture for them called *Hard to Kill*. It would be a revenge action picture with the twist of Steven coming out of a long coma to exact his revenge. When I walked into the room, he was seated behind his desk talking on the phone. He motioned for me to sit down. He was dressed in black, the trademark ponytail in place, and he was speaking Japanese to whoever was on the other end of the line. At that point, I knew some of the backstory about him must be true because who else speaks Japanese?

He finished the call, said hello and thanked me for coming. He then shifted in his seat a little, reached behind his back, and drew out a large handgun which he put on the desk in front of him.

I was not accustomed to having firearms brought out in a Hollywood meeting. I thought, "If I just ignore that there is a gun on the desk, he's going to think I'm afraid of it." So I just said, "What're you gonna do, Steven? Shoot me?"

He smiled and told me it was hurting his back a little and now he was more comfortable. The moment passed and we continued as if the gun was not there. I think he just wanted to see what I would do.

Steven seemed to have an active mind. He was interesting and spoke carefully. He said something nice about *Halloween 4*. He particularly liked the performances and mood. He was a sphinx, though. I had no idea what he was really thinking.

I had brought my own kind of gun into the meeting: a small cassette tape player–boom box.

"What's that for?" he asked.

"I've been thinking about your film, and I've come up with a way to begin it and set the tone." I had cued up one song that I thought could capture the feeling of what the movie could be. He looked eager to hear it. I had picked out Bob Dylan's "Political World." I put the boom box on his desk and told him, "Press play." Dylan's scratchy voice flooded the office.

This was a wild risk as I had no idea what kind of music he liked, but I felt it would come across as proactive and creative. I thought the lyrics would reflect the kind of themes he had been reaching for in *Above the Law* and might be in his wheelhouse.

He loved the song. It was "anti-establishment," and from his generation. Despite the austere clothes, the Aikido, the years in Japan, and God knows what else, he was a Midwesterner from Michigan and I was able to reach him. We talked about the production of *Halloween 4*, movies we both liked, and just hung out for 45 minutes until his assistant came in and ended the meeting. I left with a hopeful feeling that maybe I could get my first studio movie.

I was so encouraged that I took a little of the *Halloween 4* money and bought my first car in ten years. The "student film" Datsun was about dead. My trade up was only to a Toyota Corolla, but it was new. I also bought a few new clothes for meetings, plus a new TV and VHS player. I figured with these purchases, I was good to go out and take on Hollywood.

But it was not to be.

It turned out that Warner Brothers had big plans for Steven and they were not going to entrust their new action star to the *Halloween 4* guy. They had a director who had done a big-studio Sylvester Stallone film, and they were going to have him direct Steven's movie. This was all like an acid flashback to the time Henry Winkler had tried to get me a job. My agent told me they were "going another way," and there was no call from Steven.

I honestly think he was embarrassed that he didn't have the clout to make it happen. I was disappointed but not crushed, as I had been when I was younger. I was getting tougher and more resilient.

One thing I had learned over the years was to always have a Plan B since more often than not, Plan A just doesn't pan out.

I had been putting off a meeting with the notorious B-movie producer Menahem Golan of Cannon Films, ever since his office had called a few weeks earlier. Golan's call was the only other thing on the table at the time. I decided to put my studio dreams on hold and go meet him.

* * *

In its heyday, Cannon Films was making 50 movies a year. Menahem and his cousin Yoram Globus were called the "go-go" boys and they flooded the international market with action movies and thrillers all through the '80s. Charles Bronson, Chuck Norris, Jean-Claude Van Damme, Michael Dudikoff. They overpaid the actors and then made the movies for cheap. A winning formula. But they had also made a few quality films along the way. John Cassavetes' *Love Streams*, Andrei Konchalovsky's *Runaway Train* and *Maria's Lovers*. They had even made films with Jean-Luc Godard and Norman Mailer, so I thought there was a chance to make something other than another B movie.

One day, while Menahem was reading the classifieds on the way to his London offices, he came across a public announcement that the estate of Gaston Leroux had passed into the public domain. That would mean that Menahem could now make a version of *The Phantom of the Opera* for free. Andrew Lloyd Webber's adaptation was still on Broadway raking in a fortune. This was how independent producers acquired "branded" entertainment: wait a very, very long time. Roger Corman used this approach with the Edgar Allan Poe titles: *Pit and the Pendulum, The Masque of the Red Death* and more.

Menahem was directing a movie in Budapest, *Mack the Knife,* based on *Threepenny Opera* (another "public domain" property). He had constructed enormous London period sets on stages in Hungary. Moving quickly on *Phantom*, he had made a pay-or-play offer to Robert Englund to play the title role. Robert was one of the biggest horror stars in the world because of the *Nightmare on Elm Street* franchise in which he played Freddy Krueger. Menahem hoped to amortize the cost of his sets by making a second movie on the same stages. Now he just needed a director. He saw that *Halloween 4* was #1 at the box office so he had called me.

The only unusual part of the meeting was that he wanted to meet me in a hotel bar in 48 hours in Budapest! It's hard enough to get to meetings in L.A., but going to Budapest seemed really "across town." My passport was current, and I wasn't doing anything else that couldn't wait. So I flew off to Budapest thinking, "This guy wants to make a Robert Englund horror version of *Phantom of the Opera*? Really?"

As I arrived in the Hungarian capital, there were Russian soldiers at the airport with machine guns. There was also a general feeling of gloom. Before the fall of the Berlin Wall, this was still Cold War Eastern Europe.

I arrived at night and the landscape felt like a production design from Carol Reed's *The Third Man* with Orson Welles. Streetlights haloed in fog. Stone apartment buildings from before the war. Cobblestone streets and people moving like ghosts past ancient streetcars.

With the time change and jet lag, I managed maybe two hours of sleep before my 7 a.m. meeting with Menahem. He was an effusive man with a thick Israeli accent. He might have had a dodgy reputation for his business dealings, but he was a legitimate film fan. He really loved the movies.

He bragged about his new company, 21st Century Films, and declared that *Phantom* would be a flagship production for them. He had had a falling out with his cousin Yoram Globus after all those years and was striking off on his own without Cannon. With Robert Englund, the "*Halloween-4* guy," and a branded title, how could he go wrong?

All I wanted to do was read the script, but he said, "Not to worry, it will be ready for you in L.A. when you get back." He wanted me to spend the day with him first. Another salesman, Menahem wanted me to see the sets and the production value in Hungary before reading the script.

Built on stages on the far outskirts of Budapest, the sets were phenomenal. The place was called FOT Studios and it was owned by the government, like everything else in a socialist country. There were London storefronts and winding streets, authentic-looking mid–eighteenth-century buildings, rooftops and alleyways. Menahem introduced me to his DP and crew and showed off the world he had created.

Who said *Phantom* had to take place in Paris? Why not London? Same story, just English. Then we could fly over actors from England and cast the whole thing without having to deal with the U.S. at all (except for the two leads). The filmmaker in me couldn't resist the idea of standing on those beautiful sets and calling "Action." Menahem knew what he was doing. He had me hooked. Plus, he was offering me some real money.

Then, back in L.A., I read the script. As I suspected, the script was a disappointment. It was creaky and old-fashioned, and it read like a Vincent Price horror movie from the 1960s. It wasn't scary and the dialogue was pedestrian. But I had been in this situation before, and I knew that there was a film hiding in these pages, so I made a pitch to Menahem. "Let me have a writer and I'll do a draft which I can commit to directing."

He was already pregnant with Robert Englund, so he quickly agreed.

Three. Into the Great Wide Open

Dwight Little and Robert Englund filming *Phantom of the Opera*.

Duke Sandefur had written the *Nightcrawler* script that I prepped for Sam Arkoff and I thought he had a good genre sensibility that would work for *Phantom*. We came up with an angle to make the whole thing feel a bit more fresh and "of the moment." We decided to make Christine Day, the protagonist, equal to the Phantom. She would be a young Juilliard student living in present-day New York. Our Christine would be transported back in time, after finding an original, unproduced opera composed by the Phantom, buried in the school music library. This was a bit of a gimmick to be sure, but it gave us a chance to reach out to a younger Robert Englund demographic. And the story would end up back in contemporary New York, creating a full circle for Christine and the audience. The school librarian ended up being played by the young actress Molly Shannon, who went on to be a huge comedy star on *Saturday Night Live*. Everybody starts somewhere.

Since we had Robert in place for the Phantom, all we needed was Christine, and fast. We had to get to Budapest quickly while the sets were still up and the stages available.

Jill Schoelen was a young actress who had made a strong impression in the successful horror thriller *The Stepfather*. She famously had a "husky" voice and was very pretty and talented. She also loved to sing and would be able to vocalize the *Faust* opera staged in the movie. She seemed a perfect fit for the movie and Robert loved the idea.

Pulling from relationships I had forged in the past, I put the elements together. I hired Misha Segal to compose the score and an opera. Misha had written the score for *KGB* and he was Israeli like Menahem, so a perfect fit for this project. The DP, production designer, and set decorators would all be from Hungary, with the AD department and other key department heads from Israel. Very international.

My first creative concern beyond the casting, music, wardrobe, script, locations and a hundred other worries was, how would I get Christine from contemporary New York back to period London without it being completely cheesy? I thought if I could get the audience over that hurdle, then I could make the rest of the movie work. The script just said that Christine was knocked on the head when a stagehand dropped a counterweight sandbag from the catwalks, and woke up in the past. I didn't think that was going to be enough.

As I began prep in Budapest, I had a few random encounters that led me to a useful solution. One day while watching Menahem finish shooting *Mack the Knife*, I saw that he was using a horse and carriage in a scene. As they did take after take of a shot, the carriage kept going past the same building again and again. While I watched this, I started to see it in slow motion, and the whole picture seemed to feel to me like a clock unwinding, going backwards in time.

And then, back in the city, everywhere I went there were mirrors. Big, gilded mirrors, small porcelain mirrors and ceiling mirrors. I saw myself distorted in the aged, centuries-old glass of the mirrors and thought some more about bending time. What if the mirror glass was shattered and the pieces were broken apart in a kind of fractured space-time? I could maybe make time stand still if I shot the mirror in extreme slow motion. I put all these ideas in my head and combined them with what the script said, I pitched a time travel sequence to the DP.

Elemer Ragalyi, a brilliant Hungarian cinematographer, was up for anything. He told me we would need a special high-speed camera that was not available in Hungary, but there was one in Berlin. He agreed to help me realize this crazy cinematic idea: While singing the Phantom's newly discovered opera as her audition for Juilliard, Christine would be hit by a falling sandbag. Then we would see her spinning and falling, reflected in a full-length stage mirror that would shatter into slivers of fractured time. While the glass was falling, the horse and carriage would circle a center fountain and "unwind time," until she collapsed on a stage floor amidst broken glass in the London of some 150 years earlier.

We would be shooting the reflection in the mirror at hundreds of frames per second, so we would need lots and lots of light. The high-speed camera didn't arrive from Berlin until the end of the shoot, but it did get

Three. Into the Great Wide Open 53

there. The producers didn't want to spend this money, but I hounded them for weeks until they relented. I couldn't imagine pitching an idea like this to a studio. They would have said no before I'd even opened my mouth to speak. One of the advantages with independent movies is that there are generally less people around to say no. The producers just want to get something into the theaters and collect their advances.

The final "time travel sequence" was quite stunning and got the movie off to a strong start. Christine did in fact travel back in time in a way that seemed organic to the movie, and it was visually seductive. None of this was in the script and just grew out of being on location and letting the creative elements come naturally. Sometimes you have to close your eyes at night and just dream it.

We were lucky in the casting and booked several first-class English actors, including the great Bill Nighy (*Love Actually*). The production design and wardrobe were beautiful and we found stunning locations to enhance the sets.

A great perk of the movie business is the luxury of being a VIP tourist all over the world under the guise of location scouting. For *Phantom*, we explored Turkish bath houses, centuries-old cathedrals, ancient graveyards, timeless baroque cafés, Old World opera houses and massive government buildings. We used them all.

Kevin Yeager was, and still is, a top-of-his-field special effects makeup artist. First, he helped us design the grisly deaths that the Phantom carried out in the name of love (the Phantom eliminated all who stood in the way of his obsession, Christine). R.I.P.: the opera star, the critic, the stagehand, the street thug, and on down the line.

Next, he helped design the Phantom himself. The horror concept of the movie was that the Phantom used the skin of his victims to create a "mask" which covered up the facial burn scar placed on him by the Devil in a Faustian pact. The Phantom traded his soul for immortality through music.

This was the theme of our movie—immortality through art—which was our own spin on the material. Our mask was not the classic "Phantom mask" from the movies and musicals, but rather a kind of throwback to the Lon Cheney horror monster of yesteryear. "Only love and music are forever," was the movie's tagline.

Robert himself had found a bust of Beethoven in a souvenir shop and he showed me the little knockoff sculpture. The wild head of hair and high forehead and dominant chin. We decided this would be our Phantom, a kind of Beethoven-looking dandy. Kevin's team made the Phantom real every morning as Robert sat for hours in the makeup chair getting ready for his first shot of the day. I would always have to plan several hours of work early in the morning that did not need Robert, so that they'd have a chance to get him ready.

One day at lunch, I was walking alone in the fields outside the sound stages. I needed to think and clear my head after a frustrating morning. The language barrier, the cultural differences, and my own lack of sleep, were all wearing me down. Plus, the actors were demanding and the schedule impossible. I needed to walk it off and just breathe.

There were some old, abandoned sets still standing in the badly overgrown grass. These were the barracks and buildings created for the long-forgotten John Huston movie *Victory* with Michael Caine and Sylvester Stallone. Windswept and derelict, the sets were reminders of the lives of these great film artists who had tried their best to create cinema magic but came up short on that project. It had been a critical and commercial disappointment. But I could hear that gruff John Huston voice echoing through the timbers like the wind itself. I was following the footsteps of the Gods.

Looking back toward the stages, I could see the trailers and RVs and tents of our production company crowded into the parking lot outside the World War II era Soviet-built sound stages. I realized that a film company doesn't just *look* like a circus, it *is* a circus.

Film schools have now been normalized in our society and degrees are given out as you would to students of law, or dentistry, or medicine, but it is a bit of a false promise. Before any parent shells out 70 grand a year for film school, they should realize that they are sending their children off to join the circus.

Many things went right while making *Phantom,* but on this movie I made the one mistake that a director should never make, especially on a distant location. I fell for the star, and she fell for me.

The director's relationship with the female lead is a kind of love story itself. Trust, intimacy, long hours together, fights, make-ups, flattery, seduction. The actress needs your approval and prodding and encouragement and tough love. You need her to be at her best and open and trusting and available in order to seduce the audience. When you add physical attraction to this mix, it becomes highly combustible.

There is no seminar or awareness training or hashtag that is going to keep two people apart once the match is struck. Like Johnny Cash said, it's a "burning ring of fire." The problem is that everyone on the movie eventually knows. I tried to keep my affair unknown to the cast and crew but of course word got out pretty quickly that Jill and I were "involved." As a director, you lose all your power over the actress and you lose some of the respect of the crew. Generally, when a movie winds down and people have to return to regular life, the affair comes to an end with one party or the other being very hurt.

Three. Into the Great Wide Open

We went back to New York to shoot the modern-day ending and things were so bad between Jill and me that we were barely able to finish the movie. Jill was badly hurt and none of her later diva-like behavior was her fault. She was a delightful person and I had no business getting involved with her in the first place. But in the end, I had no control over the whole episode. We were like magnets. Magnets attract.

What I did not know was that she was engaged at the time to a young actor she had met on another movie. It is not cool to "kiss and tell," but that actor was future movie star Brad Pitt. Brad has discussed the whole thing several times publicly so I'm not breaking any confidences all these years later. I'm not the first director to fall into this love trap. In fact, it is another cliché because it happens so often. So, for the record, I did have an affair with Brad Pitt's fiancée but I had no idea at the time.

Peter Bogdanovich fell in love with Cybill Shepherd when they made *The Last Picture Show*, and they stayed together for some time but with diminishing returns creatively (*Nickelodeon*, *Daisy Miller*). Some director-star romantic pairings have created great art before the inevitable separation and acrimony. Woody Allen and Mia Farrow. Orson Welles and Rita Hayworth. Kenneth Branagh and Emma Thompson. Some have lasted and thrived. Steven Spielberg and Kate Capshaw, Blake Edwards and Julie Andrews. The only thing that is sure is that it is going to happen as long as there are movies.

There were other hurdles to clear. Like almost all independent movies, the money was a constant problem. When the bills weren't paid, the lab stopped developing our dailies and the crew was told not to report to work. Our line producer, Harry Alan Towers, was an old-school indie veteran. Harry had shot B movies all over the world and had started his show business career doing radio shows with Orson Welles in London.

I went to see Harry in his hotel suite to find out if we were going to be able to shoot for the next few days. Rumors of financial ruin had spread like wildfire. When I got to his suite, Harry was sitting on a couch having a drink and seemed calm as can be.

I was much more wound up as I saw my schedule melting away and my movie being thrown to the wolves. Harry poured me a drink and brought out a suitcase from the bedroom. He snapped opened the simple latches and there, in the bag, were stacks and stacks of cash. English pounds worth several hundred thousand dollars. He had flown to London and picked up the bag himself; then checked it through as baggage!

Harry now had what everyone in Budapest wanted: hard currency. The local Hungarian forint was essentially useless outside of the country, so Western clothes, cars, stereos and really any kind of consumer product was impossible to get. Harry had a middleman who would trade the pounds for forints on the black market and by doing that, he'd nearly triple the value of his money. Harry needed the money to spend in Hungary, so forints were fine for him. It seemed like a crazy, risky scheme, illegally bringing hard currency into the country and then selling it on the black market ... let alone the risk of having it lost or stolen.

But the next day, everyone was all smiles. The debts had been paid and we all went back at work. To this day I have no idea where he got that money. It's probably much better that I don't know. Using movies to launder money is one of the most common ways that films have been financed. In South Africa, there was really no way to get the Krugerrand out of the country. You could build a boat with local currency and sail it to a country that would buy the boat with dollars, thus washing the money. Or you could make a movie and sell it to international distributors who'd collect real money from theaters and TV stations. The investors would get hard cash back on their local investment. Money had then been safely laundered.

Financing movies has always been a dangerous trap for many otherwise smart investors. I have seen many groups and individuals come to town to take a bite of the apple. Insurance companies (Destination Films), dry cleaning moguls (Franchise Films), shopping mall developers (Mel Simon), car dealerships (Morgan Creek), wealthy family fortunes (Odd Lot). The new players are often from the tech centers; Megan Ellison (Annapura) and David Ellison (Skydance) are both heirs to the Oracle business fortune. They all come to play in Hollywood, but they don't stay around very long. The hits are few and the misses are many.

* * *

Months later, I was back again in the far reaches of the San Fernando Valley. We went out to test *Phantom* at one of the "market research" screenings which were so popular at the time. As beautiful as the film looked, and as rich as the music was, we managed to miss both of our demographics.

The Freddy-horror crowd was just not used to opera and period settings, or a complex story about love and art. The *Phantom of the Opera* fans from the Lloyd Webber musical were somewhat horrified by the Phantom's violent kills. By today's standards, it was pretty normal and could be seen in any *Game of Thrones* episode. But it was a bit much for Lloyd Webber fans. I could tell during the screening that we were in big trouble. I was very happy with the movie creatively, but a miss is a miss. And we missed by a mile. Neither audience liked it.

But Menahem pressed on with his tireless enthusiasm and decided to distribute the movie himself. He called it a "horror *Amadeus*." Menahem managed to get about 1300 theaters and a national release, but he didn't really have the marketing money to push it on TV. The reviews were not helpful. Critics didn't know what they were supposed to think. They saw it as a cash grab and rip-off of the title. But they really missed the whole texture and point of the film itself. Many years later, the film has been reconsidered. It was presented as a 25th anniversary Blu-ray and now the critics embrace it. People write books about it and parse out its meaning. Not everything that is popular in its day holds up, witness *Love Story* and *Crash*. Some films that struggled when they were first released, age better. David Fincher's *Fight Club*, Arthur Penn's *Bonnie and Clyde*.

None of the "Monday morning quarterbacking" mattered. The opening weekend numbers were tepid, and after the crazy success of *Halloween 4*, I was already back in "movie jail" with a box office bomb.

* * *

Nobody wants to hear bad news, especially agents and managers, so I decided to do the only thing I knew how to do: Go back to work. I needed to find something that would get buyers excited. My project development was not looking good. There really wasn't much new to say about Vietnam after *Platoon*, *The Deer Hunter* and *Apocalypse Now*. Not much new to say with Old People movies after *On Golden Pond* and *Harry and Tonto*. And my gangster–Western would cost a fortune to produce. Besides, my one hit had been a horror movie, so I figured that's what I needed to find.

I read outlines, treatments and spec scripts, but they were all disappointingly dull. I started to spend the weekends in used bookstores, looking for overlooked stories that might make for a good movie. This was exactly what Sandy Howard had said never to do, but I needed a spark. I thought if I could get the rights to an old paperback for cheap, I could adapt it myself. Orson Welles had famously been in a hotel lobby looking for something to pitch to a studio boss. when he saw, by chance, a potboiler paperback for sale: *Badge of Evil*. He got the rights and made a great Orson Welles movie from it, *Touch of Evil*.

When I was in my twenties, I always spent the weekends working on projects. Other people went to the beach, or spent hours at the gym or the clubs, but I figured that in the great competitive footrace of filmmaking, there was no time to waste. Others might be more talented than I was, or more connected than I was, but they weren't going to outwork me. Besides, was Alfred Hitchcock in shape? Was Welles? Coppola? De Palma? Scorsese? No, they would never be caught dead in a gym. There is an old chestnut that I've found to be true: "The harder you work, the luckier you get."

Finally, I found it. A stunning horror paperback called *Golgotha Falls*. Some young Harvard parapsychologists try to use science to detect an unholy presence inside a New England church. It was scary as hell. Unfortunately, the author, Frank De Felitta, turned out to be a serious, well-known writer who had written *The Entity* and *Audrey Rose*, meaning he was not going to be cheap. I didn't know if my agents would be able to get me a meeting with him to pitch my take on his book.

But, as I was trying to figure it out, the phone rang. "Steven Seagal wants to meet with you."

"What? Again?" This was a phone call I didn't see coming.

* * *

By this time, Steven had made his coma revenge picture at Warner Brothers and it would be coming out as *Hard to Kill*. The experience had not been a good one. Steven did not get along with the studio director and he was not happy with the movie itself.

Steven had a deal with Warner Brothers, but he had an "out" in his contract for one picture. Since he was mad, he decided to make a deal with 20th Century–Fox. Now he was looking for the right director and was ready to try again with me.

He was in business with two writer-producers, Mark Victor and Michael Grais, who'd had a huge success with *Poltergeist*. They had written a "Jamaican Posse" cop-drug action movie called *Screwface* that had made it to Steven's desk. He wanted to do it.

Once again, I didn't like the script, but I wasn't going to tell them that. I needed to get bailed out of movie jail, and fast. I tried to see what might be good about it and went to meet with Steven and the producers in a funky building in Venice.

We talked about our favorite cop movies and how much we loved reggae music. The meeting went pretty well, and Mark and Michael seemed like they would have no problem with me directing. Then, after that meeting, I needed to meet with the two heads of the studio, Joe Roth and Roger Birnbaum.

This process of meeting and getting approvals from people is generally called "jumping through hoops," which is different from a "beauty contest" because you are by then "the frontrunner." The director puts on his best outfit, arrives early, waits patiently and pitches his take on the script to whoever the gatekeeper is. I have a personal rule that I will never wait for more than 30 minutes. For anybody. After that, I leave and try to reschedule. I've only had to do this twice, but both times they caught up with me in the hallway on the way out because the executive had suddenly "become available."

Some directors take visual "look-books" with them that provide a guide to what they might be thinking visually. Others cut promo reels

Three. Into the Great Wide Open 59

Steven Seagal, Dwight Little, and an unidentified actor during filming of *Marked for Death*.

from existing movies to make an impression. My approach has always been script-driven. I talk about story and character and assume *they* know that *I* must know at least the basics of how to make a movie. Or else why am I even there?

There is a general saying that every time you have a lunch or meeting with a producer or executive, there are really three people in the room: you, the executive and your last movie. If it was a hit, every meeting is a pleasure and all you see are smiles. If it was a flop, then you have to carefully navigate every move because they already have a very good reason to pass on you.

Everywhere I went, I had to deal with *Phantom of the Opera*. "What happened with that movie?" people would ask. The only strategy I had was to try and avoid responsibility, blaming everyone but myself. "They ran out of money and there were terrible production problems." Or, "There was no money for distribution and marketing, so the movie tanked because they dumped it." Or, "The title was deceiving, and people came to see what they thought was a musical." I would try and address the elephant in the room and then re-direct the conversation back to the incredible success of *Halloween 4*.

Joe Roth had recently taken over the reins as the head of 20th

Century-Fox. (It is shocking to think that such a storied studio and American institution is now gone; owned by Disney!) Roth was a real filmmaker who had produced and directed, and had also successfully run Morgan Creek, a mini-major finance company. Roger Birnbaum was Fox's head of production and they worked pretty much as a team.

Joe and Roger were extremely wary of me, but Steven had insisted on a meeting. The picture was low-risk for them at $11 million, but with a marketing campaign for a national release, the number would be more like $40 mil. Nobody throws away that kind of money. Fox had been struggling and they were trying to turn the studio's fortunes around. (Joe hit the jackpot that same year with *Home Alone*.)

They asked me a ton of questions about the script and the tone of the film, and how I would approach the material. I think I helped myself by telling them I wanted to make a mainstream action film more like *French Connection* or *Bullitt* and not a gory, bone-crunching martial arts movie. No one, not even studio executives, want to think they are just putting out "product." They want to think it could be something actually good.

Steven called me after the meeting to say they were willing to give me a chance but wanted to make sure I was surrounded with top people in camera, stunts, casting, production design, etc. I would be getting a full "A" Hollywood crew.

There is a moment for most young filmmakers when, if you're lucky, you get a chance to move up in the ladder. This often means that you won't be able to take along some of the people you've come up with. Friends, colleagues, classmates, family will often have to be told, "Sorry, I am doing this with their people … there's nothing I can do." You don't have to be quite the asshole Kirk Douglas was in Vincent Minnelli's *The Bad and the Beautiful* (1952), but tough calls come with the price of having a little success. Don't be too sentimental about it. "Don't blame the player … blame the game." This saying is used often as both an explanation and an excuse.

So now things were "blinking green" for me to do my first studio movie with a proper star and marketing campaign. But then, trouble. It was a Hollywood movie so of course there was trouble.

Steven was a client of Michael Ovitz at CAA and they were now well aware of the Fox movie and everyone's intention to have me direct it. Ovitz was known to be competitive and vindictive, and he was not happy that a CAA client was not directing this movie. If Steven was a client, and his discovery, how could a CAA client *not* be directing this movie? The smear campaign began.

Joe Eszterhas was a famous screenwriter who had written the money-makers *Basic Instinct* and *Jagged Edge*. He wrote in his book that Ovitz had threatened him when he decided to leave CAA, venting that he would have

Three. Into the Great Wide Open

his "foot soldiers" (who walked up and down Wilshire Blvd.) ruin him. Now Ovitz turned loose his foot soldiers on me.

CAA had underlings and interns go out and find copies of all my old B movies on VHS. They put them all in a brown paper bag and delivered them to Steven's home. "Is this the guy you want controling your future? This bargain-bin B movie guy? We have five directors right here at CAA, use one of them."

I could just see Steven looking at the lurid covers of *KGB—The Secret War, Getting Even, Bloodstone* and *Phantom of the Opera* and having serious second thoughts. It is very hard to escape the past. In movies and in life.

Then I got the call. Steven said he was getting some pushback from the studio (it was not the studio) about hiring me. I told him very calmly that he could do whatever he thought was best for him but, unless he wanted to have another experience like the one he'd had at Warners with *Hard to Kill*, he would be better off sticking with me. "I'll give you a '70s classic," I said. "I'll give you *Dirty Harry*, I'll give you *Prince of the City*, not just another action programmer." I didn't really have a clue how I would do that since the script was weak, but it sounded good.

If things had gone differently with *Hard to Kill*, this would certainly have been the end of my studio chance. But Steven was tired of being told what to do and dug his heels in. He wanted me and he knew he had leverage, even over his own agency. Saying no is a gutsy thing to do in Hollywood, but Steven came from another world. He was an Aikido master and weapons specialist with tactical training. He was used to fights and actual physical confrontation, so he was not easily intimidated by some guy in a suit on a phone in Beverly Hills. Anyone else would have caved to the pressure, but not him. The deal was back on and it was time to start prepping the movie.

* * *

What a difference a budget and a studio can make! I was assigned a line producer by the name of Peter McGregor Scott, a chain-smoking Scotsman who walked like a drill sergeant everywhere he went, but he was extremely good. And funny. Peter made off-color jokes all the time, mostly about sex, and they were laugh-out-loud funny. In today's world, these jokes would register complaints. In my early workplace experience, I found that the woman could dish it out just as funny and dirty as the men. But no one tells jokes any more. Everything is pretty much off limits. Peter was great at what he did, because he had come up as a unit production manager on many independent films, and he ran a tight ship.

He helped me put together an incredible team: DP Ric Waite (*48 Hrs.*), stunt coordinator Conrad Palmisano (*Stakeout*), editor O. Nicholas Brown (*The Accused*) and many more top IA union Hollywood department heads. Pre-production was run like a fine Swiss watch. Meetings were organized, schedules kept, phone calls returned. And then the final piece of the puzzle: Peter introduced me to Jerry Ziesmer, a world-class first AD (*Apocalypse Now*). Jerry knew everything about filmmaking and studio politics. He handled the producers and the studio, answering all their endless questions, so that I could actually do my job. I had become so used to doing everyone else's job out of self-preservation that I didn't really know what working with people at this level could be like.

One of my many challenges during pre-production was to "handle" Steven. He had one idea after another about every aspect of the film. Maybe one out of three of his ideas was fantastic, and the other two were just plain bad. I had to steer his good instincts toward the movie and make the bad ones go away without stepping on his ego.

Steven kept pushing for the movie to include "Santeria," which was an African religion practiced in parts of the Caribbean. He was quite obsessed with it. So Steven, Peter and I went out to a middle-class house in the Valley to witness a Santeria ceremony for research.

Inside this nondescript Valley house was the strangest group of "worshippers" imaginable. Most of the men looked like they had just been released from a federal pen, and the women were like voodoo priestesses. The bedrooms, where one might expect to find posters of favorite rock bands and soccer trophies, were instead full of shrines and candles and creepy animal sacrifices.

To "mask" their religion, many West African slaves had taken the Catholic saints favored by the plantation owners and adapted them into their own gods. It was odd to see statues of St. Peter and St. Jerome covered with the feathers and blood of dead birds.

Out in the living room, a place was prepared where a dead relative or ancestor could be summoned, and then that spirit would "possess" a member of the group. There was eerie chanting and wailing and lots of drumming, until one random participant suddenly leapt onto the floor in the middle of the room and started writhing around, until all the members themselves seemed to be possessed. I had no idea what exactly was going on, but it was spooky and unsettling.

Steven had shown me his gun before we went in, and this time I was glad he had it. Finally, after much drama, the place calmed down and we were able to leave. I had seen enough. I had been to many ceremonies before, Hindu, Buddhist, Jewish, Catholic and Druid; but never anything like that.

But we did meet a technical advisor who was able to help us write

Three. Into the Great Wide Open

Dwight Little, producer Peter MacGregor-Scott and Elizabeth Gracen filming *Marked for Death*.

authentic rituals and behaviors for the main Jamaican heavy, "Screwface." We learned how to use rum, chicken blood and candles to put a curse on someone. When you make movies, you never know who you are going to end up rubbing elbows with.

Technical advisors are invaluable. They can provide years of experience and knowledge to any scene that requires research and expertise. Police, SWAT, and medical advisors are the most common. But it can be anything. I've had enormous help from marine biologists, opera directors, morticians and even a fly fisherman. I have been creatively and professionally involved with mobsters, cowboys, monks, gurus, high priests, KGB agents, FBI agents, tycoons, Israeli Mossad agents, Muslim brotherhood leaders, convicts, rockers, cops, Jamaican gangsters, circus performers, Appalachian moonshiners, Navy SEALS and more. It's a strange world out there and they *all* want to be in the movies!

I knew we were really on to something when we did a makeup and hair test for Screwface. The actor we had cast, Basil Wallace, was a powerful presence in his own right, tall and imposing. But after we put him in dreadlocks and colored contact lenses, he transformed completely into the mystical Screwface. In full wardrobe, he came out onto the stage so that we could do lighting tests. The place went completely silent. He was extraordinary looking. The makeup and hair people had outdone themselves. Fascinating and scary at the same time, this character would be a match for Steven Seagal.

It has been said many times, but it is worth repeating: Action movies and thrillers are successes often because of the antagonist-villain. This is also true of horror movies. The strength of the bad guy is the strength of the movie. Anthony Hopkins in *The Silence of the Lambs*, Alan Rickman in *Die Hard*, Michael Myers in *Halloween*. Who can really put up a fight against Arnold Schwarzenegger? An alien *Predator*! The thing I always think about first after reading an action or thriller script is "Who is the bad guy? Is he memorable? Is he a match for the hero? Will there be a rooting interest in watching him die?" In *Marked for Death*, we had a killer bad guy.

On the first day of principal photography, the pressure was on. We were shooting on a Mexican village set out in the Santa Clarita Valley. There was a seven o'clock call, which meant leaving L.A. at 5 a.m. How nervous was I? I had planned my first shot carefully because I knew that Day One would *have* to go well. I was a green director (to them), and the first choice of no one but Steven. Studio executives started showing up before seven and mingling around, nervously drinking their coffee. As soon as the crew was "in," I had the grips start laying down the dolly track for the first shot. The special effects team mounted the breakaway doors, and the welding machine that we would need up first was wheeled into place and tested.

By 7:30, I was ready for the "second team" (actor stand-ins or doubles) to run a rehearsal for camera. The idea of the shot was that the audience would be staring into a black screen when the main title credit *Marked for Death* would appear and then fade out. Sparks would then fly into frame from the welding machine. A lighting effect would be timed to the sparks to brighten the room.

All of a sudden, the door of the little warehouse-barn would smash down and a blast of light would flood the lens. The man knocking down the door would be Steven Seagal and he'd be running like hell. Was he chasing someone or running from someone? The camera would dolly and spin around to reveal an entire Mexican town full of cars, people, fruit vendors and donkeys. Steven would run off and disappear into the crowd. I thought this was a cool introduction to the movie and to Steven's character, John Hatcher.

* * *

One summer, I had a job in a ball bearing plant on the west side of Cleveland. One day, my job was to use an extremely high-powered,

Three. Into the Great Wide Open 65

scalding-hot steam pressure-wash machine to clean the grease off diesel engines. Next to me was a welder who was sending sparks flying everywhere around me all morning. When I had scouted the auto parts location in Santa Clarita, I decided to put in that welder as an homage to my lousy job. You never know what you might be able to use from your life when you are making a movie.

* * *

By 8:10, the shot was worked out. Ric Waite and his team would have to do a massive "stop pull" to make this shot work since it was so dark inside and so bright outside. Jerry Ziesmer called up to base camp to let Steven know that we were ready. Being ready to shoot an hour and a half after first call is pretty good on a feature. But soon the trouble began.

Ten minutes, no Steven. Twenty minutes, no Steven. I could see the studio people getting nervous as tens of thousands of dollars were being spent every hour. The extras sitting around, the crew killing time talking. The nice morning light getting flatter and flatter. I was going crazy. I asked Jerry for a golf cart so that I could go up and talk to him. Jerry told the second AD to do one more rehearsal (just to look busy for the studio guys) and took me off to the side.

"Look," he said. "Steven knows that the execs are here. He knows we are ready. This is all a big power play. If you go up there, you will lose all your power on the first day and the studio will lose confidence in you. Just wait. I promise you he will be here before nine. He knows two hours from call is pushing it. Also, it's Day One so he's nervous about his hair and wardrobe. Stay calm."

Jerry then told me a story about being a young PA on *The Way We Were* where he'd be on a walkie-talkie with another PA and they'd have to walk Robert Redford and Barbra Streisand down to the set so that they would arrive at exactly the same time. The star who arrived first had less power than the one who arrived second, because the first star would be left waiting. "Slow Barbra down a little, speed Bob up." Getting stars safely down to set at the right time is not an area of study in film school.

Then, at ten to nine, there was a mirage in the distance. Like a shot from *The Wild Bunch*. A group of people emerging through the dust with Steven in the middle. The hair stylist, the trainer, the nutritionist, the makeup supervisor, the wardrobe lady, the acupuncturist, and assorted ADs and PAs.

Steven split off from his entourage and came over to video village where I was.

"What's the shot?" he asked. No "Good morning" or "Excited to get started." No niceties.

"I've got it on playback," I said. "Do you want to see it?" I showed Steven the shot as his double had done it in rehearsal. Steven looked at the playback monitor.

"Okay, let's shoot," he said.

Steven went around to the outside of the barn and we rolled our first shot on Day One with no rehearsal. I called out, "Background action," then I waited until there was enough time for the main title and then said, "Action, sparks." The welder came alive. Then "Action Steven." He smashed down the door, ran like the wind and disappeared into the crowd.

"Cut!"

It was perfect. "Print! One more for protection."

Steven came back to me in the barn. "Okay?"

"Yes, it was great. Just one note: As you pass by the camera, slow down a little so we can keep up with you."

"You said fast," he replied, but I could tell he was happy. He knew the shot worked.

After two takes we moved outside, and the weight was lifted. The studio sighed because there was no problem between the star and director, and off we went for 55 more days.

When preparing the production board (the schedule) for a movie, it is important for the director to plan the first two days for maximum impact. The producers and the studio want to see the movie they have paid for and are scared to death of. They want to see their star. They want to see production value. They want something funny or suspenseful or exciting. They want a good performance. If they see some or all of this in the first two days, then they will stop watching dailies. They're on to their next movie and next set of problems. Don't shoot something boring or not essential. Don't be a coward and shoot a car going by or a man in a closet. Give them a taste of their movie. I had a chase, some fight action, Steven being Steven, crowds and some fun dialogue. That's the last I heard from them. They didn't send me love notes, but they didn't bother me either.

A lot comes with a studio movie including many different opinions. The opinions are coming from very experienced people, but it can sometimes be suffocating. I was shooting a scene in a department store with Steven taking on a bunch of bad guys. It was a complicated situation. The DP wanted to do the scene a particular way because it was good for his lighting. The production designer wanted another plan to save his "breakaway" props and set pieces. The AD wanted to shoot it another way because it was best for the day's schedule. The stunt coordinator wanted "still another approach."

I assessed the situation and tried to remain calm. By this time, I had done five movies and had made enough mistakes to have learned a thing or two. These were all smart people, but I had to go with my own gut. I looked at Jerry and said, "Okay, the A camera is going down there by the counter on a 180 [camera lens focal length]. The B camera is here, handheld on a butt dolly [a rolling stool]. I want to shoot in Steven's direction, and I want all the stunt doubles ready first. All the props should be replicas. Then I want the actors to be ready 15 minutes after we roll. Set it up. I need ten minutes with Steven. Let's go." Jerry looked at me with a kind of relief. No one said a thing and just went to work.

Directing is a Monarchy (I prefer this to Dictatorship) and sometimes you have to make decrees.

One of my favorite movies growing up was *The Harder They Come* starring Jimmy Cliff, the Jamaican reggae superstar. It was a coming-of-age gangster love story shot on Super 16mm film with lots of insanely good music. It was rebellious and anti-establishment and suited my political mood as a young man.

Steven had somehow been able to make contact with Jimmy Cliff and had talked him into doing a few songs for the movie. One of the songs would be performed by Cliff while Steven's character was making plans to attack Screwface's compound.

The art department dressed a warehouse in downtown L.A. to look like a club in Jamaica. When I walked in to start the day, I was escorted over to meet Jimmy Cliff.

A few times in my career, I have been able to meet my heroes. But to actually direct Jimmy Cliff while he was performing a song for my movie was just a blast!

"Mr. Cliff, do you think when you hit that note, you could turn around toward this camera and really belt it out loud?"

Jimmy Cliff looked at me. "Ya, mon!" he said.

What a superstar he was.

* * *

Some years earlier, I attended a fancy Hollywood party. Kenny Loggins was playing the piano just for fun in the living room. Blake Edwards, Julie Andrews, John Travolta and others were lounging around. But the evening got really exciting when I saw one particular man on a couch in the corner of the room, and it was my all-time movie hero, Sydney Pollack.

He had directed some of my favorites: *Three Days of the Condor, Jeremiah Johnson, Tootsie, Out of Africa*. At one point, I got up the nerve to approach him and said something very awkward about how his movies had inspired me to pursue a career in the movies. He did not seem flattered, just mildly irritated. "Oh, I'm sorry to hear that," was his answer. I think he was in a more cynical stage of his career and knew only too well the turbulent life of a movie director. I tried this one more time when I sat across from Arthur Hiller on a first-class flight to Chicago. I attempted to say something nice about *The Hospital* with George C. Scott, a film I loved, written by the great Paddy Chayefsky. He also seemed more bothered than flattered. I learned my lesson: Leave these people alone.

* * *

In Jamaica, we started off in the capital city Kingston to get some gritty shots that would show a darker side of life on the island and help the audience understand the attraction of drugs to people who had nothing. This had been my idea because I thought it was a way to put something very "indie" into a mainstream studio movie. Actors Keith David and Tom Wright would walk through a tough part of Kingston and talk about what they were seeing. "It ain't all sunshine and bikinis," David's character says. It was haunting. The faces of people who were fighting day to day just to survive. Those shots made it in the movie. A Hollywood studio movie.

As I was talking to the actors on the street, I envisioned a shot that I really wanted to get. It would be from inside a building looking out through bars on the window. I just walked into the building with the first AC (assistant camera), the camera and a tripod. I'd just operate it myself. I felt all would be okay if we worked fast. We had to step over sleeping and passed-out people to get set up near the window. We didn't have permission to be there.

"What chu want, white boy?" a big, tough-looking dude said to me.

It was not a friendly question and he had every right to be pissed. I was the one being an asshole just by being there. But I played the one card I knew would do the trick: "I'm trying to put you in this movie," I said.

That stopped him cold. I don't know what it is about movies, but *everyone* grew up with them, and *everyone* wants to be in one.

"What chu want me to do?" he said.

His whole aggressive attitude changed. I pointed outside. "You walk out there and stand next to those two actors. When you hear 'action' or see them start walking, you just walk with them. Wherever they go, you go. Just don't look at the camera. You don't know I'm here."

"Ya, mon," he said, and that was that. Outside he went.

The night before hadn't gone as well when we drove into a Kingston neighborhood looking for a club that we shouldn't have been searching out anyway. A large group of locals, nearly a mob, tried to roll our van over. Our driver made an excuse for us and handed out a few hundred bucks, and that's the only reason we were able to turn around and get the hell out of there.

You have to be very careful mixing people in extreme poverty and

Three. Into the Great Wide Open 69

L.A. film people with money. The same thing had happened in Bombay (Mumbai) when I was filming there and for the same reason. We tried to get some shots from the top of the van but were driven back inside by bottles and stones.

After all that effort, when we got back to L.A., we discovered that there had been a problem with the film and 80 percent of what we had shot was lost. An insurance claim was made and we had to go back to Jamaica and do it all over again.

Obstacles and roadblocks are thrown in your path every day and you just have to figure out one at a time how to solve each problem. It's no good to have a big emotion about it, the same shit happens to everybody. Some films go better than others, but it is a known fact in the movie world that, more often than not, the worse the experience, the better the movie.

The first great thing about making a movie is when you get the call that you actually got the job. The second great thing while making a movie is finally settling into the editing room with your editor for the Director's Cut. The Guild allows the director to have ten weeks to cut the film before showing it to the producers or studio. This creative time with just you and the film you shot, building a movie, is Heaven. No crew or cast or catastrophes, no power struggles. Just pure filmmaking.

Everyone will keep hounding you to "see something" because they are scared for their jobs like everyone else. They want to know if "there's a movie there." Should they start doing damage control now? Or be a cheerleader with the studio until the first test screening? Try to avoid turning over anything. But if the pressure is too great, just show them a reel (ten minutes) to whet their appetite.

Don't fall for the trick where the studio insists they need the movie for their marketing department. They will tell you it is for "their eyes only" and then proceed to show it to everybody including the head of the studio. And you aren't even happy with it yet, yourself.

The director has no one to blame in the cutting room. And you will kick yourself for not getting enough coverage or giving up on a shot that you now wish you hadn't given up on. But remember to cut the movie you made ... not the one you *wanted* to make.

I worked around the clock in the editing room on *Marked for Death* and had O. Nicholas Brown, a great editor with good instincts, working with me. To do the music, the studio had recruited James Newton Howard (eight Academy Award nominations). He was an "A" composer by any measure. His score was very unusual, and it gave the movie a real cohesion.

We took the Director's Cut with a temp mix to a screening room on the lot where a recruited audience would fill out cards. Roger Birnbaum was there along with the producers. Steven came in late and hid in the back. We didn't really need cards. The audience loved the movie. You could just tell. It was scary, funny, edgy and full of action. The movie *played*.

We opened in October, two years to the month since *Halloween 4* opened. *Marked for Death* was #1 in the U.S. and Canada three weekends in a row. A legit hit. The reviews were mixed but it didn't matter. Movie jail and *Phantom of the Opera* were now things of the past.

I went out and bought a black Ford Thunderbird SC Coupe, fully loaded, and made a down payment on a small condo in Santa Monica. I changed agents.

CAA, the company that had tried to sabotage me, now wanted to sign me. I signed with them of course. They were CAA! I figured at this point that things were looking pretty good. I had a hit studio movie, and I was only 34 years old.

But, not so fast. As they say in *Star Trek,* "The future is the undiscovered country."

Four

It's Not Your Fault But It Is Your Problem

As life would have it, my father died the week after *Marked for Death* was released. He asked for me when he knew he was close to the end. I rushed home to Cleveland to see him. Emphysema made it hard for him to talk, but I knew he loved me (men of his generation didn't tell their sons that, but we knew) and he wished me well. He loved winning, and me being #1 at the box office appealed to him. Plus, the one newspaper that he read (*USA Today*) happened to give *Marked for Death* a good review (three-and-a-half stars out of four). I hoped he wouldn't hear about the bad ones. *Variety* called it "a dim-witted revenge yarn," and *The New York Times* said it "lacks much dramatic interest or suspense." Thanks a lot. But then there was this: "A smart piece of hard-action filmmaking" (*The L.A. Times*). Smart or dim-witted? Take your pick.

When I left his room one overcast weekday afternoon, knowing it would be the last time I would ever see him alive, I went behind the old Ohio house and sat in the woods to cry. Here I was, a Hollywood director with a hit movie, sitting alone on a log, completely destroyed. I felt hopelessly lost. And yet, these were the woods where I had shot my first Super 8 movie with my brother Mark as the star. He played a soldier back from the Vietnam war having PTSD flashbacks. These were the woods I had played in, been lost in, and grew up in.

I had recreated a scene from *Swiss Family Robinson* (the first movie I ever saw), where the family rolls logs down a hill to bowl over the attacking pirates. I cut large branches and rolled them down a ravine, pretending to knock down the bully neighbor kid from across the street. These memories comforted me at that moment. Memories of movies.

When I returned to L.A., I was asked to take a meeting at William Morris. I went into the conference room and the *whole agency* was there sitting around a huge table. They applauded as I walked in. It was surreal.

Marked for Death had been a genuine sleeper. The agents smelled money and they were out in force.

The scripts came in. Every mid-budget action film was suddenly looking for a director with a hit. One project had the great actor Ray Liotta attached. I met him at a bar in Century City, and as great as it would have been to work with the star of *Goodfellas*, the script was just bad and so was the concept. Ray was surprisingly reserved for an actor with such explosive acting skills. We had a pleasant conversation, but I didn't feel a spark. The movie was eventually made and released as *No Escape*, directed by Martin Campbell, but nothing much happened with it.

* * *

Futuristic prison drama was a subject that seemed to be going around, since the next project I considered had almost the exact same premise. It often happens in Hollywood that very similar concepts are in development at the same time. Mostly this is just due to the fact that everyone is picking up on the same cues from the culture, and certain ideas are just "out there." Suddenly there are two volcano movies, or two asteroid movies, or two airline hostage movies. I do think ideas are sometimes "borrowed," and it is good to stay on your toes. When you see a development executive in the corner of the room taking notes of everything you say, it's better to hold something back so that they might still need you later.

I was once in an office at Fox pitching some project and there was a very young, almost frail-looking English kid sitting in the corner taking notes. It turned out to be Peter Rice, who many years later became the *head* of 20th Century–Fox. *His* notes must have been impressive.

* * *

Christopher Lambert, the French action star from the *Highlander* movies, had some value in the foreign market, and he was attached to a different futuristic prison drama. I never met with him because I couldn't get through the script and didn't know how to fix it. Eventually made as *The Fortress*, directed by Stuart Gordon, it came and went.

Jean-Claude Van Damme had a project where he would play himself twice, as twin brothers. *Double Impact* was eventually made and went quietly to video after a disappointing theatrical release.

It was becoming pretty clear that the only thing I was going to be able to get was another genre action film with a B-level star. I was hoping for something more, but directors and actors are meant to "stay in their lane." I was no longer the *Halloween 4* guy, I was the *Marked for Death* guy.

My agents were getting restless with me for being such a prima donna all of a sudden. "The kid got lucky with one picture and now he's all picky?" They knew the heat from *Marked for Death* would wear off quickly and they wanted to book me into something soon. They needed their ten percent.

* * *

The studios were still making action programmers because the foreign revenue for this genre, combined with the VHS-cable sales, could still cover a domestic flop. Studios typically calculated 30 to 35 percent of their revenue from foreign sales as long as it was action because "action travels." Today many studios look to get 70 or 80 percent of their money from foreign, which is now politely called "worldwide." Numbers from China were never even heard of then, and now movies often open in China first.

I once saw a *Pirates of the Caribbean* movie on a small screen in the Fijian town of Suva on the same day it opened in New York and Los Angeles! That meant Wall Street investment bankers and Fijian fisherman were watching the same movie on the same Friday night on different sides of the world and in different hemispheres. How do you make a movie that will play to both of those demographics? Digital projection was making this "day and date" strategy possible. The arrival of new technology is the one constant of the film business. It changes and develops all the time and the "content" changes to serve its needs. Theatrical, VHS, laserdisc, DVD, pay-per-view, streaming, downloads, premium cable, Blu-ray, VOD, SVOD, etc.

When scouting locations, I am often invited to walk through people's homes to see if we may want to shoot there. The smallest apartment in a struggling neighborhood still manages to have a 42-inch flat screen TV in the middle of the living room no matter how tight the space. America may not always have a chicken in every pot but it has a flat-screen in every living room.

* * *

I received baskets of muffins and cheese from my agents. Gifts of wine arrived by messenger from writers' agents. The phone was ringing. I should have been giddy with excitement; instead I was slightly bored with all of these projects. I was no virgin. I knew what was involved in directing a studio movie, the pressure, stress, conflict, and physical exhaustion. I needed something I thought I could do well. Something that might actually make for a good movie.

Then my agent called with something interesting. Joe Roth and Roger Birnbaum, my two supporters over at Fox, had decided to make Brandon Lee an action star. Brandon was "branded" in the most perfect way possible: He was the son of legendary martial arts star Bruce Lee. Brandon had done a low-budget Dolph Lundgren movie that no one had seen, but the studio was exposed to his potential. Brandon was funny, handsome, young, and had all the training to pull off real martial arts action. He was a fresh idea and I thought maybe I could introduce something new into the action genre. I was flattered that Joe and Roger wanted me, and my agent said they were willing to pay.

I read the first page of the rough script they had in mind. It opened with "EXT THAILAND – DAY." I didn't read any further. I called my agent and said I was interested. I loved to travel and, more importantly, I needed to get out of town to distract myself. Thailand would be fine. After the death of my father, I needed to go to work on something good. Life is too damn short.

The first thing I did was get the studio to hire screenwriter Alan McElroy to reinvent the script. This kind of action was right in his strike zone and he'd make their uninspired script work. This was becoming a pattern with me: say "Yes" to a movie where the script still needs work, and then hire a talented writer and fix it.

The second thing I did was to go see Brandon. He shared a small (two-room) apartment up above Hollywood Blvd., off a one-lane asphalt driveway. There were heavy training bags hanging from the porch beams. He drove an old black hearse, which seemed appropriately quirky to me. One picture on his wall was an 11 × 14 of him and his dad. Bruce Lee was

Al Leong, Dwight Little, Tony Longo and Nick Mancuso filming *Rapid Fire*.

holding a piece of wood and a five-year-old Brandon Lee was wearing a "Gi" (white robe) and holding his arms high, ready to smash through the wood with his hands. That was gold.

I took him through my take on the script. How it could be the next *Lethal Weapon*. I wanted to make an action movie like that, only with martial arts. Today it is standard to have action stars do martial arts, but the crossover wasn't as established at that time. Jason Statham, Matt Damon and Dwayne Johnson all do martial arts in their action movies now, not to mention all the Avengers.

Brandon and I were on the same page right away and I knew we were going to be able to make a great movie together. He didn't have the arrogance and narcissism of a big movie star. He just wanted to make sure he didn't blow this studio opportunity. The same way that I wanted Alan to write the screenplay, he wanted his fight choreographer, Jeff Imada, to do the stunts and fights. This was fine with me. We would be inspired not only by Bruce Lee and Jackie Chan, but also by William Friedkin and Richard Donner.

The first location scout took us to Thailand. In the story, a Chicago mobster goes upriver, deep into the Thai interior, to make a deal with a heroin kingpin. We needed to find the river and the boats that would take the characters into the "heart of darkness." We found ourselves standing on the bank of the River Kwai where, during World War II, Allied POWs had been forced by the Japanese to build a railway bridge, to link Bangkok and Rangoon, under horrendous conditions.

Many years before, director David Lean had been brought here to scout locations for *The Bridge on the River Kwai*. After he surveyed the area, he realized that this was no place to make a movie. The water was slow-moving and muddy, the banks were uninteresting, the light flat and oppressive. He was not interested in this reality. Lean ended up finding locations in Sri Lanka that had mountains, ravines and stunning jungle vegetation; he made his Oscar winner there.

Lean was not making a documentary. He was making a poem about what that ordeal might have been like; but with music and heroism and fascinating characters. "Paul Revere's Ride" by Henry Wadsworth Longfellow is not about what really happened the night the British were coming. It is about the spirit and emotion of what happened. The same is true of Tennyson's "The Charge of the Light Brigade" and, in song, Gordon Lightfoot's "The Wreck of the Edmund Fitzgerald." The poems are repeated so often over the generations that they become a kind of accepted mythology. *Apocalypse Now* is a poem about Vietnam. *Erin Brockovich* is a poem about an activist, *Philadelphia* is a poem about AIDS. Movies are not real, but they are so immediate that people do often accept them as reality.

Lean's visuals are world-renowned and carved into our collective memory. But it is still the whistling of the soldiers and the famous Alec Guinness monologue that many people remember best from *The Bridge on the River Kwai*. These words spoken by Guinness stuck with me: "There are times when suddenly you realize you're nearer the end than the beginning and you wonder, you ask yourself, what the sum total of your life

Dwight Little and Denis Stewart filming *Rapid Fire*.

represents, what difference your being there at any time made to anything … or if it made any difference at all, really."

Script and actor always win out. But then again, the *Bridge on the River Kwai* movie itself is all but forgotten now.

Sri Lanka was not an option for me, so we took long wooden river boats with outboard motors up the River Kwai. As we moved away from any visible civilization, a feeling of remoteness and isolation set in. Everything was becoming mysterious and somewhat threatening. Then we came to a narrow canyon with rock cliffs on each side. The boatman had us climb up the side of one cliff to meet a Buddhist monk who lived alone in a cave overlooking the river. The boatmen would bring him supplies, and visitors like ourselves would leave a few baht. In return, the monk blessed each one of us and our movie.

The incense was burning in the cave and this ancient holy man sang rhythmic Buddhist chants that echoed off the walls. It would be convenient to think he was crazy, but his eyes were clear and he seemed completely lucid. This was a life being led by a human being, on planet Earth, about as far removed from my life as possible. I was happy to have the blessings.

When we filmed the opening of *Rapid Fire* in Thailand, I used those same wooden boats to carry my Chicago gangster (Nick Mancuso) upriver to meet with the bad guy (charmingly played by the great character actor Thai Ma). After some searching, I was able to find a different river (the Chao Phraya) up north of Bangkok that was far more interesting and accessible than the River Kwai. The location was an ancient city called Ayutthaya. The ruins of this great trading post dated back to 1350 and we had permission from the Thai government to shoot in and among the many beautiful ruins.

While filming an opening fight sequence there, the Thai sun finally got the best of me. I was standing next to Denis Stuart, my first AD, when I started to show the signs of heat stroke, dizziness and nausea. When I knew I would no longer be able to tough it out, I grabbed Denis by the arm. "Finish the day," I said to him. I knew that he knew most of the shots since we had prepped so carefully, and that Tai Ma could direct himself just fine. And then I collapsed.

The crew rushed me into a bus that had the only air conditioning for miles. With heat stroke, the key is to bring the core body temperature down as quickly as possible. The team used old-fashioned smelling salts to revive me, then wrapped me in towels which were soaked in ice from coolers meant for cold drinks. I had all the symptoms: confusion, fever, rapid heart rate, vomiting. But by that night, I was on the way back to the hotel and slowly on the mend. The Thai and American first aid crew had undoubtedly come to the rescue. I was never too worried because I knew we had a killer opening to the movie. It would all be worth it.

Alan had written a very complex script in which his ingenuity for action set pieces was on full display. There were gunfights, martial arts battles, explosions and car chases. One night in L.A., we had to film a scene where a car is struck by a shotgun blast, blows up, flips over and catches on fire. These kinds of stunts have to be very carefully planned out and executed so that no one gets hurt. *Rapid Fire* was loaded with stunts. Motorcycles through glass, zip lines into buildings, high falls onto train tracks and other show-stopping theatrics.

The best way to approach these sequences is to have the production design team build very simple cardboard models of the streets and buildings where the stunts will take place. Miniature toy cars are used to show exactly where each driver and stuntman will be when the cameras roll. It works well to gather all the stunt team and key camera crew members around a folding table in the middle of the location where the scenes will be filmed, so that they can examine these models. All questions can be asked and answered. Distances and real perspectives can be measured against the models and toy cars.

Dwight Little and Ric Waite, along with an unidentified photographer, during filming of *Rapid Fire*.

A part of my job is to explain to everyone what the "story" of the stunt is. In this case, Jake Lo (Brandon Lee) had been told to meet with his FBI handler (Raymond Barry) in a lonesome alley in Chicago. Jake soon realizes that the Feds are crooked and dives away from certain death just in time. Jake fights back and is rescued by the honest Chicago cop (Powers Boothe). Boothe was both a star and a great character actor and we were

Four. It's Not Your Fault But It Is Your Problem

Powers Boothe and Dwight Little filming *Rapid Fire*.

lucky to have him. He had real chemistry with Brandon. This sequence would set up their father-son relationship for the rest of the movie.

Powers had jumped to stardom with his Emmy-winning performance as Jim Jones, the Guyana cult leader who infamously had all his disciples "drink the Kool-Aid." Several starring roles followed: *Southern Comfort, Red Dawn, The Emerald Forest, Extreme Prejudice, Tombstone, U-Turn, Sin City* and many others.

Explaining the story to the technical crew helps to get everyone thinking about the film we are making and not just the mechanics of the stunt. I also have a chance to communicate exactly what I want to have happen as far as the action goes. I prefer this hands-on approach to computer models and animatic pre-visualization.

For this particular stunt, the stunt team and riggers put a section of a telephone pole into the picture car and attached it to a huge explosive charge. Then they installed propane in a special breakaway tank to be detonated in perfect timing with the car flip. The blast of the charge is so powerful that the telephone pole slams into the concrete street below the car, and the "counter force" flips the car up into the air, end over end. The driver, secured in a metal roll cage, wears a full fire suit and helmet. When he gets up to speed, he has to hit the ignition button himself; then at the same time, push the propane ignite button, all while driving the car!

The last job for the director is to place the cameras. I wanted a long lens at the end of the street running at 72 frames per second. This camera would be operated so that no matter where the car went, or wound up, we would have something on film. A "B" camera was set at street level for a more profile shot on a wider lens. This camera would be a "lock off," meaning it was too close and too dangerous to have a cameraman there. The assistant turns on the camera and runs away. Another camera is placed in a "crash box" somewhere near where we think the car is most likely to skid to a stop, still on fire. We hope the camera doesn't get destroyed but it might. The camera placement has to make the stunt dynamic, provide good cutting angles to extend or reduce time later in the cutting room, and also avoid actually showing that the driver is wearing a helmet and sitting in a roll cage. Our car flip was saved for the last shot of the night (five in the morning) because there could be no take two. We already had as many other pieces of the chase as we could get. The gun blast, the squealing tires, the actors driving and reacting, the point-of-view shots, etc. When the time comes for the stunt, the tension is very high. Everyone is aware that there is a man in that picture car taking a risk. For a dangerous stunt, the stuntman always gets a "bump" in his pay depending on the degree of difficulty and level of risk.

Finally, we are close. The stunt coordinator checks and double checks with his team and with the special effects captain. The fire crews go to their preassigned "out-of-shot" places, the ambulance is fired up and standing by. When I get the "all clear" from the stunt coordinator and first AD, then, as director, I tell the DP, "Roll cameras." The assistants run into the shot and turn on the unmanned cameras. We then wait for the confirmation that the cameras are on and working. More assistants run in to "mark" each camera. This is the famous "clapper" or "slate" that all movies use to identify the shot. The slate also provides what the editor will need to sync up the sound and picture back in the editing room. "A camera marker!" "B camera marker!" "C camera marker!" Each assistant marks his camera. "Everyone clear!" the AD shouts.

The AD gets an OK signal from each department, and then turns to me. So now the cameras are rolling, the driver has given the thumbs-up that he is ready, and I turn to the AD. We nod at each other. Crossing my fingers, I say, "Action." The AD repeats on the walkie-talkies, "Action. Action." The driver gives one more thumbs-up and the car starts rolling down the street. It's a night shot and the camera department has had to flood the scene with enough light to get a proper exposure with the high frame rates for the slow motion. Everyone has to be pulling together for something like this to work.

Four. It's Not Your Fault But It Is Your Problem

We see the car picking up speed, though it is hugely weighed down with the metal crash cage, propane and telephone poles. When it's two-thirds of the way down the alley, we hear the huge concussive blast of the telephone pole explosion. A fireball erupts out of the back of the car and the car flips, as designed, end over end.

The last part is always the hardest for me. I have to watch the car crash, land, slide and come to a stop. In my mind, I have to calculate how many frames I will need in the cutting room before going to the next shot. If I say "cut" too early, we lose some of the coolest part of the stunt. If I say "cut" too late, it puts the driver in danger. There is no course in film school titled "When to Call 'Cut' During a Dangerous Stunt 101."

I watch the car come to a rest … one, one-thousand, two, one-thousand, three, one- thousand … and then I yell "Cut!"

The AD screams "Cut!" The fire team runs in with extinguishers and starts hosing down the car. Two other stuntmen run in, grab the driver and pull him away from the burning car. He wobbles like a drunk, a bit shaken up, but then he puts up both thumbs and everyone bursts into applause

Holy shit. We did it. Congratulations all around. That's a wrap. See you in ten hours.

And so it goes.

There have been many stunt accidents over the years. Vic Morrow and

Brandon Lee and Dwight Little during filming of *Rapid Fire*.

the kids killed on *Twilight Zone: The Movie*, Sarah Jones on *Midnight Rambler*. A paraglider on *XXX* crashed into a bridge. A pilot went down on *Top Gun*. It is unfortunately a long list. In the end, the responsibility always goes back to the director, which is why we have to be very careful, know our stuff, and hire the best people.

On *Rapid Fire,* we shut down a portion of the El train in Chicago for a crazy fight on the tracks with an oncoming train. We filmed an assault-siege sequence in front of a restaurant with SWAT trucks and rocket-fired grenades in the middle of downtown Chicago. We choreographed fights, one with Brandon paying homage to his father's famous single-shot "take down" (in which he takes out multiple opponents while standing in essentially the same position, all filmed in a single take) in *Enter the Dragon*. It was all mostly fun, and the studio was supportive—until we started spending too much money. Finally, after weeks in Los Angeles, Thailand and Chicago, we wrapped. Thank God. Now off to the editing room.

After a long shoot, I like to comb through material by myself with just a marker and a legal pad. I look at the footage for "highlights"—moments I remember. I find it astonishing what I am able to remember from the shoot. Every take of every shot is pretty much seared into my head. Only the director really knows what is in the material. I "pull" all

Dwight Little (right) filming *Rapid Fire*. Director of Photography Ric Waite is behind the camera on the crane; others unidentified.

Four. It's Not Your Fault But It Is Your Problem

these moments, not even knowing where they will go or if they have any value. Maybe the actor looked over his shoulder and the light caught his eyes in some cool way, or the B camera did a "whip pan" and caught the oncoming car in perfect focus. Or a line was read perfectly in an otherwise useless take. I grab all these pieces and put them in a bin, and I will try to find a home for them later.

The most important thing is: Don't get discouraged. The saying is, "Your movie is never as good as your dailies, or as bad as your first cut." The first cut is always depressing. It is slow and choppy and much of the good stuff is not even in it.

The trick is to just dive in. I try to identify scenes that I know will eventually work, and those that just seem to have died. Leave the good ones alone for now and try to fix the bad ones. Then, go back and start cutting the movie from the beginning. Finish one reel (about ten minutes of material) at a time. Get it working great and then move on. And work in as many of those highlights as possible. When you re-screen the movie four weeks later, your spirits will be lifted.

The *Rapid Fire* dailies had been good and the studio was starting to have some hope for this little action movie. They scheduled a mid–August weekend for a wide release and were already asking us for materials so that the marketing people could begin on the campaign. I showed the producers and our creative executive a couple of reels of the film and they were pumped up. Chris Young from *Getting Even* would be coming in to do the score. Title genius Wayne Fitzgerald and I had dreamed up a very cool opening title sequence and the studio agreed to give us the money to do it. All the lights ahead were blinking green. But then the call came that we never expected.

Joe Roth was leaving the studio. He was going to Disney and Roger Birnbaum was leaving to start a new company called Caravan. This meant that our biggest champions inside the studio would be gone when it was time to release the movie. This is a disaster for the filmmakers.

The new regime is in a "can't win" position regarding the films that have been green-lit by the prior bosses. If *Rapid Fire* is a huge hit, they get none of the credit. If it is a bomb, they and their new marketing team get all of the blame. A $12 million movie is really nothing in the grand scheme of things to a major studio and the "nobles" in the castle need to establish their new power more than they need to protect any particular movie. The only way for them to proceed would be to dump this "orphan" with as little fanfare as possible and hope the ancillary value will eventually help the film to break even, or at least not lose too much.

I went to see the new head of marketing for the Peter Chernin era at Fox. I sat in her overstuffed office in the executive building. Flower baskets were pouring in as all the big players around town were seeking her favor. The interior designers were still working on the details for the antique furniture and hand-sewn carpets. The meeting itself was chilly. She politely explained that she had heard some good things about the movie and that "they" looked forward to screening it and evaluating its commercial prospects. When I left that meeting, I knew for sure that the new regime wanted little or nothing to do with *Rapid Fire*.

The movie was released in August and performed badly. There were a few ads and TV spots but by the second weekend it was all over. We had put so much of ourselves into this movie and it was heartbreaking to see it wither away. It wasn't really my fault, but it certainly was my problem. I was just issued a one-way ticket back to movie jail.

All the agents and managers who thought this movie would be a great career move for me disappeared. Suddenly everyone is "in a meeting" and will get back to you (but don't hold your breath). All the love is gone in an instant.

I went back to the drawing board. What did I have that could get people excited again? I had been so involved in *Rapid Fire* that I didn't really have a lot of new ideas and material. The final shock came while I was driving down Sunset Blvd. to some pitch meeting when the car phone rang. It was our first AD Denis, who was off on another project.

Denis told me he had some bad news. "You better pull over," he said.

I pulled over to the side of the road. Brandon Lee had been accidentally shot and killed on the set of *The Crow*, a movie he had been offered thanks to *Rapid Fire*. I couldn't believe it. Jeff Imada had been on the *Crow* set and I knew how good and careful he was. It didn't make any sense. I was deeply saddened. Everyone was. I think Brandon would have been a huge star and would have been in almost every tentpole movie of the last 20 years.

The tragedy was so eerie with the death of his father, also at such a young age. I went to the memorial service where Melissa Etheridge sang "Ain't It Heavy." On top of everything else, Brandon, was engaged to be married.

* * *

All these years later, these are the "facts" that I have been able to gather, though I'm not sure I have the full story. The night before the accident, the second unit was doing some shots on a different set from the main unit. There was a big (close-up) shot, looking up the barrel of a gun. The camera people were worried that the barrel might be seen to be empty, so a "slug" or "dummy bullet" of some kind was put into the barrel to keep light from getting through. When the second unit wrapped, the gun was put away for the night. No one remembered to take out the slug.

Four. It's Not Your Fault But It Is Your Problem

Brandon Lee, Gerry Olson and Dwight Little filming *Rapid Fire*.

When the first unit needed the gun the next day, it was taken out and a blank charge was put in for a set-up. No one from the first unit crew knew that the slug had been put in the night before and no one checked. When the actor aimed the gun at Brandon, the blank went off and the slug discharged. The slug hit Brandon in a main artery in his abdomen and he lost consciousness almost immediately.

Two things. One, the prop man or AD always looks down the barrel of the gun to see that it is clear. (The prop man is obliged to show the director that the gun barrel is empty.) Two, the actor with the gun is instructed never to aim the gun at the other actor directly. The shot is always supposed to be "off angle" and the lens and composition makes it "look like" the gun is aimed properly. How all these mistakes could have been made in succession is almost impossible to imagine. The odds of Brandon being shot and killed by this forgotten slug were so long that of course the speculation about a "curse" began.

On the Internet and in newspapers, theories ran wild about the "Lee family curse." One was that Bruce's own father (a theater actor) had been involved with the Chinese Mafia, and Bruce had refused to do films for them, making the Mafia angry. Just before his death, Bruce received (from a woman other than his wife) some medicine that caused swelling in his brain. Speculation increased that he may have been murdered. Bruce Lee was then on the cusp of stardom; and his soon-to-be-released movies *Enter the Dragon* and *Game of Death* did make him an international star.

To make things even more strange, in the posthumous *Game of Death*, Bruce's character is shot by accident with a gun on a film set. This was so close to how Brandon actually died that one does begin to wonder.

In *Dragon: The Bruce Lee Story*, there is a sequence where a demon comes after Bruce and shows him his own headstone while trying to kill him. Bruce tries to protect his son Brandon from the demon and fights it off with nunchucks. Bruce yells, "Run, Brandon, run!"

Demons, curses, the Mafia and unlikely coincidences that are especially eerie all play a part in the mythology of how these two gifted men each died so young and both on the very verge of stardom. Bruce and Brandon are buried side by side in a graveyard in Seattle, 32 and 28 years old respectively.

Tragedy strikes in every walk of life, but the lives cut short in Hollywood seem particularly cruel because the dead are often so beloved by the public. River Phoenix, James Dean, Heath Ledger, Marilyn Monroe, John Belushi, Paul Walker, Natalie Wood, Philip Seymour Hoffman, James Gandolfini, Jean Harlow, Freddie Prinze, Chris Farley and too many others.

* * *

The money from *Rapid Fire* was dwindling and now I had some actual expenses beyond a rent-controlled apartment and an old Datsun. I had a mortgage, a car payment and life insurance!

There were a few meetings with mostly fringe players. Scripts were slow to come in, if at all, and there weren't really any development deals in the hopper. My champions at Fox were now gone, and the new regime saw me as pretty toxic in terms of box office.

I did write a story that would later become *Broken Arrow*, and I talked to the *Marked for Death* producers about a Stephen King original called *Sleepwalkers*, but nothing came of it.

In career moments like these, you realize there is no "job" of filmmaker or film director. You can't search for openings like "director wanted" on the Internet. You can't polish up your résumé and send it in with a cover letter. Sometimes movies come together, and mostly they don't. Only when they do will you get a fee. Unless you are "on the floor" yelling "Action!" you are not making money. Many filmmakers have had to hold second jobs to get them through the down periods.

Some film directors do commercials. Some direct TV shows. Some are paid as writers and others get paid to act. Many directors find work in casting offices, agencies and production companies. Some have family trusts to live off. I have even known directors who have practical skills and do construction work. For novelists, the standard way to survive was to teach while writing novels. Film directors can't teach and raise millions of dollars at the same time.

* * *

Out of the blue, there was a very strange phone call from a guy over at CAA who knew I needed money. How would I like to direct the first-ever live-action, interactive, point-and-shoot video game? *What?!* A company in Palo Alto had been commissioned to make a game for SEGA CD on a new video platform and they wanted it to have Hollywood production values and excitement. CAA had pitched me to them because they knew I was out of work and fit the profile of what they were looking for. I had experience in action *and* horror movies.

I agreed to fly up to San Francisco to meet with these guys. They had real money and were prepared to pay. That was all I needed to know.

When I arrived at the office building of Digital Pictures (that's what they *actually* called themselves), it felt like a trip to another world. This was Silicon Valley, not Warners or Paramount or Universal. Everything was cold and "architectural" with no history of anything. Just a fancy office park which they called a "campus."

Computer engineers and software designers ruled this planet and I was a classic luddite, confused by the technical computer-speak. They had an idea of what they wanted to do (some version of *Invasion of the Body Snatchers*) and so I did what I had done many times before: I pitched them a better version of their idea. We called it *Ground Zero Texas*.

Back to L.A., I called Alan and we cobbled together some movie ideas we'd been working on. Aliens taking over a small Texas town and the military coming in to stop them. The Reticulans could hide in the bodies of the townspeople, so the shooter had to be very careful about destroying an alien. The game had battle cams, particle beams, motherships, weapons caches, storm troopers and a big nuclear blast—all the building blocks of nearly every single point-and-shoot game of the last 30 years.

I was able to get Peter Collister to help out as the DP and I recruited Danny Trejo and some other character actors I had worked with to fill out the cast. We went up to the movie town where we had shot *Marked for Death* and created a new entertainment model.

Alan had to work the script out like a math problem. Each of the alien deaths had to be shot in multiple versions so that the game could be interactive. In one take, the stuntman would die and fall, in another take he'd die and then reanimate as an alien. In other takes, he'd be replaced by a civilian townsperson and in another he'd stand back up in a green suit (like a visual effects green screen) so the computer engineers could blow him up. The script was in a huge three-ring binder and the script supervisor and I had to go through all these variations to make sure the game designers had what they needed. The "story" elements of the game could be filmed as if it was simply a movie with Jeeps, stunts, dialogue, the works.

We were in completely new territory since this kind of "live-action" video game had not really been tried before. The project was so complicated and so technical, and yet … it was kind of fun too. The main thing was that they paid me a good fee and I was back on my feet again. The game itself was a bestseller in the U.K. and was named Best Sega Mega-CD Game of that year. How many directors have *that* on their résumé? Did we make a difference? I think so. Many gamers, designers and marketing gurus have come up to me over the years to say how much *Ground Zero Texas* had informed how they thought about first-person shooter games. *Call of Duty*, *Halo*, *Grand Theft Auto*, these are the descendants of *Ground Zero Texas*.

It was a pivotal time for video games. Everyone suspected that this new medium might be the future. The studios, unwilling to be left behind, were interested in seeing how they might be a part of this coming entertainment revolution.

* * *

Richard Donner and his wife Lauren Shuler Donner had offices at Warner Brothers and were making big Hollywood movies. Dick Donner's résumé was legendary: *The Omen*, *Superman*, *Lethal Weapon*, *Scrooged*, *The Goonies* and many more. Lauren had her own hits with *Dave* and *Mr. Mom*; and this was before her long run as the driving force behind the *X-Men* franchise. Together they were Hollywood power players.

Producer Jenny Lew Tugend had worked on many of Dick's movies and had her own office on the Warner Brothers lot. Jenny had been asked to find out about this new game phenomenon and had called an agent friend at CAA to see if they knew anything about it. The one guy CAA knew, who had actually done this, was their client … *moi*. So off I went for a meeting with Jenny.

Here I was driving back onto the Warner Brothers lot. I hadn't been here since my first meeting with Steven Seagal many years and heartaches earlier. I had my black Thunderbird and a new jacket from Neiman Marcus that I'd purchased with *Rapid Fire* money. Appearance is important. You can go to these meetings as a "raggedy creative type" in torn jeans as long as you're still in your twenties. I was now in my mid-thirties and I needed to be a bit more grown-up and *look* like I was successful. It wasn't lost on me that I hadn't been invited onto the lot because of some movie I made, I was there because I was the video-game guy.

Jenny and I discussed *Ground Zero Texas* and I told her as much as I could about the project, how it was shot and how it all came together. Behind Jenny's desk was a huge poster of the family hit *Free Willy*. Jenny had brought the *Free Willy* concept and script to the Donners and they had set it up with Jenny producing at Warner Brothers. The movie was a surprise hit. I told Jenny how much I had liked it. She said they were making a second one.

"Who's directing?" I asked innocently.

"We're still looking," she said. "We're down to about three candidates."

"What about me?" I asked.

Jenny looked at me in a funny way. She clearly hadn't even thought about this, and certainly on paper, I was not the right guy for this job. I was still an action director and had no experience with family movies.

"Well," she faltered, "I'm not sure Warner Brothers would see the 'fit.'"

"I understand," I said, "but I think I'm perfect for it. Can you ask?"

"Sure," she said. "I'll bring it up in the room."

And she did bring it up in the room. I damn sure needed a break, and my serendipitous video game, of all things, proved to be the Trojan Horse that got me in the door.

The great TV producer David Wolper (*Roots, North and South, The Thorns Birds*) once told me in a meeting, "Your job is to knock on as many doors as possible until one of them cracks open. Then, you put your shoulder down and push your way in."

Five

A Game of Thrones

When my name did come up "in the room," it was Dick Donner who thought he recognized it. "Why do I know that name?" he asked. Jenny said, "Dwight directed a Brandon Lee movie called *Rapid Fire*."

That's when he connected the dots. Dick had been interested in having Brandon appear in one of his *Lethal Weapon* movies. His agents sent him a print of *Rapid Fire* and he screened it at his house. He had liked Brandon and also thought the film was well-directed. What an insane bit of good luck! Not that many people had seen *Rapid Fire,* but Dick Donner had.

Dick was the director whose "picture" you'd see if you looked up "director" in the dictionary. He was at least 6'2" and had a booming low-end voice that went with a big personality. He was funny and charming, and it was easy to see why he'd started off as an actor. He really was "larger than life." Dick called everybody "kid" no matter how old they were. It was explained to me that he called everyone "kid" because he met so many people and couldn't remember names.

There wasn't really a script to read at this point so I didn't know what my angle would be when I finally had a chance to meet with Lauren Donner, who was producing *Free Willy 2* with Jenny. I studied *Free Willy* and made notes about all the things I had liked about it and kept quiet about what I didn't like.

In these director "beauty contests," there comes a time early in the meeting when you have to show your cards. You can't just wait and try to figure out what the studio likes and then say, "I agree!" You need to offer your own opinions, then gamble that what you are thinking will match what they are thinking. It's a poker game. You show your cards first.

The initial meeting was at Lauren's Warner Brothers office. Mega-producer Joel Silver was across the courtyard, Michael Crichton and Sylvester Stallone were mingling about, and Mel Gibson was wandering out of Dick's office. Clint Eastwood and his Malpaso offices were around the corner. I was hangin' with the cool kids.

Five. A Game of Thrones

Michael Madsen, Lauren Shuler Donner, Jason James Richter and Dwight Little filming *Free Willy 2*.

I didn't just tell them how much I "liked" *Free Willy*, I broke it down for them, describing what I admired about certain scenes. "I love how Jessie just pulls up on his bike and throws it down when he goes to see Willy," I said. "He doesn't have time to park it properly. It speaks to his character."

"I loved that too," Lauren said.

Okay, one down, keep going. "I thought it was gutsy to have the whale go through the car wash. It was a little over the top, but the kids loved it." (*The Goonies* had been a big hit for Dick, and I was sure a gag like that must have been his idea.)

"Right," Lauren said. "We can't forget it's a kids movie."

That was two "Yes I agree" moments so I kept my foot on the gas, trying to describe scenes that I thought worked in the film and why. When I left the room, I knew that the meeting had gone well. To top it off, Lauren was also from Cleveland. I didn't meet people from Cleveland very often in Hollywood. As the saying goes, "It's a good place to be from … far from."

But there was a long way to go. Other directors were in the mix and I had come in near the end of the audition process. I knew the names of some of the other contenders and they were all very qualified. Also, there were three companies involved: Warner Brothers, New Regency (who were putting up half of the money) plus the Donners' company. Everyone would have to sign off on whoever the director was going to be. I left the meeting feeling good, then tried to just forget about it. Landing this assignment was going to be a long shot.

Out of the blue, another project came up thanks to my CAA agents. Savoy Pictures (a start-up New York company with deep pockets) wanted to make a sexy dance thriller with Emilio Estevez and singer-dancer Paula Abdul. Emilio and Paula were a couple. Then Savoy enlisted another couple, producers Chuck Roven (*12 Monkeys, Heart Like a Wheel*) and Dawn Steel (*Flashdance, Cool Runnings*), to put this indie feature together. Their script *12 Bar Blues* was about a stripper who gets caught up in a mob operation and has to outsmart the men who try to keep her down. (The script was very similar to Jennifer Lopez's later hit *Hustlers*.)

Savoy didn't know if Paula could act and they wanted to do a screen test to find out. CAA had put me forward to shoot three scenes, which would in effect be an audition for me as well.

Dawn Steel was a 1980s uber-producer and the second woman (after Sherry Lansing) to run a Hollywood studio. She was a very blunt, colorful New Yorker, but also capable of charm. While at Paramount, she had overseen a string of hits including *Fatal Attraction, Footloose, Beverly Hills Cop* and *Top Gun*. No one makes that many consecutive hits today, except maybe Marvel.

I met with Dawn and Chuck at their impressive Beverly Hills home. The driveway climbed up from a side street near Coldwater. Lawns and trees and orchards passed by my window for several minutes, and this was all private property! The house was tasteful and Tuscan and the impression of money and influence was everywhere.

From Malibu to Holmby Hills, Beverly Hills, Hidden Hills, Bel Air and the Pacific Palisades, I have been to many Hollywood estates. The view of life from these trophy homes is very different from the estates of the Midwest, which I also know something about. In Hollywood, the money is a reflection of the owner's recent successes. In the Midwest, the money is often many generations old, from our Industrial Revolution past. In Cleveland, it's coal and shipping and steel (my mother worked at Republic Steel). In Hollywood, it's a few hit movies or popular TV shows. There are legacy Hollywood estates from the "founding fathers" like Zanuck, Goldwyn and Mayer. Some from the silent era (*Sunset Blvd.* anyone?) but mostly it's actors and producers and musicians with a few recent hits. No wonder the politics are so different. Red state, blue state.

Dawn wanted me to push Paula creatively to see if she had any comic timing and/or dramatic weight. We picked three scenes from the script that might each showcase a different side of the character, and of Paula.

While we were organizing the screen test, Savoy suddenly decided they wanted to do more work on the script. They came up with some money to send the writer and me to New York to do location scouting, and to interview some real-life club owners and strippers. At this point, I didn't even think I was the director, so I was confused.

"Just go," my agent said. "It can't possibly hurt, and you'll get them more pregnant."

We were obligated to go to strip clubs around the city for "research." Imagine telling your significant other that you're going to spend all day in strip clubs for "work." But we did learn some things.

During the day, when the clubs are closed, the reality of the whole stripper fantasy is exposed. Without the lights and the music and the girls, what you see are just cheap faux leather seats, tacky stages with stripper poles, empty bars and dirty floors. This is the same feeling one often gets coming back from lunch on a sound stage. The sets are naked, the lights are off and hanging on stands, the cameras pointing nowhere. The dream factory is very lonely after lunch. The crew wanders in and they are already tired and depressed because they still have six, often seven hours to go before wrap and they've already been there since seven a.m.

* * *

Workplace hours are a continuing problem for the film and television industries. In no other business that I can think of, are everyday workers expected to work 14 or 15 hours with a ten-hour turnaround. (There would be protests in the streets!) By the time a crew member drives to work (in L.A. traffic) and gets home late in the evening, there is no time left to play with a kid or help with homework, or talk with a partner. The problem is that the technicians get hooked on the overtime and start making more and more money as they rack up overtime hours. A bigger house in Santa Clarita, a new RV or boat in the driveway. Money is wickedly addictive.

Haskell Wexler, the great director of photography (*Bound for Glory*, *One Flew Over the Cuckoo's Nest*), made an important documentary about this, *Who Needs Sleep?* It details the circumstances surrounding the death of a cameraman who crashed his car and was killed on the way home from work after an 18-hour day. The documentary is an accurate look at life on set.

Since that film came out, some things have changed for the better. Generally, the day is now kept to 12 hours plus lunch, which is 13 hours plus travel. Still, this is 50 percent more work per day than would be asked of an employee in almost any other profession. Lawyers and doctors sometimes put in those kinds of hours, but not every day. Agents and managers have to go out for drinks and attend screenings most evenings, but that is still a bit different than pushing a dolly or running cable for another five hours.

Directors don't have to stay and put up the equipment after wrap, but we do have to arrive at least a half-hour early, and when we do get home, we have to prep for the next day. Most other "civilians" do eight or nine hours, then go home and have family time.

To try and stay awake while driving home from yet another all-nighter, many times I've had to roll down the car windows and blast the music. A drive from Long Beach or Valencia back to L.A. is a haul. I did fall asleep at the wheel once, but I was already off the freeway, close to home. I rolled into a ditch which woke me up.

I've often wondered where the unions are in all of this. Why can't they protect their members? And of course, the answer is *money*. In Atlanta, Albuquerque, Wilmington, Toronto, Shreveport, Providence, Calgary, Vancouver, Baton Rouge, etc., people will work long hours and not ask questions. I think excessively long work hours are the great black eye on the film business, which sees itself as a progressive community.

* * *

Everyone walking around a strip club at 11 in the morning is some "made guy" from Brooklyn, Queens or Staten Island. Big guys, little guys, old and young, but all clearly "mobbed up," and not happy to have outsiders poking around. Sure, they'd all love to be part of a movie but photos were not to be taken, and many rooms were out of bounds. A strip club is a cash business and therefore a perfect place to launder money. Who knows where all those dollar bills come from or how much the bar till has? Maybe the script wasn't so far-fetched after all.

Paula Abdul's screen test was done deep in the Valley, in an old sound stage with a standing bar. I was very attentive to Paula as I knew how stressful this must be for her. She was a singer-dancer, not an actress. While the lights were going up, I read the scenes with Paula and Emilio and gave her notes and positive encouragement. Emilio was a consummate pro. He'd been a very big star in lots of movies in his day (*The Breakfast Club, Young Guns, St. Elmo's Fire*) so he didn't need much from me. He was just worried about Paula.

When it came time to shoot, I immediately realized that she was a bit stiff and mannered. I tried to get her to improv a bit to loosen her up, but I didn't see a lot of magic happening. It was also strange that there wasn't much chemistry between her and Emilio even though they were a couple in real life.

Screen chemistry is a mystery. Some stars hate each other during filming but make very successful and convincing love stories: Ryan Gosling and Rachel McAdams, *The Notebook*. Patrick Swayze and Jennifer Gray, *Dirty Dancing*. And then some, like Ben Affleck and Jennifer Lopez, a real couple in life, went out and made a turkey called *Gigli*. Go figure.

Five. A Game of Thrones

When the dailies for the screen test came in, I made sure I cut the scenes together to try and give Paula the best possible chance to prove herself. I was hoping to get a movie out of it myself. Chuck, Dawn and Paula's manager Bob Cavallo (*Purple Rain, City of Angels, 12 Monkeys*) came to the screening. I tried to look at what we had done with fresh eyes.

To be honest, it wasn't very good. Paula was ordinary and didn't really connect with Emilio. Everyone said all the right things when the lights came up: "Better than I expected," "She's got something," "She's charming" and so on. They all thanked me and said they'd send the screen test off to the studio. I figured that would be the end of it.

It had been "radio silence" at Warners for a couple weeks until one day my agent called to say that I needed to meet with the New Regency executives and the Warner Brothers production people. Remember, this is part of the "jumping through hoops" process and it meant that the Donners had come down to their final choices; and I was one of them. Others would now weigh in with their opinions.

These meetings are mostly just a personality test. The studio wants to see if you're sane and can be trusted and know what you're doing. It was an $80 million dollar decision ($40 million to make the movie, $40 million to market it), so the stakes were high. I made sure I was prepared and hoped for the best. Whether it's actual production, or just job interviewing, preparation is the key to everything. Even if you think you can wing it, don't. You can go with your gut after you've prepared the hell out of it.

One random morning near the Christmas–New Year's holidays, I had calls from Lauren Donner, Dawn Steel and various CAA agents all coming into my home office at the same time. Apparently, Savoy had *liked* the screen test (big, fat surprise) and now they wanted to make a deal with me.

Just a month ago, I had been "the video game guy," and now two big-time producers were calling me at home. What if both films wanted me? Which one would I do? Feature films rarely come together so this dilemma never really materializes. Just go after each one as hard as you can. The answer will be presented to you.

And then, as if on cue, I got a call from Chuck Roven. There was a problem with *12 Bar Blues*. Emilio and Paula were breaking up! Two nights earlier, I had been out to dinner with both of them and they were very "handsy" and affectionate with each other, so this news seemed out of the blue.

But, then again, who knows what is really going on between two people? After the writing and the scouting and the screen test, it didn't really matter. This film was a dead duck. Now I just had to hope that I would win the beauty contest over at Warner Brothers for *Free Willy 2*. Otherwise, I was really going to be in a world of hurt. I was running out of money, again.

* * *

Several years later, I ran into Dawn Steel, who was then having cancer treatments. We spoke briefly about what "might have been" with *12 Bar Blues*, but of course it was quite awkward. Dawn was very sick. Her reality was a million miles from a Hollywood fantasy. It was sad that ovarian cancer took her life at an early age. She had many more films to make. Good ones, I believe.

* * *

One night a few days after the *12 Bar Blues* news, a production assistant showed up at my door. She had a stuffed orca plush toy, some balloons and a bottle of wine. That's how I learned I had won the job at Warner Brothers. This was a $40 million, prized studio sequel, and I had been selected as director.

I'm not sure what I said or did that turned the trick, but maybe it helped that at the last minute I had cut an audition tape together. I knew they must be thinking, "How can this action and horror guy pull off a family film?" so I took some softer family scenes from *Halloween 4* (a movie I was 100 percent sure none of them had ever seen) and cut them together into a reel. Bonding scenes between the two sisters and one of the other family members at breakfast. I also changed the music. Without Michael Myers, *Halloween 4* kind of looked like a family movie with female energy. I don't know if that last-minute extra push made a difference, but, as my father would often say, with his faux Yiddish accent, "It couldn't hoit."

* * *

Free Willy 2 was a Warner Brothers movie with important producers, and the scale of the production was crazy. In pre-production, we had access to the Warner Brothers jet, which took us back and forth to the scenic San Juan Islands off the coast of Washington state for scouting trips. The San Juan Islands were right in the path of migrating orca pods (family groups), so the location made perfect creative sense. But logistically it was a challenge.

Paul Sylbert (*Shampoo, Kramer vs. Kramer, Gorky Park*) had been brought in as production designer. His twin brother Richard was also another world-renowned production designer (not to mention, studio head), and they both had landmark films to their credit. Paul and I spoke at length about the tone of the movie we were trying to create.

"What are you making?" he asked. "You're the director, give me a direction."

"I want to make *The Black Stallion*," I answered. "A boy and his whale, instead of a boy and his horse. Something beautiful and poetic."

Five. A Game of Thrones

"You know they want to make *Lassie*," he laughed.

"I know," I said, "but let's try to sneak in as much *Black Stallion* as we can."

Even though Paul had been engaged by the Donners, and was very close to both of them, he loved the idea of making a stealth art film out of a $40 million studio franchise sequel.

I was no longer a student of first-person shooter video games, but now a student of orca whales. I learned about how they moved in pods and how their feeding and hunting habits took advantage of sophisticated communication skills, which in turn shaped their social groups.

We met with marine biologists, whale watchers and wildlife activists. All I kept hearing over and over was how they were *mammals* and carried their young to live birth. They were smart like wolves or bears. They were *not* fish! It was all quite interesting, but I had a million other questions on my mind. Like, "How the hell are we going to shoot this?"

On Lopez Island (one of the smaller San Juan Islands), we found a summer camp that could be used for many of the film's early scenes when the family is on a summer holiday. We would then have to move to one of the larger islands for different parts of the story.

Not since *Halloween 4* had I felt so close to the material. I had gone to summer camp and knew what the tents, campfires and canoes should look like. I knew how 12-year-old boys acted, and a little bit about 12-year-old

Dwight Little and Jason James Richter filming *Free Willy 2*.

girls. I had also been a canoe guide in Canada, and a group leader for the Youth Conservation Core, a government program that took troubled kids into the wilderness.

The kids under my supervision in the summers were not much younger than I was, and I had to keep them in line and hard at work building outhouses and clearing trails. I think having been in these leadership positions from an early age has helped me lead a 200+-person crew for weeks at a time.

Some directors know the grit of New York city streets (Scorsese, Lumet), some know the bars, valleys and freeways of L.A. (Tarantino, Michael Mann). But luckily, I knew the outdoors. I knew how to handle boats, and I knew something about Native American lore. I grew up with Ohio stories about the Algonquins, Iroquois, Hurons and Shawnees. It was not exactly the same as the Haida culture in *Free Willy 2*, but it was close. On *Free Willy 2*, I was in my element.

All in all, we moved the entire company five times, including to Astoria, Oregon, and San Diego. Nothing could move forward until I found locations I liked for each sequence and could commit to creatively. Then Lauren and Jenny would have to tell me if it could work in terms of money, transportation, etc.

I have always been very practical about picking locations since the most creative choice in the world will have no value if you can't get a film company moved in close to your dream.

I know where the trucks and motor homes will have to go, and where the backlight will be best for most of the day's shooting. I know how far base camp needs to be from the location so that actors can get to set quickly. Every single choice needs to take efficiency into account. Getting the crew from set to lunch and back quickly is essential. Then a one-hour lunch doesn't turn into a two-hour lunch (or more).

The director needs shooting time more than anything else. Time is the indispensable commodity. This is true on a little indie or a big studio movie. No matter what location you choose, remember that most of the time, you are going to be filming a close-up of an actor's face.

The *Free Willy 2* logistics were dizzying. Crews would have to be ferried to location every morning from Friday Harbor where there were motels and restaurants. Makeshift buildings would have to be set up for props, wardrobe, special effects, the art department, etc. Housing would have to be arranged for the stars and producers and the army of Hollywood executives.

With each company came one or more "creative" development executives. This meant that there would be "notes," often "group notes" on everything from script to casting to locations. Since each company had some skin in the game, their notes would have to be read.

Five. A Game of Thrones

The problem with studio notes is that the creative entities are often pulling and pushing in different directions, and this leaves the director caught in the middle. Make Regency happy but upset the Donners. Make the Donners happy but upset Warner Brothers. Or make them all happy and be unhappy yourself. This is the funhouse of studio filmmaking. A hall of mirrors with people shooting at you, just like Orson Welles' *The Lady from Shanghai*.

All these notes didn't address what I was really panicked about: the god-damn whale! The actual Willy (an orca named Keiko in real life) was still stuck in a tank in Mexico. Reality is a buzzkill. Keiko did not jump over a rock jetty to freedom.

"Wait until you meet Walt Conti," everyone kept saying. And then, one day, I did.

Walt Conti was an engineer from Northern California who had designed and built three full-scale animatronic orca whales. These whales were to be operated from enormous barges with their own power generators. Multiple long pneumatic tubes ran from the barges out to the synthetic-rubber whales, and operators could manipulate their movement from control areas on the barges.

The first time I saw the whales, they were up on tractor trailers in a parking lot with their mechanical guts hanging out. It was surreal. These were the stars of my movie?

Each animatronic whale had been designed to portray one of the characters in the script. There was "Willy" with the bent dorsal, "Luna" the mom with the "crescent moon," and "Little Spot" the brother with the three "spots" under his chin. Maybe with these whales, I would once again have a seal who could do a "fucking trick!"

All the producers seemed very excited and impressed and couldn't wait to see the "movie whales" in action in the water for a test the next day. I kept it to myself, but I was worried.

I kept thinking of the legendary stories about Steven Spielberg's shark in *Jaws*. They never really got that thing to work right, and when they did, it looked fake. Not that anyone seemed to care. But Bruce the Shark would never make it today. In the '70s, Spielberg & Co. got away with it. The director famously shot around his fake mechanical shark with quick cuts, POVs and a great score.

The next day the producers and I assembled on a dock looking out over the calm water of an inlet. The rubber whales were in the water and our first AD was talking to the engineers on the barge by walkie-talkie.

The whales skimmed across the surface and water shot up into the air from their blowholes. The producer group looked excited when the whales disappeared underwater, only to pop up later a few hundred feet away. Everyone was thrilled.

The problem for me was that the whales looked like submarines diving below the surface in a World War II movie. They were just as stiff as they looked on shore. The swimming motion was always at one speed, so it seemed to me more like a black torpedo than a whale.

"It's gonna be great!" I exclaimed, knowing Warner Brothers had spent millions on these replica whales. Another test up by the dock with the open mouth and moving tongue was better, but still, how was I going to survive this mess?

I knew that Warners had commissioned the great wildlife photographer Bob Talbot to go out and shoot real orca whales on 35mm film for *Free Willy*. My assistant, David Eichler, discovered that Talbot had also gone out and made some shots for *Free Willy 2*, in case they ever decided to make the sequel. Plus, there were shots filmed for the first movie that they had never used, and they were just sitting in a Warners vault.

* * *

Bob Talbot had grown up in Southern California. In love with the ocean from an early age, he almost went into oceanography, but then realized that he had a talent for photography. Bob made a huge name for himself with iconic pictures of whales and dolphins. He would wait in the open ocean for days and often weeks for the chance to capture the perfect photograph. Through Bob, we were able to meet and consult with Jean-Michel Cousteau of the famous underwater Cousteau family. These were fascinating people.

* * *

I asked David to dig up Bob's 35mm footage and have the editors go through it shot by shot. I needed the best pieces pulled and sent up to me. My plan was to see exactly what I could use from Bob's wildlife footage, then combine it with the miniature and animatronic whales.

I did storyboards to show how all these moving parts would fit together. For example, a sequence might start with a miniature whale (an eight-foot-long fiberglass replica) swimming toward the surface (shot in slow motion in a huge pool), then continue with a Bob Talbot shot of an orca breaching the surface. Next, there might be a cutaway to one of our characters on the shore. After that, we would follow with an animatronic whale with water shooting up from its blowhole. Then a diving shot from wildlife footage, and a final miniature of the orca near the ocean floor.

Once all of these elements were cut together, it seemed like a fluid and natural orca event, even though it was made up of many different pieces, some real and some not.

Five. A Game of Thrones

Bob's footage really was magical, and it helped sell the Walt Conti animatronic orcas. Careful prep, detective work and old-school storyboarding made the whole thing work.

I figured out a good plan for the orcas, and the table readings with all the cast members had gone well. But the weather was a bitch. It was cold and gray. We were making a happy movie based around a summer vacation. Nothing is ever easy and the bad conditions caused a ripple effect that almost cost me my job.

I knew that I was inheriting much of the crew from the first movie. I had asked for Ric Waite, my DP on *Marked for Death* and *Rapid Fire*. He had stumbled once with me when we were in Jamaica, but most of his work had been excellent. On *Free Willy 2*, there was a lot of pressure on Ric to make the film look "beautiful" and the actual conditions on the ground were not pretty at all. It was only April in the Pacific Northwest and the weather was drab. Ric got ahold of a new Kodak film stock (that he hadn't used before) and started to play around with various coral filters. He was trying to come up with a look that would "outsmart" the weather. Instead he outsmarted himself.

The first day's dailies were okay but seemed a little underexposed. Everyone said they could bring it up in the lab. The actors had done fine, but the photography was only average. The second day there was a peek of sun. We were all so excited because there was just enough natural light to get a nice, pretty shot of the campground on the water. When we were watching dailies after work in a location tent, there was a collective gasp when the footage seemed fine at first, and then suddenly went dark. *What was going on?*

Somebody "stopped down" on the aperture, but why?

Would we have to reshoot? By the third day, the producers had lost confidence in Ric. There was so much money at stake and somehow, he wasn't getting the exposure right. In fact, he was shooting through so many different kinds of "glass" that the light meters were tricked in some way, and the lenses just weren't letting enough light through.

At the end of the day, I got the call that production would be suspended until the camera issues could be resolved. In this case, "resolved" meant "replacing Ric." Bottom line: The studio was not happy with the dailies. Heads were going to roll.

After all this work and prep, it began to dawn on me that if they were going to replace the DP, and the DP was my guy, I'd probably be replaced as well. And they'd just start fresh with a new director.

Later, I discovered that it was the first AD, Jimmy Van Wyck, a real industry veteran and close to the Donners, who came to my defense. He told the producers that I was prepared and working well with the actors. He recommended they boot Ric and spare me.

There was nothing I could do to save Ric. He had messed up big time, and if I was going to keep my job, I would have to go along with the firing squad. I was reminded of a song by The Band that went like this: "Save your neck or save your brother—looks like it's ... one or the other."

Truer words were never set to music. Again, another example of, "It wasn't my fault, but it sure was my problem."

The producers flew in another DP from Los Angeles. As Ric and most of his crew packed up and went home, I headed off to meet the new man. It turned out to be none other than Laszlo Kovacs, one of the great cinematographers of all time. Dick had worked with Laszlo on *Radio Flyer* and had called in a favor.

I took Laszlo on a tour of the location to catch him up on where we were in the filming, and what we were planning to do next. I immediately felt a kinship with him and knew that his intention was to help me make the best film possible.

* * *

Laszlo and his colleague and lifelong friend, Vilmos Zsigmond, had famously escaped Hungary during the Soviet occupation of Budapest in 1956. Laszlo and Vilmos had a 16mm camera and film that they had procured from the national film school in Budapest. They covered the camera with a brown grocery bag and cut a small hole where the lens could stick out unnoticed. The young film students managed to get footage of tanks, soldiers, protesters and overall chaos. They escaped on foot with the film, crossing farmlands and climbing fences until they were able to sneak into Austria. It was a harrowing story: two young refugees who just loved movies, making it out of a Communist country by the skin of their teeth.

In America, they both found tremendous success in Hollywood. They remained close friends their whole lives. It is a powerful story that any aspiring filmmaker needs to know. They risked everything, including their lives, to follow their dream.

Laszlo shot *Easy Rider, Five Easy Pieces, Paper Moon, Shampoo, Ghostbusters* and numerous others. Among Vilmos' credits are *Deliverance, Close Encounters of the Third Kind* and *The Deer Hunter*. That is as good as it gets.

* * *

On the first day back, Laszlo made the single decision that would save me for the rest of the movie. We were setting up a shot where Jesse, the lead boy, must break away from some greedy businessmen and run up a dock to warn the whales. There was a posse of people at video village: Producers, studio people, many heads department were there because this was our first day back since firing Ric.

Jimmy Van Wyck was giving me advice on how to shoot the scene, when an associate producer came down from video village and said there had been a "suggestion" that a Steadicam be used in the shot. I looked up the hill and could see that Dick Donner was sitting there, a great and experienced director. What was I supposed to do? If I used a Steadicam, then the cameraman would have to run backwards up the dock. Two grips would have to hold his belt to guide him so he wouldn't stumble and hurt either himself or the camera. At the same time, the young actor, Jason James Richter, would have to chase him, controlling his speed so that he wouldn't catch up and run smack into the camera. Instead of acting, Jason would be thinking about the camera.

Maybe Anthony Hopkins would have the concentration to do something like that, but not a 12-year-old kid. I wanted the character to run as fast as he possibly could in order to save the captured whales. I wanted the cameras back and out of the way so that Jason could really cut loose and act. I was not just being stubborn, I really thought Steadicam was not the right approach.

Preparing to film during the making of *Free Willy 2*.

Laszlo could see how torn up I was, since everyone was trying to tell me how to direct, and I had no power since my last DP had just been fired. If I did what they said, then I'd be surrendering all creative control for the rest of the movie. And if I didn't listen to someone like Dick Donner, then I'd be poking the bear and giving everyone another reason to fire me.

Laszlo took me gently by the arm and walked me over to the side of the dock. He looked right into my eyes and said, "Just tell me … what do *you* want to do?"

I looked right back at him with a deep sense of gratitude. Here was a world-class DP saying to me, "Sonny, this is your movie and I will shoot *your* movie. But you have to tell me what you want."

I told Laszlo where I wanted each camera to go, which ones on dollies and which on telephoto lenses.

Laszlo turned to the AD and told him exactly what I had just said, then everyone went to work. In other words, he was saying, "I'm shooting this guy's movie, and I'm Laszlo Kovacs, and you all need to get on board."

From then on, Laszlo and I worked together hand in glove. He had come from a world where the director was king and always had the last word. There used to be an ironclad rule that was for everyone on the set: "When you have a question, rule number one is *Ask the director*. Rule number two is *See rule number one*."

Sad to say, those days are long gone, and everyone now seems to chime in whether they have any set experience or not. The big tentpole

Dwight Little and Laszlo Kovacs filming *Free Willy 2*.

movies are very producer- and executive-driven because they often involve pre-designed "universes" where the special effects will reign supreme.

One day we had a fairly simple dialogue scene to do at the base of a waterfall. We were in a beautiful woods; the morning sunlight was dappled and perfect. I was working with a fine actor and great human being, August Schellenberg. Augie was a Canadian actor, part–Swiss and part–Native American, and a genuinely spiritual man. He also had a biting sense of humor.

His character Randolph was supposed to approach an old growth tree and carefully remove a perfect piece of moss which had medicinal properties that would help heal the whales if prepared in the old Haida Indian tradition. Of course, this was a movie and I had the art department take some very tiny tacks and fasten the moss to the trunk of the tree where we would need it for the scene. Augie looked at the guys with their hammers as they nailed the moss onto the tree, and yelled out, "The environmentalists are killing the fucking tree!" The whole crew cracked up.

Later, looking through the lens of the Panavision camera at the sun-drenched waterfall, I realized that I was experiencing that rare perfect moment. Here I was, a studio director, filming a story I believed in, with actors and crew I liked, in an environment that inspired me. When fighting all your battles and trying to stay sane, it's important to remember that sometimes you have the best job in the world.

For me, this was always the goal. To create cinema and tell good stories. The agents and managers, lunch at The Palm, and screenings in Westwood are all part of the process, but making "pictures" ... that is the ultimate goal. On this one sunny day somewhere in the Pacific Northwest, I realized that dream.

Much later in the production, I had another "full circle" experience. After we finished all the principal photography and the underwater live-action work in a huge tank in San Diego, we still had one piece of the movie left to do. We needed to shoot the miniatures.

In the story, a huge cargo ship crashes against the rocky bottom of the ocean floor and oil begins to leak. We were all set up at the Olympic swimming pool south of USC near the Coliseum, where the art department had built an ocean floor on the bottom of the pool. They also rigged a 30-foot tanker hull with leaking oil and other special effects. We needed to see dailies every night to be sure that the lighting and underwater photography were working. The closest screening room was the Norris Cinema Theatre on the USC campus.

One evening I arrived at the theater after a long day of shooting. At this point, we had been going nonstop for months. I was worn down. But as I entered the lobby of the theater, an avalanche of memories came back.

Dwight Little, Mary Kate Schellhardt and Jason James Richter during filming of *Free Willy 2*.

This was the room where, as a student, I had seen John Cassavetes and Gena Rowlands speak about their approach to indie DIY (do it yourself) filmmaking. I had listened to James Bridges talk about his approach to *Urban Cowboy* and had seen a fresh 35mm print of *Days of Heaven*. And also the evening with Orson Welles where the man himself had come slowly down the aisle and climbed the stage. There he was, the creator of our modern film language, old and weary but full of life and enthusiasm when he talked about cinema.

Welles pointed to the big white screen behind him and told us how impossible it was to make that static "bitch" come alive. The very act of projecting images up on the screen tended to slow everything down, he said. He advised directors to use a stopwatch when rehearsing their actors. Tell the actors to go as fast as they can, and then check the time. Whatever it is, tell them to do it 30 seconds faster. Although it may seem rushed on the stage when filming, the scene will slow down to the right pace when edited and projected. If the actors complain about missing a chance to "create a moment," tell them the audience doesn't have time for their moment. Here was actual directing advice coming to us from Orson Welles. I was a long way from Cleveland that evening.

In the Norris Theater lobby, my Chicago Film Festival award for *Americano* was still behind glass in the elegant trophy case. Minutes later, as I watched the *Free Willy 2* dailies dance across the screen, I also took a minute to remember *Americano* itself playing on the very same screen 15 years earlier.

The screening of *Americano* had been the culmination of my time at USC film school, and the film had "worked" for the audience. As they say, "it played." A *Hollywood Reporter* writer who'd been there that evening singled out my film from the others for excellence. Sandy Howard had seen that article and, as Robert Frost wrote, "it had made all the difference." And to top the evening off, the great director Stanley Donen had come to the screening and was enthusiastic about the film. (Of course, his son Josh had been the editor!) Stanley had nearly invented the Hollywood musical with *Singin' in the Rain* and perfected the Romantic Comedy with movies like *Charade*.

The good news was that the *Free Willy 2* miniatures looked good and it was now back to the business of editing 70 days of shooting into a coherent movie that would move audiences and make Warner Brothers some money.

Free Willy 2 was the last feature to be cut on film at Warner Brothers. Going forward, all the editing for feature films would be done on computers. I was lucky to have a great editor, Robert Brown (*The Client, Lost Boys, Flatliners*), working with me. We pored through the material. We cut and recut the scenes over and over trying to find the balance of comedy and drama, message and heart, and—most importantly—make the whales believable.

Dick and Lauren got restless after a month or two and asked us to show them a cut of the film. I stalled as long as possible, but I knew they deserved to see their movie. Robert and I went across the lot to a screening room with a work print "rough cut" and temp music. Showing this cut of the movie to Dick and Lauren, Regency and Warner Brothers was terrifying.

Even after all our cutting, the movie played long. There was a scene where Jesse had to give a salmon to Willy for the first time since discovering him in the wild. The boy is out at the end of a dock and the animatronic whale is in the ocean next to him. I had shots of Willy and shots of Jesse. Masters, over the shoulders, singles, cutaways, close-ups and then more coverage of the family and Randolph watching. It was a slow burn to see if Willy would trust Jesse again after all the time that had gone by since the first *Free Willy*.

Watching it on the big screen, it did seem to take a bit long. (Welles was right, things did seem to slow down when projected.)

Dick Donner finally said out loud, in the middle of the screening, "Just give him the fucking fish!"

I was horrified, but of course he was right.

Later, after the screening, he said to me in a very supportive way, "It's all in there, kid, just cut out all the crap."

Again, I thought about what Welles had said: "The audience doesn't have time for your moments" ... and that included mine.

After some re-cutting, we played the film for a recruited audience in the Valley. Many of the composite shots and special effects were not ready but we screened it anyway. The movie tested great. It "played," and Warner Brothers seemed to be ready to push full steam ahead for a July release. But then, as always, trouble reared its ugly head.

Early on, there had been a lot of discussion about trying to have one group or another move Keiko the real "Willy" from his tank in Mexico to a much larger facility in Newport, Oregon. In fact, the new "tank" was actually being built with money and donations generated from the first film. But now, it seemed like the plans had stalled. There were complications with moving the orca since his health was not good, and they were worried that the stress of the move might actually kill him (talk about bad publicity). Plus, there were construction delays on the tank and the July target was going to come and go.

Meanwhile, as the early press began to get out to the public that Warner Brothers would be releasing a *Free Willy* sequel, many students and teachers were starting to ask questions. Keiko had been embraced by grade school kids all over the world, and now they had to be told that he was still in a tank in Mexico. For young people, it is very hard to separate the fantasy of a movie from reality. This is why so many young people thought Wakanda from Black Panther was a real place.

Warners was inundated with letters from elementary schoolchildren imploring them to take care of Keiko and make sure he'd really "get free" as promised in the first movie. I was very aware of all this because my niece was a girl of about seven at the time, and I knew that her class in Ohio was following the story very closely.

I finally persuaded Lauren that we should go see Bob Daley, the head of the studio, and bring this grass roots action to his attention. My feeling was that they should hold the movie at least until Keiko was moved into the Newport tank.

I had two huge mailbags full of handwritten letters from children and I marched them up the stairs of the executive building to see the president of the studio. I could tell that Lauren was not in favor of this meeting, but I had been pushing hard for it.

Daley's office was bright and spacious and had all the trappings of a studio chief's office. Photos of him with famous people, awards, trophies, diplomas. Expensive drapes, carpeting, furniture. I was just one of many directors working at the studio, so he had no reason to know anything about me, other than I was the *Free Willy 2* guy. It would be like Jack Warner knowing who was directing the latest *Rin Tin Tin* picture on the backlot.

I shook his hand and looked him in the eye. He looked away, which told me he was already uncomfortable about this meeting. He did not want to be confronted about a whale problem in the middle of his morning.

* * *

I have one "golden rule" for dealing with people in the entertainment business, and in life: Never look up or down at anyone, always straight across. You never look up to the studio head or movie star because they don't know any more than you do, but you give them the respect of their position. At the same time, you never look down at the craft service people or the drivers or the cable person. You may be the director but you're not better than they are, and their jobs are also important. There used to be a saying: "Don't be the kind of guy who kisses up and pisses down." I respected Bob Daley, but he didn't know any more than I did, and in this case, he knew less.

* * *

Lauren and I explained to Daley that lots of schoolchildren had been writing to Warner Brothers about the fate of Keiko. Kids had been pitching in their allowance money, nickels and dimes to help "Free Willy."

He seemed unmoved. "Listen," he said, "Warner Brothers is in the movie business, not in the marine mammal business." He suggested we go talk to the people at New Regency. Maybe they'd give us some money to finish the tank and move the whale but it wasn't Warner Brothers' responsibility. He assured us that the July date was the right time to release the movie. He never looked at a single one of the letters I'd brought in. Not one.

I realized what I should have already known: You don't get to be the head of a major movie studio by being sentimental. About anything. And certainly not whales. Decisions are made every day based on what is best for the studio and the shareholders. Corporations are not necessarily evil. They just have their own interests to protect, and that's how it is. If you don't want their money, don't take it.

If releasing the movie while Keiko was still in a Mexican tank was Strike One against our movie, then the next sequence of events would be Strike Two.

Michael Jackson had written several songs for the first *Free Willy* movie and they were so beautiful that they really elevated it. His childlike voice and melodic arrangements made the audience feel like a part of the film in a way that melted millions of hearts.

Michael was coming out with a new album and had agreed to write new music for *Free Willy 2*. The problem was that he was already being whispered about as someone who had acted inappropriately with young children. Lawsuits were being drawn up and legal action was looming. I discussed this with Lauren; she said there'd be a studio meeting about the issue and I was welcome to attend.

Off I went to another meeting in the Warner Brothers executive building. This time there were people attending from Michael's record company and his management team. Also present were the Warner Brothers marketing chiefs, Dick and Lauren Donner, and a battery of lawyers. This was a big meeting.

The people on Michael's team jumped right in. They talked about the projected sales for Michael's new album and that at least two *Free Willy 2* songs would be on it. This would mean that music videos would be financed and filmed promoting the album *and* the movie. The Warner marketing people piped up with their estimates of what Michael would bring to the movie in free marketing dollars. Millions.

I knew I was very "over my pay grade" but at some point, I joined the conversation: I naively offered, "Is there any concern that the current problems surrounding Michael and children might be a negative to a family audience where the parents help choose what movie to see?"

The looks around the room were acrid. "If looks could kill" barely covers it. I had just basically suggested that all these people—lawyers, managers, agents, executives, producers—give up millions of dollars in fees and commissions. That was not going to happen.

"Those are wild accusations," one lawyer scoffed. "There is no merit, and this will all be a memory by June."

"Michael is not giving in to extortion," said another.

"None of these so-called witnesses will hold up in court," fumed another.

This was before the age of Times Up and MeToo, when slick lawyers could make almost anything go away, sealed in an NDA (non-disclosure agreement) somewhere downtown. I was shut down with extreme prejudice. Even Dick and Lauren would not make eye contact.

Of course, what all these "suits" didn't understand was that back in Ohio, and places where people actually buy tickets, Michael Jackson was already becoming tarnished goods. What I witnessed was the brute force of money over any kind of common sense. Michael Jackson would end up with two major songs in the movie. The audience would literally cringe when the songs came on, and so would I.

One day while I was mixing the movie, my assistant David came up to me and said, "Michael Jackson is on the phone for you."

Five. A Game of Thrones

Uh-oh. Has something gotten back to him?

But he was very pleasant and said how much he liked the movie. Then he tried to persuade me to put a third song into the movie and play all of them loud over the dialogue.

I told him how much we appreciated everything he had done and that I would try to use as much of his music as possible. I actually used less. The songs were not as good as what he had written for the first film. In fact, I didn't like either of them.

While scoring the film on a huge, historic scoring stage on the Sony (former MGM) lot, a bit of the real world crept in. We were all giddy with excitement about what the live orchestra was playing. Composer Basil Poledouris (*RoboCop, The Hunt for Red October*) had really outdone himself and the scenes on the screen were coming to life. It was thrilling. Suddenly, someone ran into the scoring stage and told us to turn on a TV. There had been a bombing in Oklahoma City and hundreds were dead, including children.

Here we were, putting the final touches on a beautiful film about children and wildlife, while in the real world, bombs were going off in daycare centers. We tried to watch the reports, but it was just too upsetting. The day was cancelled, and everyone went home.

On *Rapid Fire*, I was mixing the film in Burbank when the L.A. riots broke out. By three in the afternoon, the studio shut down the session and told us all to go home. The streets were getting dangerous and no one knew what might happen next. As I was cutting across the city trying to use Mulholland Highway, I looked off to my left and could see smoke coming up from the city. Black smoke and flames rising up into the blue sky.

And then again, some years later while driving very early in the morning down the 405, I heard on the radio that a small plane had crashed into the World Trade Center. By the time I pulled into the Manhattan Beach studios, the full story was coming out. It wasn't a small plane, it was two fully loaded passenger jets and thousands of people had likely been killed.

The producers gathered us on the set of *The Practice* and told all actors and crew to go home. Manhattan Beach was the center of many defense and aerospace companies, and there was good reason to think that a war had started. As everyone now knows, it was 9/11.

There were more world events that crept into my alternate world of moviemaking. I was in Chicago for the fall of the Berlin Wall. Then there was the first Iraqi invasion, the bombing of Baghdad, the death of Osama bin Laden, the hanging of Saddam Hussein, the 2007 financial meltdown, the unlikely elections of Barack Obama and Donald Trump, and the Coronavirus, among many others. The world keeps spinning on its axis. As

Billy Joel sang, "We didn't start the fire, it was always burning since the world's been turning."

As we all geared up for *Free Willy 2*'s release, the signals were good. The test screenings continued to go well; ditto for the screenings for the theater owners and exhibitors. The producers rented a stretch limo that we'd use the Friday of opening weekend to sample theaters around town.

I knew that the inclusion of Michael Jackson's music and the continued captivity of Keiko were two real-world issues that were going to hurt us. The studio felt that the affection people had for the first movie, along with the marketing campaign, would still prevail. Maybe so, but there was a Strike Three that no one saw coming.

Two movies, nearly unknown to the studio, were scheduled to come out on the same weekend. There was a little sleeper made in Australia called *Babe*, about a farmer and his pig. It was completely under the radar, but had been quietly testing very well and was going after our exact demographic. Instead of a sequel, this was a brand-new movie.

There was also a "tween" movie called *Clueless* that was going after every girl over the age of nine.

The *Free Willy 2* reviews were all over the map. "The Perfect Family Movie," raved *The New York Times*. But there was also Two Thumbs Down from Siskel and Ebert in Chicago.

I should have bolted when I had the chance.

During the long post-production of *Free Willy 2*, I had been developing my own original idea at 20th Century–Fox. While doing research on an action movie, I had come across a fun fact from the military. It turned out there was an actual expression created for use in the unlikely event that the Air Force would lose a nuclear bomb. The fiasco would be called a "Broken Arrow." "That's a movie!" I figured.

I set up a meeting with a Fox executive I knew from the *Marked for Death–Rapid Fire* days and pitched him the basics. The executive saw the potential and set me up with a writer with whom they already had a deal. His name was Graham Yost and he had hit it out of the park with an action flick called *Speed* starring Keanu Reeves and Sandra Bullock. The film had been a big surprise hit for Fox and they were understandably very high on him. Graham and I hammered out the treatment and he wrote several drafts of the script while I was editing. Graham later went on to be a bigtime TV showrunner with winners like *Justified*, *The Americans*, *John Adams* and numerous others.

All of a sudden, the Fox executives realized they didn't have a Christmas movie, and out of all their movies in development, they decided *Broken Arrow* was their best bet. But they'd have to film right away. This meant that I'd need to leave *Free Willy 2* and turn the movie over to the studio and the Donners to finish. What to do? Have a heavyweight meeting at CAA, of course.

The CAA building in Beverly Hills was an architectural masterpiece situated imposingly on a wraparound corner of Little Santa Monica Blvd. The reception desk was manned by the most beautiful assistants one could imagine (stone cold blondes) and the waiting area was populated with famous writers, stars and directors who were there for meetings. The agency handled most of Hollywood's major movie stars as well as directors. After the obligatory half-hour wait, a new assistant would finally come down and escort you to your meeting. In my case, I walked into a conference room with about ten people. There were the two men who were called my "day-to-day" agents, a more senior agent from the Motion Picture Literary Department, the "covering" agent for Warner Brothers; and assorted assistants to all of these people, taking notes. Sparkling waters and cheese plates were everywhere, along with the fruit salads and fresh-baked cookies. (The urban legend was that the CAA elevators were bugged so that the agents could hear what the opposing team was thinking right after a meeting. People can't help themselves from talking in an elevator. My rule is always wait for the parking lot.)

The main point of the meeting was to decide whether or not I should stay and finish my movie at Warner Brothers and be loyal to the Donners, or run off to Fox and start prepping *Broken Arrow*. Calculations were made about money vs. loyalty. No need to piss off Warner Brothers, who had a huge stake in *Free Willy 2* and had taken a chance on me. But then again, here was an opportunity to do a new movie at Fox.

We went around the room and everyone offered their perspective without actually saying anything definitive. The main point of these meetings for the agents is to stay on the right side of their bosses, so every thought is conditional and full of ambiguity.

When it came to the biggest fish in the room, the senior agent, he looked at me and asked, "What do you want to do?"

All this industry experience, and in the end, they wanted *me* to decide anyway. It's like having six doctors with medical degrees from Ivy League schools asking you which treatment *you* think they should proceed with.

I figured the buzz on *Free Willy 2* was good, and I had another script at Warner Brothers that I preferred to do anyway. Plus, the *Broken Arrow* script was not really ready. So I decided to stay with my Warner Brothers movie and finish it properly, hoping it would become the hit everyone thought it would be.

20th Century–Fox immediately put Hong Kong action master John Woo on *Broken Arrow*, and he turned it into a hit with John Travolta. Shows what I know.

My big studio franchise sequel flopped, I missed out on the chance to direct a movie based on my own idea, and the storm clouds blew in. Those agents, whose job it was to protect me, should have had the sense to pull me out of Warners and put me into the Fox movie.

But as William Goldman famously said about Hollywood: "Nobody knows anything."

Six

Three Strikes and You're Out

Somewhere in Morocco, Wesley Snipes and Jean-Claude Van Damme were preparing to do a big Warner Brothers action movie. I'm not sure whether it was a clash of egos or a clash of schedules, but at the last minute, Snipes dropped out. The studio freaked and looked everywhere for an action star to replace him. Plenty of studio money had already been spent on construction, locations, crews and logistics.

It turned out there were not many "A" level stars willing to sign on for a film starring Jean-Claude Van Damme. Van Damme was a martial arts action star who was trying to find his way into mainstream studio movies. He had made decent moneymaking B pictures and was hoping to build on his box office success. He was making a name for himself with theatrical performers in *Sudden Death*, *Timecop* and *Hard Target*. Despite the money already spent on pre-production, Warner Brothers was not able to replace Wesley, and eventually they just pulled the plug. The movie was shut down and everyone went home.

The catch was, Warner Brothers had a pay-or-play deal in place with Wesley for $10 million, plus a million more for his "perk" package (trainers, chefs, drivers, security, etc.). They'd have to move fast and secure him another movie or pay the $10 mil and not have a movie to show for it.

The executives were instructed to see if they could find a decent, ready-to-go script for Wesley. Lorenzo Di Bonaventura, the head of the studio, brought the problem up to his partners at New Regency (a supplier for Warner Brothers). It turned out New Regency had a little detective thriller called *Executive Privilege*. And guess what? The *Free Willy 2* director had been developing it and they thought it was pretty good. It had a hooky premise: "What if a woman is murdered in the White House?"

The original idea was to have one or more of the Warners stars read it: Russell, Costner, Gibson, Stallone *et al.*, and see if the script got any

Wesley Snipes, Diane Lane and Dwight Little filming *Murder at 1600*.

traction. But now it appeared that *Executive Privilege* might be the project most likely to solve Warner Brothers' big Wesley Snipes problem. Maybe it could be turned into a vehicle for him.

Lorenzo called me into his office in the executive building. He was a very bright, Yale-educated production chief who always seemed to be thinking about 20 things at the same time. After a reasonable wait (under 30 minutes), I was sent into his office.

"I hear you've got a thriller over at Regency," he began. "Would you make it with Wesley Snipes?" I had had some interaction with Lorenzo on *Free Willy 2* so he was aware of me, at least a little.

I had never considered an African American for the lead detective role, but if that's what the studio wanted, then of course I was on board.

"That's really interesting," I said. "I think it's even better." And then, for some reason, I just blurted out, "Black man, White House."

Lorenzo was up on his feet with enthusiasm. "Jesus. That's brilliant! Black man, White House!" he echoed. Warner Brothers never used this tag line in the marketing, it was deemed "too controversial."

The marketing department didn't like the title *Executive Privilege* either and they focus-grouped the now well-known title *Murder at 1600*. I thought it was lame. I liked *Executive Privilege* much better.

* * *

Six. Three Strikes and You're Out

When I originally signed on to do *Marked for Death*, the script was called *Screwface*, which was horrible. Thank God they changed the title. In those days, Steven Seagal was branding himself with three-word titles. *Out for Justice, Above the Law, Hard to Kill*. During production at Fox, we shot the Brandon Lee movie as *Moving Target*, and then later as *Chasing the Dragon*, before the studio finally settled on the generic *Rapid Fire*. Now *Executive Privilege* was being rebranded as *Murder at 1600*.

The studios have their marketing teams go to shopping centers and test various titles. They stand there with a clipboard and stop shoppers to ask, "Which of these three titles do you like the best?" They don't even say what the movie is about or who's in it; just "Which title grabs you?" Fifty-five percent of random shoppers at a generic mall in the San Fernando Valley liked *Murder at 1600*. So that was that.

* * *

Lorenzo told me the movie had to go into prep right away, and I needed to make any script changes that would be required to accommodate Wesley. Plus, we'd have to get Wesley to sign off on the script and me. "I'm going to put Arnold on it," he said. Arnold was legendary producer Arnold Kopelson (*Platoon, The Fugitive, Seven, Falling Down*), who had a deal on the Warner Brothers lot. Lorenzo knew that getting a big star to sign off on me might be a problem since my last two movies had tanked. But Arnold was an Oscar winner and he liked the script. He had also seen some nice reviews of *Free Willy 2* in the *Hollywood Reporter* and *Variety*.

Arnold talked to Wesley's agents and a meeting was set up for me to go to New York and talk to Mr. Snipes. There was no time to waste and I was off to the airport the next day.

Wesley's apartment was in trendy lower Manhattan and I had a hard time finding it. I panicked at the thought of being late because I am obsessed with being exactly on time. I had a football coach who taught me the following rule: "Early is on time, on time is late, and late is don't bother." (I even show up on time for dinner reservations.) Remember this rule and break it at your own peril.

Thanks to a fruit seller, I finally located the address and made my way up in the elevator. Wesley's loft was on a high floor of a pre-war building, and he opened the door himself. There were no agents or managers or security. He was pleasant but reserved. This was the star of *White Men Can't Jump, Demolition Man, New Jack City, Passenger 57, Money Train, Rising Sun* and many others. A legit movie star sitting casually on his zebra couch in a beautiful room appointed with heavy African decor.

Wesley had questions about the script and the tone. He knew political thrillers were popular, but I could tell that something was holding him back. He thought *Executive Privilege* was too confusing, a bit overwritten, and not enough action. He was not sold on the project. (P.S. He was not wrong about many of these criticisms.) I knew that if I left this room without Wesley on board, the project would be toast. Warner Brothers would just find him another script.

I needed to change the direction of the meeting—and fast. Knowing Wesley might be a tough sell, I had brought along a VHS copy of *Marked for Death* as a kind of Plan B. I took the video out of my black work bag and placed it on the coffee table. I turned to Wesley and said, "If you want to get a sense of what *Executive Privilege* might look like, you're welcome to keep this copy of *Marked for Death* and have a look at it."

Wesley saw the familiar red cover with the silhouette of Steven Seagal and he sat up straight. "You made this?" he asked with some excitement.

"Yeah, man, it's *Marked for Death*," I casually answered.

"I know what it is," Wesley said, "The brothers loved this movie."

Of course, by "brothers" he meant the African American community. "Steven Seagal is a bad motherfucker," he smiled.

"We can have a hit like this," I said, trying to keep his enthusiasm going, "We just have to pump up the action in the next draft."

* * *

I always found it a little strange that *Marked for Death* had so much support from the African American audience, and yet we were often criticized by white reviewers for being "racist" because the Jamaican bad guys were … well, Jamaican. I have worked very closely for many years with African American colleagues; writers, actors, craft technicians, drivers, executives, producers, you name it, and never had the feeling that whites and blacks hated each other. The media pushes the narrative that we are all racists; but I think it's a con job to create conflict, generate outrage and get ratings. Most people in show biz, I would say 90 percent, are respectful, grateful and appreciative of everyone's contributions and friendship. Anyway, that's my experience, as naïve as it may sound.

* * *

I was astonished that Wesley knew about *Free Willy 2* (a bomb), and maybe about *Rapid Fire* (a bomb), but didn't know about my hit, *Marked for Death*. (Never assume that your agents are going to do their job. You are your own best and often *only* salesman.)

When Wesley picked the videotape up off the coffee table, the whole tone of the meeting changed. He wanted more information on *Executive Privilege*. He asked about possible co-stars, where the movie might be shot,

Six. Three Strikes and You're Out

and when we were set to start. These were now the questions of somebody who was seriously thinking about doing this movie.

I decided to vacate the apartment as quickly as possible while he was still upbeat. I told him I had an event to go to at Lincoln Center, and that I hoped he would decide to be "Harlan Regis," the lead detective. "Leave them wanting more," as the old show biz saying goes.

The television soap opera *The Guiding Light* was having an anniversary celebration party and I was going. My wife at that time, M.J. McDonnell, was the youngest woman ever to direct a daytime network television show, and one of the first female directors in the genre. Everyone was dressed beautifully, and the setting was elegant. It seemed that even this little corner of the entertainment business had its very glamorous moment.

I had never seen so many pretty faces packed into one space, not even in L.A. However, behind the glamor, it was easy to see, as an outsider to this world, the reality of the actual occasion. There was endless jockeying for position, constant flattery, snubs and seductions as careers were enriched or stalled. The older soap opera stars were mostly the center of attention, trying to hang on to their 15 minutes, until the young beautiful ingenues and their publicists arrived; then the swarm of cameras shifted to the fresh and new.

Even the guests clustered to the brightest new lights, just like in Hollywood. The planets always revolve around the sun and other bright stars.

But my mind was not really focused on the jostling for power at a soap opera party. I was pondering my own future with the upcoming yes or no from Wesley Snipes. I felt positive about the meeting, but I had been fooled too many times before to start celebrating. As the Tom Petty song goes, "The waiting is the hardest part."

The next day dragged on. I kept checking my messages to see if anyone had phoned. Then, late in the afternoon, a call came in from Arnold. Wesley was in! He liked the meeting. At last, some good news.

Arnold told me to keep working on the script, because the movie was now a "blinking" green light. We still needed to land the female Secret Service agent and the bad guy.

It was terrifying to think that this whole movie might not be going forward if I hadn't brought a copy of that old film with me. Such a slender thread held my career together.

We screen-tested several actresses for the part of Nina Chance. We read well-known names like Kelly Preston, Anne Heche and Marisa Tomei. I had my heart set on Diane Lane, and I finally got to meet her for lunch in Beverly Hills.

Diane did not want to play "the girl," which was understandable. I explained to her that this was not a "love story" relationship or flirtation part. This was an equal partnership between a cop and a Secret Service agent, and she'd have plenty of action of her own.

She was in.

Finally, Arnold put me on the phone with Alan Alda to help persuade him that his part would not be a clichéd villain, but rather a career Intelligence man who was 100 percent sure he was doing the right thing for his country. This was Alan Alda! I was not going to be able to bullshit this legend, but I did sell him a little "sizzle," as Sandy Howard had taught me years before. I told him we were making *Three Days of the Condor* and needed a "Max von Sydow" to balance the movie. Von Sydow was one of the world's great actors and I figured this comparison would appeal to Alda, who never really got to play a bad guy. No actor is above flattery. No director either, for that matter.

The director wears many hats, and selling big stars on your movie is one of the most difficult. You have to be complimentary but not over-flatter. Enthusiastic yet realistic. Confident but not arrogant. With Wesley, Diane and finally Alan all on board, we were ready to go.

The budget was crunched, dates were moved up, script notes poured in; but we were still making the movie.

The real question now was: What kind of movie did I want to make? With any script, the director has many different approaches to choose from. It is the director who has to have the vision for the "look" of the movie and set the tone.

Was this a gritty *French Connection*-style docudrama about a killing in the White House? Maybe a glossy thriller like Tony or Ridley Scott would make? When it comes down to style and approach, it is often *time* that will dictate many of the creative choices. Since this was a studio movie, I'd have more days to shoot than an independent feature. But once

Dwight Little and Alan Alda filming *Murder at 1600*.

Six. Three Strikes and You're Out

you have big stars, the pace slows down by half and the shooting time ends up being about the same.

Here is a sample of how the director might plan his day and approach the agreed upon style: Let's say you have three scenes to do on a particular day. In the morning, a scene in an interrogation room; a "two-hander." Blocking will be easy since the actors are sitting at a table. Lighting should be straightforward since it is a controlled set. By this time, you have arrived at a lighting concept with your DP. Did you decide the story would be best served by moody noirish lighting with deep shadows and hard blacks? Maybe natural lighting with outside light entering through the windows and a little soft "fill" for the actors' eyes. Or "studio lighting" where the actors are lit to look their very best and their most glamorous at all times. But wait. What about "documentary lighting" where only practical lights are used: lamps, overhead fluorescents, flashlights. The lighting plan has to be consistent all through the movie. The chosen style of lighting will influence the pace of the shooting, so figuring this out with the DP is important both artistically and from a production point of view.

While the lights are going up, there will be many questions from the stars about their motivations and decisions. Explaining everything to their satisfaction will take time. Let's say you and your first AD allow five hours for the interrogation room scene. This assumes that the star will be on time and know the lines and not question or argue about every little thing. (You must know your script inside and out and be able to answer *every* question.)

So now let's assume the following: If it takes two hours to set up, light and rehearse the scene, and two hours to shoot the standard coverage of masters, close-ups and over-the-shoulders, then there might be one hour left to do something a little out of the ordinary. I call these more creative shots "specials," and I try to work at least one or two into every scene. If I had only three hours to shoot this same scene (say in television, where everything must go faster than with films), then I'd have to get the coverage but be out of time for anything else. The studio or network will always expect proper close-ups of their million-dollar actors.

A "special" might be an ECU (extreme close-up), say of ice in a cocktail glass. The ice goes into the glass, the actor takes the glass to his lips, sips the drink and looks over, reacting to a sound at the door. The camera has to follow all this in ECU so the focus is "pulled" to keep the long lens sharp at each stage. This kind of close-up can really increase the tension of a scene, but it is very time-consuming to achieve. The actor, operator and focus puller have to be in complete sync or the shot will be "buzzed" (out of focus).

A well-known example of a "special" is evident in the opening title sequence of *Murder at 1600*. I suspended a camera on a crane looking down at an extra-large oak dining table. The actor playing a maintenance man, had polishing towels wrapped on his knees, hands and feet. Then he "swims" across the surface to do the dusting and polishing of the huge table. This shot was much discussed by film fans. It took hours to accomplish. The "style" of the shot was only possible because we luckily found the time to do it.

* * *

Paul Greengrass is a director who came up making documentaries like *Bloody Sunday* about the Irish "troubles." When he directed the *Bourne Identity* movies, he brought a relentless, hand-held, shaky camera style to the films. Even the dialogue scenes were hand-held.

Greengrass was able to pull off this look to great effect because everything is unsettled in the *Bourne* movie world. Action, fights, double crosses, sabotage. The "look" of the *Bourne* films was so successful that many other directors copied this approach for years. Shaky hand-held camerawork was suddenly applied to multiple movies for no particular reason—and it just didn't work. The style of a movie has to fit the material. Period.

Ridley Scott and Michael Bay come from the world of commercials and their images reflect a kind of constant seduction. Backlight streams in from everywhere all the time—smoke, rain, telephoto lenses, filters, etc.— the exact opposite of Paul Greengrass. These directors each have a certain style, and the producers generally expect their signature look when they hire them. A producer wouldn't hire Wes Anderson (*The Royal Tenenbaums*) and expect the finished film to look like it was directed by Danny Boyle (*Slumdog Millionaire*).

* * *

So … imagine the interrogation scene is done a little before lunch (only 30 minutes over schedule), and the afternoon's work lies ahead. We will be shooting the exterior of a police station. The movie's two stars, Snipes and Lane, arrive outside their precinct building and have to walk through a throng of reporters to get into their offices—all the while bantering with story exposition.

Some of the crew members start moving the equipment outside (we still have 20 minutes before lunch), and I tell the camera and grip departments where I want the crane to go. (Cranes are very time-consuming because the camera has to be attached to the "jib arm" in a very particular way.) The soaring camera will be operated from a video monitor on the stage floor below. The grips will work through lunch so that the crane will be ready first up after the break.

Six. Three Strikes and You're Out

* * *

My first encounter with a crane was on the Bruce Jenner movie *Can't Stop the Music*. The Village People were having a free concert in San Francisco and I was with the behind-the-scenes unit filming alongside the main movie unit as the concert proceeded. The auditorium was packed with gay men who were very high on amyl nitrates (or poppers) and myriad other drugs, and the crowd was, as they say, "going wild."

I was a young associate producer with the documentary crew, pushing through the throngs carrying an ARRI handheld 16mm camera, trying to get some B-roll shots of the stage. Many of the men wore leather pants with the backs cut out so that their asses were showing. There were chains and leather whips and all kinds of odd S&M wardrobe on display. I suddenly felt myself being grabbed on the crotch and humped on like a dog, even though I had a camera on my shoulder. This was unchecked male sexual energy literally on steroids. I was feeling some concern about my safety when I looked up and saw a Louma Crane (remote control camera arm) swing into action just over my head. The sweeping camera was being retrieved by a camera team from the main unit so that the Panavision camera could be reloaded.

I shook off some of my assaulters in the crowd, brushed past other rowdy partygoers and climbed a nearby scaffold. When I reached the top, I called out to the crew guys. I told them I was with the "featurette unit" and asked, could I please stay up with them, high above the crowd, for a while? They quickly saw my situation and gave me a hand up. I spent the rest of the concert safely up off the floor with the crane operators. And I have been very partial to cranes ever since!

* * *

By lunch, the extras have already eaten, and the second ADs carefully block and organize them so that they'll make the most impact in front of the lens. One hundred extras can look like many hundreds with the right lenses and choreography.

Assume you and your AD have allowed five hours for this second scene of the day. The crane shot will have to be done multiple times for timing and focus and will test the actors' patience. So, an hour and a half for the master crane shot—and then three and a half more hours to do all the dialogue as the heroes pass through the crowd. Better not to lay dolly track for the dialogue since this will take time and the extras will trip over the metal tracks. Here is a good opportunity to have the Steadicam "pre-rigged"; you can jump right into the dialogue work with the actors after the crane shot. The second camera, from the crane, can be taken down and put into "handheld mode" for crowd reactions.

When it gets dark, there is still one more scene left to shoot with your hero on the phone on a street corner. If you've made your schedule so far, then you'll have two hours to grab this last shot, assuming you're going to stick to a 12-hour day plus lunch.

During lunch, you ran over to this location and "spotted" where the "picture car" should be parked and where the scene would be played. The electric crew will then be able to lay down the cable and pre-light the area before you get to location and save you some time for shooting. This dance goes on all day every day. (There is no time to sit in your trailer and catch your breath, even at lunch.)

Furthermore, if you don't make your day, if you don't complete all your assigned scenes, you will get a call from the head of the studio in the morning and he will "rip you a new one."

Given my 45-day shooting schedule and major stars, I decided I wanted to make a movie like the one I'd pitched to Alan Alda: *Three Days of the Condor*, a "stylish" movie, but not "stylized." Director Sydney Pollack (*Out of Africa*, *Tootsie*) was a genius at this. His camera was always in the right place at the right time and doing something interesting. At the beginning of *Three Days of the Condor*, there is a shot where an umbrella is placed in a trash can in the foreground of a street scene. Then the camera "pulls focus" to reveal that this has been a signal to a man across the street that the assassination attack on the office building is a go. It's not backlit rain (Tony Scott), or blue reflections in the lens (JJ Abrams), or soft orbs of colored light (Adriane Lynne), or lyrical dolly push-ins (Steven Spielberg), it's just a thought-out, interesting shot that tells the story.

I knew I was making a mainstream studio thriller, and I had a plan to make it "stylish" wherever I could. But then, as Mike Tyson said, "Everyone has a plan until they get punched in the mouth."

One early day in Washington, D.C., I really boxed myself into a corner. For the opening shot of the movie, I wanted an American flag to be flying right in front of the lens; then the camera would crane down to reveal a blocked intersection with a crazed gunman threatening to kill himself. There would be cops and bystanders everywhere. News crews and helicopters, the whole urban crazy. I designed this shot so that Wesley Snipes wouldn't have to be in it and I could take two hours to achieve it. This was the first shot of the movie and I didn't want to rush him or waste his time.

Since this was D.C., five different agencies plus the city had to sign off on our being there at the plaza, and the most we could get was one day of filming. We had to get permission from Justice, Treasury, Commerce, FBI and, get this, the Bureau of Indian Affairs. It was Washington Mayor Marion Barry who pushed it through—mostly because he wanted to meet Wesley Snipes.

Six. Three Strikes and You're Out

* * *

Barry had been elected mayor twice, and he was a larger-than-life political figure. A Civil Rights leader, Barry had been at the forefront of many of the Equal Rights movements of the '60s and '70s. He had been an accomplished academic in chemistry before pursuing politics; grew up in a very divided South and overcame mountains of prejudice and discrimination. It was unfortunate that his legacy was tarnished by a crack cocaine scandal, which is the one event that many people remember him for. Growing up, I was always reminded by my father: "Try not to judge people by their worst moment ... but, if you can, by their best moment."

* * *

The problem was, there was no wind at all, and the whole point of the shot was that the flag would be flapping in the breeze and create that iconic moment which would tee up the whole movie: a murder in the White House. We would literally wait at the monitor and if a gust of wind started, we'd roll the camera and try to move off the flag quickly—but no luck. In order to save the location for the day and to get Wesley's work done, I might have to give up my opening flag shot.

The special effects captain had overheard the various conversations and he approached me. "Give me 20 minutes and I can figure this out," he said.

I didn't have 20 minutes but I said okay, hoping I wouldn't lose my job over this. Once again, tens of thousands of dollars were being spent every hour.

I decided I should use the time to rehearse the scene itself where a disgruntled bureaucrat threatens to kill

Dwight Little and Marion Barry filming *Murder at 1600.*

himself and is saved by the quick thinking of our hero. I told my first AD, "Ask Wesley to come up for rehearsal."

There were two base camps on this movie. One, about a mile away in a parking lot, was for the cast and crew, with trailers and trucks and catering. There was another, completely different base camp that we called Wesleyville, where all of Mr. Snipes' people were. Gym, catering, wardrobe, production trailer, pop-out trailers, security, the works. Wesley's security was handled by some trained members of Louis Farrakhan's Nation of Islam security team. These guards went with him everywhere. I figured it would take 20 minutes for Wesley to get up to set anyway.

* * *

The Nation of Islam was a political and religious movement that presented itself mostly as an African-American empowerment group. The problem was that there were multiple expressions of anti–Semitism that seemed to be a part of their teachings. They held Jews accountable for participation in the African slave trade, had referred to Jews as "termites" and floated some Holocaust denial ideas. The group's leaders had largely denied these allegations, but they were pretty much in the public record. In any event, Wesley seemed very involved with their organization, and although I am not Jewish, our DP was and there was unnecessary friction because of it. My job was to keep everybody working together towards one goal, but the air was often thick with suspicion.

* * *

The special effects captain put a very thin wire along the top of the American flag that would artificially help support it. Then he put a medium-size wind machine up on a scaffold just out of the camera shot. When he turned on the wind machine, it would flutter the flag, which was already partially supported by the wire. (We should have done this from the beginning!) The flag went up the pole for a test and it more or less worked.

"Let's shoot it," I cried, hoping that Wesley wouldn't be too mad if he got up to set and we weren't ready for him. (Calling a star to set when you're not really ready is a *number one* no-no that directors must avoid. Sydney Pollack once said, "Stars are like thoroughbreds ... they are high-strung, and finicky, and injure easily. But when they run, it's a beautiful thing to see."

I was able to finally get some version of my opening shot that I thought I could live with. I looked around for Wesley to start a rehearsal. Where *is* he, dammit?

The first AD said he hadn't shown up yet; and we had called him

Six. Three Strikes and You're Out

45 minutes ago. It was already late morning, I had indulged my opening shot, and we were never coming back to this location. I ignored the advice of Jerry Ziesmer from the Steven Seagal days, and decided to go get Mr. Snipes myself. My ego could no longer be a factor. My future power or control over the movie didn't matter. I had to make this day, or I'd be fired.

A transportation van dropped me off at Wesleyville. I went past the gauntlet of production people and approached his huge punch-out trailer. There was a military-looking security man standing at the door. He was Wesley's private bodyguard and a member of the Nation of Islam.

I told the man, "I am the director and it's important that I speak with Mr. Snipes right away." I was very direct and clear with him. "Not in ten minutes, not when he's available ... *now*."

He took a long hard look at me to gauge my character. We locked eyes. After a moment, he said, "Wait here," and went inside the trailer.

When he came back out, he was relaxed and not at all confrontational. "Sure, go on in." He gestured to the open door.

* * *

My maternal grandfather was a six-foot-two Irishman by the name of James Murphy. I am almost always calm and accommodating, and I believe you always get more mileage with sugar than vinegar. But when something gets my Irish up, I just don't back down. This can be an asset when you've had enough of being pushed around, but it is also a liability because it is possible to piss off some higher-up.

There was one time when a writer insulted me during a pitch meeting and I stood up and squared off with him fully ready to "go there." The horrified executives intervened and the meeting ended. I was never invited back to that company. It's not about being a tough guy, sometimes it's just about standing your ground.

* * *

I went into Wesley's trailer and down at the very end where the bedroom was, I saw him very calmly playing a video game. He seemed intensely involved.

"What up?" he asked as if my entire life was not hanging in the balance.

"Wesley," I started, "we're all set up for you. We just got a great shot for the opening of the movie and I need your scene. Because of the politics, you know we can't come back out here."

He looked at me briefly like we had all the time in the world. "Oh, you ready?" he said casually.

"Yep, all set," I replied calmly.

He acted like production hadn't been calling him for the last 45 minutes and this was the first time he was hearing about it.

Now this was a very smart man with tons of movie experience, so clearly, this was all just some kind of game or maybe a weird power move. But I did have one card to play, and I played it: "The mayor is up there, by the way, and he'd love to see us shoot in his city."

This got Wesley's attention. I knew Marion Barry was due on set any time, and even though he hadn't shown up yet, I was rolling the dice that he'd be there when we got back.

"Marion Barry?" His eyes lit up.

"Yeah," I shrugged. "The mayor."

"Yeah, I know who he is," Wesley said as he put down his controller. I could tell he was moving now and would be coming up to set.

"Okay, thank you, Wesley" I said. "I'll meet you up there for a quick rehearsal."

On the way out, I thanked the security man, who was very pleasant, and a man I would lean on for help with Wesley many times during the production.

When I got up to the set, to my amazement, Marion Barry *was* there, and I wouldn't look like a liar. I had gambled and won. When Wesley and his entourage arrived, another half-hour got killed while he chatted with the mayor. These were two powerful African-American men, one from the world of politics and one from the world of movies. They greeted each other like two heads of state.

I put Barry in my director's chair and offered him my headphones. He seemed very pleased. And as long as the mayor of Washington D.C., was sitting there, no one was going to fuck with us.

It was one o'clock by the time we finally got to the scene. All the lunches had to be "walking lunches," since we had limited daylight. By now, the cop cars were set, the extras blocked and rehearsed, the cameras in position with various lenses and points of view. And not only was Wesley there but also the great comedian, Dennis Miller, who was playing the sidekick. (Dennis had done lots of stand-up and hosted "Weekend Update" on *Saturday Night Live*.)

After the first rehearsal, I went to give Dennis a note on his character. He asked, "Dude, do you want more or less Dennis Miller? That's all I've got."

A pretty clear answer from a guy who knew who he was.

* * *

Dennis had a very sharp mind and he was always "on." But he was not very comfortable with physical action and he was, after all, playing a cop. One night on stage, Dennis was supposed to bring out his gun and return fire toward a bad guy who had discovered our heroes in a White House tunnel. I was doing take after take trying to get Dennis to hold the gun properly. Wesley was on stage watching all this.

"Jesus, Miller," he finally said, "you just gotta hold your piece better than that."

Dennis was completely unfazed. He looked right back at Wesley and didn't miss a beat:

"Yeah, Wesley," he said, "me holding a gun is like you hosting a talk show."

It was so funny and so biting that even Wesley knew he'd been owned. When working around that kind of firecracker wit, you better be on your toes.

* * *

When he finally went to work that crazy afternoon in D.C., Wesley was perfect. He was funny and charismatic. He knew his lines and added some great ones of his own. He was a thoroughbred and now he was running. I had somehow managed to get him out in front of the cameras for five hours of shooting and that was enough. The scene *played* and the studio loved the dailies. I was going to live to fight another day.

Things sailed along pretty smoothly from that point forward until a regular Monday morning about halfway through the shoot. Up until then, Wesley had been *mostly* on time (30 to 40 minutes late by my watch); and though he was not exactly easy to work with, he was not impossible either. That Monday, he was in a dark place. He wouldn't chat with Diane Lane or with me. He was just far off and not happy. He seemed to be playing the scenes by the numbers, which was not like him. At lunch, I mentioned Wesley's bad mood to several people in production, but no one was aware of any changes that might be affecting him. I also sought out Wesley's driver and stand-in and decided to ask them if they had a clue what was up.

It turned out Wesley had shot a movie with Robert De Niro called *The Fan*. It was directed by Tony Scott and was expected to be a big hit. *The Fan* was going to get Wesley a solid spot up on the "A" list. I hadn't been following the release, but it turned out the movie had come out the Friday before … and bombed. I think Wesley had all the air taken out of his sails. This was a big studio film with a big co-star and because it flopped, Wesley was in a nosedive.

One of our East Coast ADs had worked on the film. He said that Tony Scott had insisted on shooting a big night baseball game in the rain. The producers and crew explained to him that in America, baseball is not played in the rain. The field is covered with tarps and everyone waits until the rain has passed before they continue.

Wesley Snipes and Daniel Benzali filming *Murder at 1600*.

But Scott wouldn't budge. He thought it would look cool. Scott was from England and he just didn't understand the nature of "America's favorite pastime" with its hundred-year-old traditions.

The AD was convinced that this mistake was why the film flopped. Details matter and sometimes things need to do better than just "look cool."

My communication with the star started to break down. What began as a very good working relationship was now strained. Wesley would not listen to notes or suggestions and, more alarmingly, was just going through the motions. I had a good relationship with Wesley's stunt double, Jeff, and I finally asked him, "What's going on?"

He explained, "Wesley is in a strange, troubled place, and has become uncomfortable taking direction from you while his posse is around watching."

I was shocked and I didn't know what would have brought this on, since we had been doing fine for weeks. I didn't think I could make a good movie without being able to talk openly and creatively with the lead actor. Was it the Nation of Islam thing? Did he assume I was Jewish? I never found out.

I asked Jeff what he thought I should do. Jeff suggested, "Give all your instructions to me, and I'll communicate them to Wesley."

It would look to the cast and crew like Wesley was just talking to his stunt guy and not the white dude director. I agreed to try this approach. From then on, Wesley did every single thing that was asked of him as long as he was being spoken to by Jeff and not me.

Six. Three Strikes and You're Out

Did I care? No. I was getting everything I needed. I'd say something to Jeff like, "I need Wesley to come down this ladder as fast as he can ... stop at the first laundry station ... steal some clothes off the rack ... then duck in behind the guard."

Sometimes in rehearsal, Jeff would do the action and actually say the lines. We would set all the cameras, then Wesley would come in and do the exact same thing. I still don't really know for sure what was bothering him, but Jeff had performed a miracle and the movie kept going.

There is no way to see the unexpected curve balls coming. That's why they are called unexpected.

One night after shooting, I found myself in Diane Lane's trailer with a bunch of her friends who were also in Toronto shooting: Rob Lowe, Tate Donavan, Emilio Estevez (who I already knew) and some other lesser-known actors. They were hanging out, telling stories and partying; and I was there with them. These were actors that were part of what would come to be known as the Brat Pack. From *The Outsiders* to *Young Guns* and *About Last Night* (and many others), they were the center of the universe for a short while. When you think about going to Hollywood when you are very young, this is the exact fantasy that enters your mind. One day you will be the director of a studio movie hanging out with movie stars, partying after a long day's shoot. Now you're one of the cool kids, right?

The reality is that when you are the director, you don't get to be a cool kid. You are weighed down with so much responsibility that you can't just *fit in*. While they laughed and shared gossip, I had to head home to deal with the next day, or the train would come off the rails, and that derailed train would hit me. Questions to answer.

> "The prop man needs to know where Alan Alda will be shot and how bloody you want the 'squibs'" (exploding blood bags).
>
> "Wardrobe only has three shirts, so if you need more, she has to shop for them tonight."
>
> "When Diane gets shot, do you want a cable pull, or a tramp?" (trampoline)
>
> "Special effects wants to know if you need any practical lasers for 'actor reference' during the break-in, or is it all going to be done in post? And if you do need them, you have to stop by the stage tonight and show the art department where you want them."

My assistant said I had to sign off on a cut of the "discovery of the body" scene so that it could be sent to the Warner Brothers studio head. Lorenzo wanted to see it. There were two casting tapes to review and selections had to be made for Friday. New cast measurements needed to get to wardrobe ASAP. Also, there was a problem with the "B" camera focus

Diane Lane and Dwight Little filming *Murder at 1600*.

in the previous day's dailies. "Can you use what we have? Or do we have to reshoot? Plus, you need to pick the temp music cues for the promo trailer…"

And on and on it goes. Script notes to answer, political fires to put out, feathers to unruffle. Long talks with the lab. There is no time to hang out with the cool kids. It was a nice idea, though. I said a quick and early goodbye and bailed out of Diane's trailer.

As production wound down, the studio was high on the dailies, but also felt something seemed to be missing. Lorenzo asked our producer Arnold Kopelson, "What can we do to have even more excitement for the trailer?" Arnold replied immediately: "You need a fucking *helicopter* and something to *blow up*."

Arnold told me he'd never really had a successful movie without a helicopter: *Platoon*, *The Fugitive*, *Se7en*. He also knew we had to have an explosion in the trailers and TV spots in order to get asses in the seats. All these years later, this was no different than what Sandy Howard used to

Six. Three Strikes and You're Out

say about his movies: "More guns, more explosions, more helicopters … and hot girls!" (The recent wave of programming at Netflix seems to indicate that, whatever the delivery system, the old Hollywood entertainment rules still apply.)

I received a phone call from Lorenzo: "We have an extra $500,000 we are going to add to the budget. We want you to shoot a sequence with a helicopter and come up with a way to have a big explosion in the sequence. Figure it out." *CLICK!*

So, now what to do? The studio wanted to spend more money (a good sign) but adding a helicopter and explosion at this late date seemed very arbitrary. After several false starts with multiple writers, we finally came up with a way for the Secret Service to chase Wesley and Diane from their hiding place in a motel room. The Secret Service would use a helicopter with a searchlight (like a real-life high-speed chase). Our heroes would shoot out the gas tank of an FBI car to create a diversion, and *voila*: big explosion!

We talked to the Toronto stunt team and they knew good people locally who could execute a stunt and explosion like this. The bigger problem was that there was a scene with Wesley and Alan Alda that would directly follow the chase, and it had already been shot. I looked at the cut footage of that scene and changed things around so that we stayed in wide shots longer. We would have to change all the dialogue with ADR (additional dialogue recording, also known as looping) and explain the new helicopter explosion scene before matching back into the close-ups. After much agonizing, we finally figured out how to plan, shoot and edit this new helicopter-explosion sequence to fit seamlessly into the movie.

The biggest obstacle turned out to be the weather on the night we were shooting. The location was down at the edge of Lake Ontario and the temperature had plummeted. It was so cold, we couldn't actually record sound: Every time the camera or sound people would move on the frozen ground, it crunched and sounded like firecrackers. The actors' wardrobe was barely enough to keep them warm for two minutes at a time. The wind whipped up so strong across the lake that the helicopter pilot had to wait for it to calm down before he could fly. Somehow, one shot at a time, we managed to put the pieces together. Wesley was super-friendly this time and acted like there had never been any kind of problem. Don't ask me.

All was well at wrap. We finished one day over schedule and almost on budget. It was time to go home to L.A.

Post-production was put into overdrive because the studio wanted to get the movie out in January or early February, and it was already October. Money was being spent for additional assistant editors, sound designers and general overtime hours.

We screened an editor's cut at the Warner Hollywood studios, and the movie played slow. Slow might be okay for European art films, but it was a disaster for a mainstream studio thriller. A lot of that expensive dialogue the studio agonized over had to go. The movie was too talky.

I was in the cutting room every day. I knew, like Dick Donner had once said: "The movie is in there somewhere." I would just have to find it.

It was nice to be back in L.A. and away from the daily obsession of shooting. There was a little time to reconnect with friends and family and re-energize for the post-production battles ahead.

One evening I was invited to attend the yearly meeting at the DGA for feature film directors. The event is held in the DGA building on Sunset. There is no press permitted, and spouses and partners are not invited so directors really do show up. I was enjoying cocktails with some of my heroes: Paul Mazursky, Michael Mann, John Carpenter, Jon Favreau, Robert Wise, Steven Spielberg and many others. They were just mingling around and talking shop. I was so proud to be there amongst them.

Some of these big directors wanted to talk to me—they wanted to know about Steven Seagal! There was a strange fascination with Steven that even captured the interest of these power players. The Aikido, the CIA, the mobsters are much more interesting than just another actor who had made it out of drama school.

I had one story I told, which was true, that everyone seemed to enjoy. At events like this, having a good story is a big plus. I described how late one night in an alley in downtown L.A., we were waiting for some lighting to be completed. At the end of the alley, there was a pile of restaurant garbage with a hoard of rats foraging in and around it. Production was trying to find a way to clear out the rats when Steven suddenly appeared with a pellet gun. He did his signature two-fisted grip and proceeded to unload on the rats. He picked them off one by one. This was from a considerable distance and his marksmanship was crazy good. He never missed. The crew and I stood there and watched this massacre in amazement. Clearly Steven had been doing something with his life besides just acting.

Now that I was the director of a mainstream studio movie, there were producers who wanted to develop scripts with me. *Broken Arrow* had been turned into a successful movie, so why not? I started to work on a Revolutionary War picture at Mel Gibson's company, Icon Films. Called *Revere*, it kind of reimagined Paul Revere as an action hero. *Revere* was never made, but Gibson used some of the ideas in his later film *Patriot*, also set during the Revolutionary War.

The only thing I really remember about the intense Mr. Gibson was that every time he took a hit from his cigarette, he would hold the smoke in so long that by the time he exhaled, the smoke was all gone. It was weird.

He was looking for a heroic vehicle for himself, and the real Paul Revere story was too complicated, too difficult to buy into, not easily digestible into a Hollywood action movie.

At New Line, I was attached to *Deep Blue*, a submarine movie written by a Washington, D.C., journalist who was repped by CAA. It was a revamped version of *Crimson Tide* and *The Hunt for Red October*. The studio was a complete hornet's nest of insider politics, but they did get movies made. New Line sent a draft of the script to Tommy Lee Jones. The note we got back was: "Mr. Jones always thought of submarines as bathtub toys, and couldn't really wrap his head around the subject."

That was a remark we didn't see coming.

At Fox, I was assigned to an action adventure project called *Tears of the Sun*, about four kidnapped Americans enslaved and forced to work in Brazilian gold mines. They all escape but only two survive. It could have been very good, but it was too expensive. I went to these meetings when I could get away from the editing room on *1600*.

Development meetings are a necessary but bizarre Hollywood ritual. There are certain buzzwords that the development execs often use to push a project forward: "We need to raise the stakes, go deeper into character, add a ticking clock, make the lead more sympathetic, find a better second act twist," and on and on. It seems like they have all read the same three books about screenwriting that are available at Barnes and Noble.

My favorite titles are *Save the Cat* by Blake Snyder, which is simple and helpful, and *The Art of Dramatic Writing* by Lajos Egri, written in 1946, which is the gold standard in this field, even today. It is best to take "studying" about writing with a big grain of salt. It is a bit like "studying" to learn how to swim. The right strokes, the correct kicks, the best breathing ... sooner or later you are just going to have to jump in the pool and almost drown. When you don't drown, you'll suddenly realize you've learned how to swim ... unless of course you drowned.

There was one producer on the Warner Brothers lot, Joel Silver, who had a system known as the "Whammy Meter." Joel had produced the huge action movies *Die Hard*, *Lethal Weapon*, *Predator* and *The Matrix*, so he couldn't be completely wrong. His idea was that the audience needed a Whammy every ten minutes. A Whammy was often a huge explosion. But it also could be a big car chase or maybe a shoot-out. A Whammy could even be a sex scene if it was exciting enough. Suspense might be a Whammy, if the sequence ended with a big scare. As a script was developed, Joel insisted on one of these *Whammys* every ten pages, or else he just wasn't interested.

Generally, it is up to the writer and the director to figure out how to address all these notes since the executives are just "spit-balling" and giving you the "bad example." The best thing to do is agree with most of what is said in the room, nod a lot, and scribble down notes that you will toss in the trash as soon as you get home. Drafts are delivered and notes are written up by the "creative group." More drafts are delivered, followed by more notes. This can go on for a year or more before the script is finally approved to either go out to "talent" (actors and directors) or just be shelved. This is why the process is often called "development hell." Usually the script is just thrown out and they start all over again with new writers.

Finally, after eight furious weeks, we finished a cut of *Murder at 1600* that I felt pretty good about. I was working with two master editors, Billy Webber (*Days of Thunder, Midnight Run*) and Leslie Jones (*The Thin Red Line*). Both were insightful and had good instincts, but sometimes we'd all disagree on something in a particular scene or sequence. Since I am the one with the movie in my head from the beginning, it's important that I follow my instincts, even when my colleagues might see it differently. If the director has a consistent point of view from pre-production and casting, through shooting and post-production, then there is a good chance the movie will feel like a whole piece. Sometimes, when movies feel like a mess, especially in the theater, it's because too many people had fingers in the pie.

The Warner Brothers marketing department set up a recruited screening in one of the bigger theaters on 3rd Street in Santa Monica (a pedestrian shopping and eating mall). The executives wanted to see what they had. I sat about two-thirds of the way back in the taped-off area of the theater. Bob Daley sat right next to me and I wondered if he remembered that I was the guy who had once come to him with a "whale problem." Probably not. Terry Semel, Warner Brothers' co-president, was there as well. Arnold Kopelson of course was there with all his people. There were marketing people, executives assigned to *Murder at 1600* from both Regency and Warner Brothers, and a few publicists and studio assistants. It is the studio's millions of dollars on the line, and they are looking at you not to lose it for them. No pressure there.

When you see a movie in front of an audience for the first time, you realize that you don't control the movie at all. It is now theirs (the audience's) ... not yours. The audience doesn't know who fought with who, or how cold a particular night was, or anything at all about what you have lived through. It is just 100+ minutes of a story. Fun? Suspenseful? Exciting? Hopefully, a little of all three.

Big surprise: There were more laughs in the film than I realized. They were good laughs too. Good laughs are people laughing *with* the movie and not *at* it. Wesley and Diane had some good banter back and forth; and Dennis Miller had some funny lines that played better than I thought they

Six. Three Strikes and You're Out

would. The movie barely dragged at all, which is hard to accomplish since second acts in a dramatic thriller are so hard to pull off without the pace lagging.

There was a "button" (generally a kind of punchline) at the end of the film where Wesley asks the president of the United States for help with his housing problem. It was funny, and we had set the joke up at the very beginning. Most gags work best when you can apply the "rule of threes." That is, when you set up the joke first, then expand on it second, and pay it off third.

In our case, we find out in Act One that Wesley's landlord is going to throw him out of his apartment, along with all his precious artwork, if he doesn't get help from the government. In the second act, Wesley asks the Speaker of the House at a Washington dinner function if maybe he can help, but he just gets the runaround. The third and final part of the gag (the payoff): Wesley gets a chance to ask the president himself, and finally gets some action. It worked as an upbeat "button" to the movie.

The screening went well but we wouldn't see the cards until the following day. Bob Daley said something like, "Good job," and then quickly left, as did all the other execs. I couldn't find Arnold Kopelson, so I didn't really know how everyone felt. I think they didn't want to express an opinion until they had seen the cards.

At the studio the next day, there was some buzz that there had been an encouraging screening in Santa Monica of a little Wesley Snipes programmer. Thirty-eight million dollars (before marketing) was a small budget for a big studio. The cards came in around midday and Arnold told me we were in the high 80s for "very good or excellent," so the studio was happy. I was relieved beyond belief. But the very fact that we'd had a good public screening actually turned out to be our undoing.

Warners' biggest star with the longest history at the studio was Clint Eastwood. He had his own company, Malpaso, with a building-bungalow on the lot. While we were making *Murder at 1600*, Eastwood was directing and starring in his own White House thriller, *Absolute Power*. It was based on a bestseller and had a stellar cast: Gene Hackman, Ed Harris, Scott Glenn, Laura Linney, Judy Davis and more. I'd been told from the very beginning that I shouldn't worry about *Absolute Power* since they were planning to release it in the spring-summer—the "Clint Eastwood slot." We were being marketed to come out quietly in the dead zone, movie graveyard of January, well before *Absolute Power*.

Several Malpaso executives heard through the grapevine that Warners' "other" White House movie had tested well and they brought this to Clint's attention. As far as I know. this might have been the first time he'd even heard about us. In any event, Mr. Eastwood promptly walked into

Bob Daley's office and made it clear that *Murder at 1600* would be pushed back and released *after Absolute Power*. Period. Full stop.

Needless to say, Eastwood was one of the biggest movie stars in the world and Warner Brothers quickly changed course. *Absolute Power* was moved up and locked into Easter–spring break, and we were pushed back to mid–April. Every *Murder at 1600* review started with something like, "Just like last month's *Absolute Power*..." or "On the heels of last month's *Absolute Power*..." We were finished and ready first but perceived now as the low-budget copycat version of a Clint Eastwood movie.

When April finally came around, we were still hoping for a miracle. *Absolute Power* had done only okay, and at the lower end of expectations for an Eastwood movie. Warners did put on a proper premiere for *Murder at 1600* at Westwood's Bruin theater. There was a packed red carpet and all the stars showed up. I was walked along the red carpet by publicity people and my manager. They stand you in front of a news outlet for two questions and then push you down the line for the next sound bite. The press cameras go off continuously. Just when you start to think you're a big deal, Wesley or Diane Lane or Alan Alda shows up and the photographers go crazy, leaving you in the dust. Hollywood is about the stars!

The same is true at Hollywood parties. If you're talking with someone and a guest arrives who is more important than you, then your conversation will come to an abrupt end as everyone jockeys for position with the new power guest. You'll be left holding your white wine spritzer.

Westwood had been my premiere home before. I had experienced the surprise sensation of *Halloween 4*, a subdued screening at the Village Theater for *Phantom of the Opera*, and there had been a huge premiere for *Marked for Death* that I wasn't able to attend. We had an afternoon premiere for *Free Willy 2* (also at the Village), and a big screening for *Rapid Fire* at the Avco. The big Hollywood movies today seem to premiere on Hollywood Boulevard. Westwood is not so cool any more. No idea why.

There is a Darwinian atmosphere to these screenings. Your agents and managers, and maybe a few friends, are rooting for you to succeed; but the rest of the crowd is hoping you are going to fail. This is not really anyone's fault. Competition for limited director openings is intense. As I've often heard: "Don't blame the player, blame the game."

I sat nervously in my taped-off seat and waited to see what the Hollywood crowd would think of *Murder at 1600*. These were not moviegoers. Premiere guests are agents, managers, executives, rival studio scouts, reporters, marketing and research people, publicists, movie and TV actors who want some publicity; plus, general industry people and hangers-on. They are not there to wish you well. They are there to wish themselves well. After some experience, you get a feeling for how a screening is going by the noises and body language of the audience. Our first scene with Wesley and the disturbed Washington bureaucrat was funny and the audience was laughing right away ... a very good sign! There was reasonable applause at the end ... more than just "polite" but not a standing ovation either. The movie "played." It seemed to be working, even for the self-styled cynics and haters.

The *Murder at 1600* reviews weren't bad, but they weren't really helpful either. Just a kind of "okay" response. The big complaint was that the movie changed tone at the end. Many critics seemed to feel that the film went from a conspiracy thriller to a wild action movie too abruptly. Of course, they were not wrong, since the helicopter and explosion scene were a last-minute add-on. And once again, it wasn't my fault, but it was my problem.

This paradox seemed to go right to the heart of the split between what the audience likes and what reviewers like. The very thing that gets the audience excited (helicopters, gunfire, explosions) is the same thing that pisses off the critics. I've always felt that a real success is a movie that wins both at the box office and gets the good reviews. A critically panned Adam Sandler movie that makes a ton of money is fine, and a critical darling that does no business is fine, but they both kind of miss the mark. The real breakout directors make tons of money and the critics love them: Scorsese, Tarantino, Spielberg.

I felt like this movie, which I was so proud of, was destined to die an unfair death. The competition did not help. There was a Tommy Lee Jones volcano movie and a Val Kilmer thriller to contend with. We opened soft and fell off 35 percent the second weekend. We weren't going to make even $30 million U.S., so the jig was up. I still wonder what we might have done in January without the Clint Eastwood interference ... but we'll never know. As my mother would say: "Don't look back, it's not the direction you're going."

There is a general understanding in Hollywood that you can get three "at bats" after a hit film, and then it's off to the Used Car Lot of directors. *Marked for Death* had been a hit and I had my three "at bats": *Rapid Fire*, *Free Willy 2* and *Murder at 1600*. And now the world was closing in. I had development meetings to attend, and Lorenzo at Warner Brothers set me up to meet with the great Kurt Russell to discuss *The Football*, a thriller about the Marine who carries the nuclear launch codes for the president. When I sat down with Kurt, I couldn't help but grill him about his Wyatt Earp movie *Tombstone*, a truly great Hollywood Western also starring Val Kilmer.

Kurt ultimately decided to do a plane hijack movie instead, *Executive Decision* (co-starring, of all people, Steven Seagal).

With a brand-new baby at home, I wasn't sure what the next move should or could be. My agents thought I should just keep developing and hope for the best; but once again, I could feel "my team" drifting away. It was time for them to put their energy into the next hot client. No one wants to be on the phone and talk about a "miss."

I decided to take a long weekend up in Lake Arrowhead and clear my brain. It had been a wild year. Right before I was to head down the driveway in the loaded-up Honda Accord, my phone rang.

Glen Morgan, an old pal from the Sandy Howard days, was making a name for himself with his partner Jim Wong, in television. Glen told me he was in Vancouver making a show for Chris Carter called *Millennium*, and shocked the hell out of me when he asked, "Would you like to come up and do an episode?"

Television? Really? I didn't know much about television, and what I did know, I didn't like. "Oh, come on," he said, "we'll have fun. It's a good show and Chris is great."

I turned to my wife and put my hand over the phone. "Should I do television?" I asked.

Sensibly, she said, "You should do anything you can."

"Okay, Glen, I'll come up. But you'll have to teach me."

"You'll be fine," he laughed.

There is a scene in *Jeremiah Johnson* where an old, grizzled mountain man (Will Geer) is trying to teach Johnson (Robert Redford) how to survive in the mountains. Geer explains that there are times when the grizzly bears migrate, get hunted out, or get sick, leaving the mountain man's way of life in jeopardy. "But," he advises, "if you save up their claws in the good times, you can leave them in a jar down by the river in the lean times. The riverboat captains will pick up the grizzly claws and leave cash money for them. The people in the towns below love to buy grizzly claws.

"Good thing to know ... times get hard," Geer concludes. Young Redford listens to the wise one.

If you think Hollywood is a survival game, then you will see that I needed some grizzly claws and I needed them *now*.

It looked like television might be the right move. Was this a career-beginning decision? Or a career-ending decision? I would find out soon enough.

Part 2
Television

Seven

The Writer's Revenge

On my first trip to Los Angeles, my buddy Peter and I snuck into the 45th Academy Awards. We took a taxi downtown from Hollywood and easily climbed up and over a simple chain link fence outside the Dorothy Chandler Pavilion. Then we crawled under the bleachers full of screaming fans like you would at a high school football game. No one noticed us or cared if they did; they were too busy gawking at the stars.

The screaming started with each name called out by the announcer over the PA system. "Clint Eastwood!" "Gene Hackman!" "Charlton Heston!" "Natalie Wood!" "Sonny and Cher!" Cameras flashed like machine guns as the red carpet glittered.

The first time I got a real good look at an actor, it was Darren McGavin, who was not more than 20 feet away when I climbed up onto the bleachers. I was a huge fan from his hit TV show *The Night Stalker*. It was strange to see that rubbery face in the flesh after watching it seemingly a million times on my 13-inch Admiral TV. Peter and I were barely 18, just out from Ohio, and we were mesmerized, taking in this great Hollywood ritual. It was glamorous and exciting to be there, but we were outsiders looking in.

Many years later, I found myself sitting in a not-so-glamorous third-floor attic, in the middle of the winter, in Vancouver, next to, of all people, Darren McGavin. I was directing my first TV show and Darren was the guest star, playing Lance Henriksen's father. Downstairs the crew was "turning around" (re-lighting the set so I could film in the opposite direction).

Darren knew his close-up was next and he was clearly nervous. He just couldn't remember his lines. He was extremely good when he read the lines off his script, and the dialogue was deeply moving, but he was near 80 now and just couldn't hold onto the words. I could see how frustrated he was.

The episode, "Midnight of the Century," was a beautifully written piece about Christmas, memory, regret and hope. This was the actor who was the star of *A Christmas Story*, *The Natural*, *The Great Train Robbery* ... plus a guest star on every major network TV show of the last four decades. Darren McGavin had worked with *everybody*, and today I wanted to make him shine.

I told him how happy I had been when I found out he would be playing the part of Lance's father. Then I told him about seeing him at the Oscars all those years ago, and how much that had meant to me. He was very touched by my story.

"Now, Darren," I said, "you are going to have to trust me."

He looked confused. "What do you mean?"

"We're going to go down there, and Lance is happy to wait in the other room." (I had already spoken with Lance about my plan.) "I am going to read *your lines* and sit in his chair. You just say the lines back to me. We'll do them one or two at a time. I'll cut it with Lance's reactions, and it'll play great."

"You mean you're going to read Lance's lines?" Darren furrowed his brow.

"No," I raised my voice slightly, "*your lines*. Then you won't have to worry about a thing."

"You can make that work?" He looked dubious.

"Like a hot knife through butter," I promised.

Two things were necessary for this idea to work. First, I had to have the confidence and experience from many years of directing movies to know that it *would* work, and second, I just happened to have this incredibly personal story that I was able to share with him and gain his trust. That is the #1 ingredient of the actor-director relationship: trust. After all, he'd been doing this since before I was born, and I was just a guest director on a TV show.

We went downstairs and started shooting the scene. I would say Darren's lines in a very neutral way and wait for him to say them back. I'd wait for a moment where I knew Lance's line was going to go, and then read the next line.

His confidence grew. "Let's go again," he said. Darren had begun to really feel the scene, and he wasn't even thinking about the lines.

Working with Darren wasn't the only thing that went right for me on that first episode. I hit it off with Lance Henriksen (Bishop from *Aliens*), which is always the key to survival in TV. The lead actor or actress is the biggest fish in the pond and holds the key to a director being invited back for a second episode, or conversely being given the sack. Robert McLaughlin, the director of photography, was world-class. He went on to do landmark television series, including *Game of Thrones*.

Everything that seemed to be going wrong for me in features was now

Seven. The Writer's Revenge

going right for me in television. I was supported by my old friends. The script was excellent. And I fell right into a great relationship with the cast and crew. This was certainly an omen that I had made the right decision to jump out of movies and into television. An old friend from movie days had helped me make the switch. Directing is a very *personal* business and relationships are vital.

At that time, television was still considered a step down from the feature world. I had the same resistance to my decision from agents and managers that I had had when saying yes to *Halloween 4*. "You can't do television ... you'll ruin your career," said the chorus of doubters. "Just wait a year and see what happens ... don't rush into this," was the conventional wisdom. Sometimes free advice is worth what you pay for it.

First of all, I didn't have a year to coast since money was going out and not coming in. But more importantly, I just had a hunch. I felt like television was going to have its day since *The X-Files* and *NYPD Blue* were really changing the rules about what a network show could be. Cable shows such as HBO's *The Sopranos* were just around the corner. Five years later, the stampede would really begin, and nearly every working director in Hollywood would be trying to get into television.

Meanwhile, somewhere on the 20th Century–Fox backlot, editors were assembling my *Millennium* episode. A producer from another show stopped at an open doorway in the post-production building and looked in on my Darren McGavin scene.

* * *

After the editor's "assembly," the director gets only four days to deliver his Director's Cut to the producers. The rest of the decisions concerning the final look and sound of the episode are made not by the director, but by the showrunner (head writer) and the studio. This is the huge difference between the role of the director in television vs. movies.

* * *

The producer turned out to be Robert Breech, who was David E. Kelly's right-hand man. Bob was doing post-production work on ABC's *The Practice* in the same building.

"That's a hell of a scene," he said to the editors. "Who directed that?"

The editors double-checked the crew list. "It says Dwight Little," they responded, then went back to work.

Bob Breech was a Stanford man who had studied producing at USC. Years before, I had met Bob though a mutual friend, and he had helped me produce my Emmy-winning *Spies* documentary. This was an incredible stroke of good luck, because he followed up with me and invited me to direct an episode of *The Practice*. "Better to be lucky than good," as the saying goes. But "good" helps.

Even though I had gone on to direct two more episodes of *Millennium*, it was my time on *The Practice* that taught me the real skills to survive in network TV.

First of all, you are *not* the boss and you have to just surrender to that. In all the meetings with department heads, writers, casting directors and studio executives, the key questions will be directed to the showrunner and line producer, *not* to you. The director can chime in and contribute, but the final word is not yours. Your hat may look the same, but it is a *very* different hat.

In episodic TV, there is a required pre-production ritual called the Tone Meeting. In this meeting, the director is summoned to the office of the showrunner to go through each scene in the script. At first, I didn't even understand the *idea* of this meeting. Isn't the director's main job to set the tone?

Apparently not.

The idea is that the writers have created the characters and know where they will be heading in the storyline as the season continues. There is a certain merit to this argument since the guest director might be doing an episode in the middle of a season and may not be clear about what has come before or what is coming after. "Educating" the director on the arc of the series has become a way for the writers to dictate how to direct the actors and, in some cases, how to shoot the scenes.

Most writers have very limited set experience and they believe dialogue delivered by an actor can be micro-managed like words on a page. Further, many series have somewhat rebellious cast members who know you've been instructed on what to say to them; so, you're already the enemy as far as they're concerned.

These are very treacherous waters as you will be immediately forced to take sides as either a friend of the cast or a friend of the producers. Like Switzerland, you must remain neutral.

* * *

When you've come from the world of features, this sea change in power is kind of shocking. (On movie sets, the presence of the writer is generally left to the discretion of the director, and most often the writer is just not around, *period*.)

* * *

Of course, once on set, all this hypothetical talk and "tone meeting" conversation becomes academic. Actors balk, schedules collapse, technology fails.

Seven. The Writer's Revenge

Lance Henriksen and Dwight Little filming *Millennium*.

One of the first shots on my first day directing *The Practice* was a scene in Bobby's (Dylan McDermott) office. I had a shot in mind that I had already communicated to the DP. But it meant that Dylan would have to cooperate. I wanted him to come in through the main door, hang his coat on a stand next to the camera, then go to the window to close the blinds before going to his desk. Each of these "blocking" ideas (movement of the actors within a scene) was going to motivate a camera move designed to create a dynamic opening shot.

I greeted Dylan and asked if he was ready to rehearse. He was late to set so I was already panicked about my shooting time. After I took Dylan through the first shot and politely explained everything, he just sort of shrugged and said, "I'm not going to do that."

And so, there it was. All my prep and planning thrown out the window on the whim of McDermott. But Dylan was the star, and #1 on the call sheet, so in this case he was boss. This was all played out in front of the entire crew, who just saw the new guy get handed his ass by the star. I needed to take the set back, and quickly. I figured I'd do the most obvious thing ... just tell him he was right.

"Hey, Dylan, you know what? Maybe you're right. It might be better if you went straight to the desk for pace, and then we can run it from there," I desperately countered.

"Yeah, let's try that," he grumbled. "I'll throw my coat over the back of the chair and just sit."

Lead series TV actors are in a brutal endurance contest. They shoot 12- to 14-hour days, day after day, week after week. Dylan didn't want to have to think about critical marks and lighting adjustments at 7 a.m. on a Monday morning. He didn't want to be there *at all*. He wanted to sit down in his chair and not move for the rest of the morning. He could hide the "sides" (small script pages) around his desk in case he forgot his lines. He couldn't care less about my cool opening shot. He only cared about his day and how he was going to get through it.

I learned then and there, television is not about the director, it's about the writers and the stars. Try to block every scene from their point of view. After eight days, you will be gone, and they will still be there with some *other* director who wants to do his or her own artsy shot.

Dylan and I ended up working very closely together for ten more episodes, and he turned in some amazing performances. I gained his trust with thoughtful notes; I respected his talent; and I always tried to get the best out of him. What I learned on *The Practice* about actors in television (see the world through their eyes) helped me with other stars: Robert Patrick, Chazz Palminteri, Scott Bakula, Gillian Anderson and others.

As far as the writing went, I became very spoiled. These were David E. Kelley scripts, written solely by him. And he is one of the few people I've worked with in either film or television who is a legit genius. Some of the stories were so moving, they made me cry. The dialogue was razor-sharp, and there was a topical element about each episode that was illuminating to the issues of the day, without being preachy.

One day I had to report to David's office at the Manhattan Beach Studios and I caught him in the hallway. I knew David well enough at this point to have a little fun with him. "David, I don't believe that you are writing three network shows at the same time! I think you've got an army of understudies hidden somewhere in a basement, and I want to see them!"

David smiled and said, "Come here." He led me into his office, and from his desk drawer he pulled out three legal pads. One read *The Practice*, one read *Ally McBeal* and one read *Boston Public*. Each yellow pad was full of handwritten dialogue and scene descriptions. When he'd finish a few pages, he'd push them under the door of his office and into the hall, and the assistants in the other room would take the pages, type them up and format them. He had three episodes of television in his head *at the same time,* and he wrote each one *by hand.*

At the start of a David E. Kelley show, you'd receive the white pages of the first draft. The director and producers made notes on this first draft. Then Bob Breech and three or four of us would go up to David's office and have an audience with the King. I'd ask questions about anything I was unsure of. The producers would ask questions about production issues and location complications.

David quietly listened and took notes. He didn't comment or offer an opinion. He was a Sphinx. The next day, a new "Blue Page" script was issued (the color blue is the industry standard for a second draft) and that's when we'd know what he had agreed with and what he didn't want to change. We'd then shoot the Blue Page script *word for word*. The actors knew that the lines were not open to discussion, they were not a suggestion. If a line had to be changed, Bob Breech would call David's office and get a yea or nay.

One new actor was hired for a recurring role (probably best I don't mention his name). From Day One, he was a bit difficult and started changing things. He was warned not to, but he persisted: "My character wouldn't say this," he'd argue. What he didn't understand was that it was never "his" character, it was David's. News of his contrary behavior found its way to the front office.

Two episodes later, the actor read a scene about "his" character. The character stepped out of an elevator and into a parking garage where he was machine-gunned to death by a Russian gang. David had the character literally "whacked" in a very public way. That was the end of that actor on *The Practice*. Like the horse's head in *The Godfather*, it sent a message to the other actors about messing around with the maestro's words!

The Practice not only improved its ratings year after year, it also took home multiple Emmys, Golden Globes, SAG Awards, Peabody Awards and many others. My work on *The Practice* put me on a list of approved network directors, and I found myself working steadily for the first time in my career.

Directing for television was once described as "hosting a party when you don't know any of the guests."

On my first episode of *Nikita*, I arrived in Toronto to discover that the lead actress Maggie Q and her co-star Shane West had just broken up after an intense affair. I was new to everyone and was alerted to the situation by the AD and producers. What was I supposed to do? *Why didn't they fix it?* Producers love to throw their problems at the guest director since there will be an easy fall guy if something goes wrong.

Maggie was surrounded by her posse (stand-in, makeup artist, hair stylist, nutritionist, etc.) in one corner of the set, and Shane and his posse (stunt double, assistant, PAs, etc.) were in a huddle in the other corner. The air was thick with the animosity that is created when two former lovers are suddenly hating everything about the person they were madly in love with a week before.

I went to Maggie's corner first. I said, "I'd like you to join me for a read-through with just myself and Shane." I went on to say what a good scene it was and that I had a plan on how to shoot it very quickly. "If we all pull together, we can be out of here in a couple hours." (There is no bigger carrot to dangle in front of an actor than "I'll get you out early.")

I thanked her, then said, "On my way to the airport, driving down the 405, I saw a huge billboard of you as Nikita, staring down like a god at all of us in our little cars." She lit right up.

Then I went over to Shane's camp and asked, "Do you think you could meet Maggie and me in the middle of the room to read the lines?" I figured if I made the meeting in the middle of the room, then neither combatant would be "going to see" the other.

Once he heard that Maggie had already agreed, he reluctantly accepted. It seemed like Shane was the one whose feelings had been hurt. I diverted his hard feelings toward Maggie by reminding him that we had met before on a feature called *The Wheelman* that was never made.

* * *

The Wheelman was a $25 million action film that was going to be shot in Utah, financed by an insurance company. I was hired for one million dollars to direct. The script was solid and we were attracting good actors like Marlon Wayans and Scott Speedman (who won out over Shane West). I'd put my team together and we were soon sending prop and grip trucks up to Salt Lake City. After a final scout, I was waiting at the Salt Lake airport with Denis Stewart, my *Rapid Fire* AD, when his phone rang. Denis handed me the phone, looking a bit pale. "You better take this," he said.

It turns out the company had been some kind of insurance Ponzi scheme and its beautiful offices in Santa Monica were shut down overnight; assets were seized. *The Wheelman* was dead in an instant when the auditors arrived. I got a few bucks in a settlement but the million dollars blew out the window. You can never be sure … *ever*.

* * *

I had my read-through on neutral territory and Maggie actually laughed at something Shane said, which kind of broke the ice. We shot the scene as best we could. Each time I said "Cut," the two stars retreated to their corners with their handlers. Eventually the storm passed because the other scenes that day did not have them shooting together. That was a day where I earned my fee!

* * *

Forest Whitaker was an Oscar winner. He had been celebrated for his performance in *The Last King of Scotland* portraying the brutal African dictator Idi Amin. He had also appeared in essential movies like *The Color of Money, Bird, The Crying Game* and *Platoon*.

About nine o'clock one night in Pasadena, I was seated in video village shooting a television series called *Criminal Minds: Suspect Behavior*, a spin-off of the highly rated and long-running *Criminal Minds*. Forest, the series star, sat down next to me, in front of the monitors.

"I checked out the dailies from last night and didn't see any coverage of me looking back at the hospital patient," he pointed out.

There wasn't much warm-up here. Forest had taken the time to actually look at the dailies from the previous day's work, which very few star actors do. He wasn't very happy with what he had seen and felt that close-up shots of him were missing.

I felt a wave of panic rise up from my toes and I tried as hard as I could to remember the exact set-up he was talking about. Why wouldn't I have that coverage? That really wouldn't be like me. Suddenly I remembered the scene and I also remembered that at the last minute I ordered a B camera to get a close-up of Forest at the hospital bed. I caught my breath.

"Forest, I think what may have happened was, I got that shot on the B camera and maybe the B camera was not printed properly."

He looked at me like he didn't believe a word I was saying. I asked him to give me a few minutes to try and sort out the problem.

The script supervisor was close at hand and I motioned to her: "Forest wants to know about his coverage from the hospital bed scene last night. What do your notes say?"

The script supervisor looked at her script pages with all the carefully marked lines drawn neatly with a ruler. Then she looked up with a nod of her head. "It's here … scene 64-B, takes 1 through 5. B-camera coverage, low angle of Cooper looking down at patient camera right. 75mm, slider in at the end. We printed takes 2 and 5."

* * *

The job of the script supervisor is often misunderstood. Their job is not just about continuity. As each scene is filmed, the supervisor writes down what shots are taken, which lenses are used, how long the take lasts, which screen direction the actor is looking, and which takes the director wants printed for each set-up. In addition to these notes, the script supervisor keeps track of continuity of props, continuity of wardrobe, continuity of body gestures, dialogue, etc., so that a scene will later cut together smoothly in the editing room. (A sandwich cannot be half-eaten in one shot and then sitting there untouched in the next.)

The notes of the script supervisor are invaluable to the editor and also help the producers know if the show is running long or short for time. The supervisor's notes also make reference to any mistakes that may have been evident in the shot. The audio boom maybe dipped into frame, the noise of an airplane was heard, a dog barked, a light went out, or any number of other annoying little problems. It's a huge job of organization and it takes real attention to detail. Some script supervisors are so good at their jobs that they have moved up to the director's chair.

* * *

"Call the cutting room and have them find and transfer 64-B and send it in an email attachment up here to set right away," I requested. Clearly the transfer lab had failed to print that B-camera set-up and it had not been posted in dailies.

Fortunately, there was someone still working in post-production even at 9 p.m., and in 20 minutes we had a close-up shot of Forest cued up on an iPad. I grabbed the small screen and walked it over to our lead as he was getting "touched up" (final makeup) for his next scene. I acted as cool and calm as I could, trying to project an air of confidence. Inside I was still freaked out. If I didn't have the confidence of the star, I would be screwed.

"Is this the shot you were thinking of?" I asked calmly, as if the whole thing was no big deal. Forest looked at the shot. His face betrayed no emotion.

"Yeah, that's it," he said. "Just checking."

I still don't know if he was testing me or genuinely concerned about his coverage. He wasn't really mean about it, but he wasn't a warm bath either. If you didn't get a lot of hugs as a child, don't expect to get them on a movie set.

* * *

I have been directing famous actors for my whole career. But even now, the young fan from Ohio sometimes shows up unannounced, and I get star-struck like everyone else.

"Ryan O'Neal wants to talk to you." That was the word from the AD on the set of *Bones*. I knew he had been playing a recurring role as Brennan's (Emily Deschanel) father on the Fox series. I tensed up a bit and tried to put on my game face. This was a huge movie star from the 1970s. *Paper Moon, Love Story, What's Up Doc* and *Barry Lyndon*! What did he want?!

I approached the door to his trailer and was met by his security man, who was actually very pleasant, though he had done time for armed robbery in Florida. "He's mostly bark," the guy said.

Then I heard that unmistakable voice from a slew of movies as it bellowed out the door: "You know I hate directors!"

Seven. The Writer's Revenge

Uh-oh. I climbed up into the punch-out star trailer, not knowing quite what to expect. And there was Ryan O'Neal, in the flesh, not making eye contact, fussing with his wardrobe.

"How can I help?" I said. "I'm the director of this episode. Happy to be working with you."

"You can help by getting me the fuck out of here," Ryan O'Neal snapped. "How long is this going to take?"

I did a quick read on his tone and body language to see what I was dealing with. Then I figured I'd try to mess with him a little, movie star or not. People who have some sense of humor can always be managed, one way or another.

"Well, I have one crane shot that starts way out on the street and pushes in through the restaurant windows until it finally lands on a waiter with a tray. Then we follow the waiter to the bar, circle around the bar, and finally land on a big close-up of you…"

He looked at me with the eyes of an old Irish boxer who was about to bring down the hammer until my face cracked a little, and I smiled.

"You fucker" he said, in a humorous way.

"Don't worry," I reassured him, "I'll be fast. But I have to ask you one thing…"

He eyed me warily. "What?"

"When you split off from your regiment in *Barry Lyndon,* and carry your uncle out of harm's way … was it your idea to kiss him on the forehead, knowing he was going to die? Or was that Kubrick?"

This was a detail question from a film nerd (me) about Ryan's greatest achievement, and it got his full attention.

"That was me!" he beamed. "Stanley said to try it, but he wasn't sure. Then he used it in the film! Great moment."

"Brilliant," I exclaimed.

And that was that. Ryan O'Neal, the cranky, difficult Irish movie star, was my new best bud. At the end of the shoot, he gave me a signed DVD of *Barry Lyndon*. (I still think *Paper Moon* is one of the great star performances of all time.)

* * *

While shooting my first episode of Fox's landmark series *24,* I was witness to a creative struggle which was completely opposite from everything I had learned from David E. Kelley.

The *24* crew and I had set up a night shot outside a barn on a movie set in Santa Clarita. It was time for Kiefer Sutherland to come down and join us for a rehearsal. I hadn't really worked with Kiefer very much. I was "the new guy" since it was already Season 5 and I had just started.

Kiefer walked right past me and went up to the script supervisor. He took her script and went through the dialogue with a red Sharpie.

"I'm not saying that. I'm not saying that. I'm not saying that. I'll say this instead…"

Kiefer proceeded to rewrite the scene right then and there, and this was before we had even read it with the other actor (*RoboCop*'s Peter Weller).

I looked around for a producer or writer to see if anyone was going to say something or intervene. Crickets. There were no writers around and no one else said a word.

At this point, *24* was making so much money for Fox that no one was willing to derail the money train *no matter what*. This meant Kiefer had complete power and authority over everything, including the script. He was, after all, Jack Bauer.

This of course was a completely different reality from how I'd been taught to protect the "written in stone" words of David E. Kelley.

As I was trying to decide how I was going to explain to the writer-producers that Kiefer wasn't going to say their expensive words, Peter Weller stepped up to the video village. He had been listening to this whole Kiefer performance from the sidelines.

"Listen, sport," he said right to Kiefer, "you can say any damn thing you want, but I am saying the lines I was paid to learn." There was shocked silence on the set. Peter Weller had no intention of pissing off the network by not doing the job he was hired to do.

Apparently, no one had ever pushed back with Kiefer before and it took everyone by surprise. I could tell by the look on Kiefer's face that he was as startled as everyone else.

Peter Weller was only a guest star, but he already had a substantial career behind him. He was beholden to no one, least of all Kiefer. He had starred in *RoboCop, Naked Lunch, Buckaroo Banzai, Screamers* and many other movies and TV shows.

I could feel the awkwardness of the situation and no one really knew what to do. I decided now would be my best chance to jump in and keep the episode moving forward. That was really my job, anyway. Just keep the money train on the tracks.

"Come on, guys," I said. "Let's go inside and run the scene … we'll figure it out."

My attitude was upbeat and confident and everyone just sort of went inside, relieved that someone had made a decision.

Once we started reading the scene, Kiefer said a few things not in the script, but stuck more or less with the words. I tried to be helpful, encouraging, and without judgment about, really, anything. I think the real truth

Seven. The Writer's Revenge

Dwight Little and Ryan O'Neal filming *Bones*.

was, it was just too damn cold to stay in that barn forever. Also, Peter Weller was a formidable presence and I believe he reminded Kiefer of his father, Donald Sutherland.

It was pretty well known that Kiefer had had a difficult time growing up because his father was away most of the time, not to mention insanely famous. Donald Sutherland was a genuine 1960s arthouse icon for a whole generation of filmgoers. *M*A*S*H*, *Klute*, *Don't Look Now*, *1900*, *Animal House*; he was like a rock star and must have cast a hell of a shadow over Kiefer.

I think Peter had unknowingly taken on the persona of the stern father and, unwittingly, Kiefer just fell into line. We managed to finish the night and walked away with as little blood spilled as possible. Floor plans? Shot lists? Storyboards? Forget about it. On a night like that, you just hope to get out alive.

* * *

On a Western movie set, a few hours outside of Calgary, I was having another problem with a big TV star, Tom Selleck. I had been hired by TNT to direct a movie called *Monte Walsh*. TNT had liked my work on *Boss of Bosses* and had put me forward to Selleck. Tom had wanted his *Quigley*

Down Under director, Simon Wincer, to do the film, but Simon was not available, and they had to go forward right away or lose their window with the network. Selleck agreed to have me direct.

The prep period had been rocky because the ambition of the script was bigger than the budget, and tough cuts had to be made. By this time, I was used to collaborating with producers and stars; but on this movie, I was chafing.

I had agreed to script changes that were indulgent and ill-advised. I had agreed to their casting choices, which were all cliched and basically friends of Tom. I agreed to locations that served the production more than the story. I agreed to their DP and composer (who were not my first choices), and now it was becoming clear that Tom and the producers wanted to dictate to me how to make the movie. I resisted. My ideas may not always be the best, but I'm hired to *direct* and I have to stand by my experience and talent at some point.

There was a dialogue scene ready to shoot on a cabin porch. The AD told me that "they" (Tom and the producers) wanted to put a dog on the porch and wanted me to get a separate shot of it.

"Well, let's get the scene first and then see if we need the dog," I replied.

"They want the dog," the AD insisted. This whole situation was so trivial and petty, but it was no longer about the dog. I was now being told what shots to get, and that was a bridge too far.

* * *

Back in film school, we learned about editing by cutting dailies from the TV show *Gunsmoke*. Marshal Dillon was having a fistfight on the porch of a cabin and there was a shot of a barking dog on the porch. This is where the expression "Cut to the dog" came from: When something didn't match or play in the scene, you could cut to the dog to get out of editorial trouble. I knew that they wanted to "cut to the dog" and I just couldn't do it. I was a TV director now, but not *that* much of a TV director.

* * *

"Is this the hill you want to die on?" the AD said when I continued to resist.

"Yes. It ends now or I am shit out of luck for the rest of the shoot. I'm going to die on this *exact* fucking hill."

The AD looked worried and walked back to the set. His head was down.

A few minutes later, there were arguments and heated exchanges; and I knew, even as I was having them, that I was going to be fired. A few frantic phone calls were made to the agents and network executives, but I was done.

It was a strange experience to be fired because it had never happened to me before. I was a bit surprised but oddly complacent about the whole thing. I really just didn't give a shit.

The drama continued when I got home. The network offered to pay me for the time I'd put in during prep and the shooting days that I had completed. I told the agent that was a non-starter. "I want 100 cents on the dollar ... the whole fee."

Phone calls went back and forth. I wanted *all* the money, or I was going to get the DGA involved and make a stink. Sure enough, I found out that Simon Wincer had become available and they were bringing him up to replace me. Until now, Simon had only been signed on to be the second unit director.

When I was on the phone with my friend Peter, he said, "They can't do that!"

"Can't do what?" I asked.

"Replace you with the second unit director. It's clear in the DGA rule book."

"No shit?" I said. I had no idea.

I immediately called my assistant in Calgary, who was still in the office packing up my gear, and told him to quietly get ahold of the deal memo between the company and Simon. This assistant had worked with me before on a different movie in Calgary, and he was very loyal. Stealth and espionage ensued.

When my agents advised the producers that they couldn't hire the second unit director per the DGA contract, they immediately claimed that there was never a deal signed with Wincer, and therefore he wasn't ever the second unit director.

I told my agent, "I've had enough. I'm going to the DGA."

I knew that if the producers ever tried to claim that there was no deal, I had them dead to rights with my stolen deal memo. I had a real smoking gun.

Suddenly the network, not the producers, became very involved and asked my agent if I'd cease and desist all further complaints or actions if they paid me the full amount on the contract.

I said, "Hell, yes!" I didn't really care about this TV movie, I just wanted the dough.

The final twist was a damage control call from TNT. The head of the network wanted to see if I had any projects that might be of interest to them. This was the most naked ploy I'd seen yet. A dressed-to-the-nines, over-slick TV executive tried to convince me that the network wanted to work with me on something. The game was, as long as they kept some sort of carrot dangling out in front of me, I'd be a good boy and not say anything negative about them or Tom around town.

"I wouldn't worry about it," I told the executive. "It's a creative business, shit happens. I don't mind that I was fired, I mind that you tried to cheat me." Then I stood up and left the room, hoping to never see any of them again.

The thing was, Tom Selleck had an end game. *Monte Walsh* was a passion project of his and he wanted the comparison to the Emmy-winning series *Lonesome Dove* which had been capably directed by Simon Wincer. And in fact, the *Monte Walsh* poster stated at the top, "From the Director of *Lonesome Dove*." The problem was, though Simon had done a perfectly respectable job, it was the writing of Larry McMurtry and the acting of Robert Duvall and Tommy Lee Jones that earned the Emmy, not Simon Wincer.

Point made again. The director must get the script and casting right if he or she wants to shine. Tom Selleck and Keith Carradine were not going to create the same level of movie as Robert Duvall and Tommy Lee Jones, whether it was Simon or me calling the shots.

The final bizarre twist to this story was that Simon knew my wife Sandy quite well because he had directed my stepson Jason Richter in *Free Willy*. An awkward situation to be sure, but in Hollywood, it's "every man for himself," and we all kind of understand that.

When people ask me what television means to me, I usually answer, "German cars, private schools and Caribbean vacations." If something artistic breaks out once in a while … it's a bonus.

Within a few weeks of getting home, I picked up a feature at Sony/Columbia that I would have missed if I'd been still working on *Monte Walsh*. So, as the believers say, "When God closes a door, He opens a window." Don't walk past it, though. You have to see that it's open and crawl through it, usually over broken glass.

Managing stars is one of the biggest challenges facing the TV director. You really have no power over the show you are doing, but you have to pretend like you do. And don't step on any toes, or you will be out on your ass. I had won over Dylan McDermott, Ryan O'Neal, Maggie Q, Forest Whitaker, Don Johnson, Lance Henriksen and David Boreanaz. Played to a draw with Kiefer Sutherland. Lost to Tom Selleck.

As much experience as I was now getting as a television director, there were always new situations that came up and I would have to improvise to stay alive.

* * *

One morning I found myself on the set of a show called *Citizen Baines*. I had been shooting for a few days, but this day was my first with the star James Cromwell. The first AD came up to me and said, "Jamie wants to talk to you."

Well, okay, I thought. He's the *star* and wants to talk to me about the plan for the day. Fair enough.

I was escorted up a flight of stairs at the back of a Warner Brothers sound stage. Cromwell was waiting in a tired old dressing room. (I decided not to mention that his little family movie *Babe* had messed up my box office on *Free Willy 2* some years before.)

"Sit down, mate," he said when I stepped in.

Having worked in Australia for a while, I always found the expression "mate" somewhat hostile, and not a term of endearment.

Cromwell, a tall (6'6"), imposing man, came from a storied show biz family. I took a seat on the cheap sofa and tried not to shrink into it.

"Listen, mate," he announced. "I'm not going to say *any* of this dialogue the way it is written, and I just thought you should know."

Okay, I thought, this is a real shot over the bow.

First of all, he was way too sophisticated not to know that the TV series director has almost no say in the lines as they are written, especially when he or she is new to the show. Second, the actors usually get the script at least a few days before shooting, so if they have a problem with the dialogue, they can bring it up with the writers in advance. This is generally what the table read is for.

I vamped for a minute so I could think of an answer that wouldn't bury me with this guy. "Well," I said, "I think the 'A' story is really good and very compelling." I was trying to lead with something positive. Then I made a passive-aggressive chess move.

"I'll tell you what we'll do … you show me where you want to go, and I'll set up the cameras and call 'Action.' Then you can say whichever words you think are best and you can work it out with John later."

"John" was John Wells, one of the most respected and successful television writer-producers in recent times. He'd written and produced *ER*, one of the longest running shows on television *ever*. I knew from the David E. Kelley days that it was easy to intimidate a guest director, but John Wells would be a different matter.

Also, the way I answered was not disrespectful or impolite but, if I'm being honest, there was an implied "Fuck you" in the words. What I was saying was, "Look, pal, I've been around the block, this ain't my first rodeo. Don't try and push me around on Day One."

Cromwell looked at me with those piercing star eyes. He was trying to read me since we were now playing some kind of Liar's Poker.

"Well," he said, drawing out his words, "let's run it as is and see how it plays on set."

Cromwell was softening his tone a little. As I stood up, I offered a parting good will gesture. "*L.A. Confidential* is one of the great films of all time and I just wanted to thank you for your amazing performance."

He knew he was being played, but he also knew that it was kind of true, and after all, he was an *actor*. I had called his bluff and survived.

The rest of the episode with Jamie went very well. He ended up saying the dialogue pretty much as written after all. The bigger problem was the three actresses who played Cromwell's daughters. I had never seen such dysfunction on a set in my life, and I had done many episodes by this time.

The actresses fought the dialogue, fought the producers, fought me, and fought amongst themselves. I couldn't understand what was going on. One actress was Scotch-taping her lines to the back of books. Then she'd go around the room grabbing them off the shelves and *reading* her lines! It was crazy.

I never was told what all the upset was about. I thought the scripts were solid and the production team was first-class, but the actresses were just unhappy. Bad chemistry, I guess. But you'd think *any* actor would be excited just to be *on* a John Wells show; work on the Warner Brothers lot and get rich. How hard can it be? Just say the fucking lines!

I was invited back to do a second episode—which is the best you can hope for as a TV director. But I got a call from my agent a few days before I was set to start. "They've shut down the show," he said, sounding amused. "You don't need to go in."

"What do you mean, they shut it down?" I couldn't quite believe my ears.

"The network cancelled it."

"Were the ratings that bad?"

"No, it was John Wells."

It turned out that running this show with all the difficulties and push-back from the cast was just too much of a headache for Wells. He was enormously wealthy and I think he just felt, "I'm too old and too rich for this shit." Anyway, this was a first. The showrunner cancelled *his own* show. I think it's safe to say the cast overplayed their hand on *Citizen Baines*.

There's a strange rumor mill in Hollywood where you hear about certain actors being monsters and you're encouraged to stay away from them. On the flip side, you also hear about the good ones who *everyone* wants to work with. The problem is that the rumors are often wrong.

I was told very clearly by many people not to work with Don Johnson because he had behaved so badly on *Nash Bridges*. And yet when I did work with him on *Just Legal,* he was a pleasure. Very funny and a good actor.

Seven. The Writer's Revenge

On my first day, Johnson walked right up to me with a fairly confrontational attitude.

"How do you see this scene?" he demanded.

I looked him square in the eye and said without hesitation, "I see it clearly."

Don took one more measure of me and then a crack of a smile crossed his face.

"Okay, where are you going to put the fucking camera?"

And that was the end of it. He just wanted to know if I was prepared and if he was going to be in good hands. As the saying goes, "Fail to prepare ... then prepare to fail."

David Boreanaz, who had been doing television for years with *Buffy the Vampire Slayer* and *Angel,* had a reputation for being "challenging." Yet when I worked with him on one episode of *Bones,* I found him to be smart, funny and the consummate actor. David and I became personal friends, and I directed 23 episodes of *Bones* which were shot in town on historic stages at the Fox lot. When all is said and done, it always ends up being about chemistry and personality.

* * *

I loved shooting on Stage 6 and Stage 9 on the Fox lot because they had small, engraved plaques displayed outside the main doors. The plaques

Jay Baruchel, Dwight Little and Don Johnson filming *Just Legal*.

listed some of the movies and TV shows that had been filmed there since 1930.

Stage 6 had been the home to *The King and I*, *The Poseidon Adventure*, *Gentleman's Agreement*, *Hush…Hush, Sweet Charlotte*, *Big Trouble in Little China* and many, many others.

Stage 9 was better known for its TV shows. *M*A*S*H*, *NYPD Blue*, *Peyton Place*, *Batman* and of course *Bones*. For the 12 years I worked on those stages, I always felt like I was part of the Hollywood story in my own small way.

* * *

It's not enough to just figure out how to manage actors, writers and showrunners. The television director must also find ways to shoot beautiful episodes that feel like *movies* on impossible schedules. It has always amused me that every time I'm in a room with a showrunner, and I mean *every* time, they sooner or later say….

"We want this show to be very cinematic … have you seen the pilot? It looks like a movie!" What you will never hear is a feature film producer or director saying, "Have you seen our final cut? It looks just like television!" Enough said.

To stay on time and on budget, creative solutions to problems are essential to survival. Despite all the second-guessing and political drama, it is *you* who is going to have to make the scenes work and stay on budget.

With each new crisis comes a chance to learn. Boy, was I going to have to learn. And quick.

Eight

Too Many Cooks in the Kitchen

Vancouver has a lovely period train station, built in 1919, that has been shot for film and TV many times. The beauty of directing is that each director can "see" the detailed architecture and rich atmosphere of a location like this with their own fresh eyes. It's like each generation discovering the world for the first time, as if no previous generation had ever seen it. Like my father said, "Every generation thinks it discovered sex!"

We were filming at the train station in the early hours of the morning for my second episode of *Millennium*. The last part of the sequence would feature a train pulling away from the station, a spectacular shot for the end of the episode. All the permissions between the city, the province, the train company and insurers had been carefully agreed to and paid for by the production company. By 3 a.m., we had finished a touching "goodbye scene" that preceded the train shot. We were now set to give all of our attention to the last shot, which had to be done by 4 a.m. All the trucks and gear had to be packed up and moved out by 5 a.m., and there was no way we were ever coming back to this location because of the huge expense and tight schedule.

At the end of the platform, I noticed a little huddle of people. Not happy people. The first AD, the line producer, the location rep—they were all packed together whispering and pointing. Whatever was happening couldn't be good. The first AD shook his head in apparent defeat, then broke off from the group and walked over to me.

"The train can't leave," he said.

"What?!" I nearly shouted. "How is that possible?"

"Down the track somewhere, there's a problem with a switcher and it's not safe."

If this had been Thailand or India or Hungary, I would have known what to do: Just pay the money. It would have been a last-minute extortion attempt. But this was Canada, and if someone said the switcher was down, the switcher was probably down.

We had spent all kinds of money on extras, camera cranes and lighting gear. We were counting on this train shot to finish the episode. Everyone stared at me like *I* should know what to do.

"Get every single piece of dolly track off the trucks and bring it all up here," I said in a panic. Years before, in India, I'd had a similar problem with a train. I knew from that experience that there was a simple trick to solving our problem. In movies, the audience only sees what it is shown, and in spatial perception terms (relative motion) there is no difference between a train moving and a camera moving. This simple trick of the eye goes all the way back to the earliest days of cinema. *The Great Train Robbery*, *The Birth of a Nation*, *The Kid*.

I showed the grips where to start putting down the dolly track. Then I went to the special effects captain and asked him if he had any steam. He did. When we were all set up, I had the dolly camera move slowly toward the actress waving from the window. I continued pushing the dolly towards her, then kept going past her, while turning the camera around in a panning motion. As she continued to wave goodbye, we kept pulling back on the dolly. I had the special effects team blast steam in front of the lens. Add a train whistle in post, and suddenly we had a lovely shot of a train leaving the station. I called "wrap" about 4:30. Crisis averted.

Reshooting or dropping scenes, adding to locations, missing coverage—none of these things is an option in television. There is no margin for error.

The schedule in television is so tight that while you are shooting, another director is already hard at work prepping the next episode. The day after you wrap, the next episode starts. If you don't "make your days," it throws the schedule off for the entire series. The networks and studios are very unforgiving about this. Solutions must be found.

* * *

On a cold, rainy day in Vancouver, I found myself looking out the fifth story window of a turn-of-the-century downtown hotel. My job was to stage a fight in the room which would end with the bad guy being thrown out the hotel window to his death five stories below.

I had asked production for a realistic, life-sized dummy of the bad-guy actor, complete with wig and wardrobe. My plan was to stage the fight so that in the last shot, the villain would fly past the camera (two stuntmen would catch him before he got to the window). Then I would cut to the hero; over his shot, TV audiences would hear the sound of glass and wood breaking.

Then I would throw the dummy out the window and film it falling from street level, in slow motion. We had stunt pads ready to "catch" the dummy since it was a "rental" and we didn't want to ruin it.

The first AD told me that the dummy had arrived on the fifth floor and I asked to see it. *It was the stupidest dummy I had ever seen!* The wig was ridiculous, the arms were frozen solid, and the legs were like broomsticks. I was shocked. Normally the art department on this TV show knew what they were doing but something had gone wrong.

* * *

In retrospect, this was all kind of my fault. I should have asked to see the dummy a day or two before, so that we might have had time to fix it. The director just has to *assume* that everything is going to go wrong and try to anticipate as much disaster as possible. This is why directors become control freaks: years of disappointment.

* * *

There was no time to get another dummy and we were losing the light. (It gets dark very early in Vancouver.) I thought for a moment and considered my options. The location was too expensive to come back to, and there was nothing in the budget for a reshoot. Then I had an idea.

I turned to the DP and asked him if he had an Eyemo camera on the truck.

"Sure," he said, and he sent one of his guys down to get it.

Made out of cast iron, the Eyemo is a crash camera that was originally designed for combat situations. It uses 100-foot camera rolls that can last a couple minutes. They are practically indestructible.

My idea was to set the camera at 120 frames per second (extreme slow motion) and we would throw the camera itself out the window and hope to "catch" it in the stunt pad below. The shot might give us a strange falling point-of-view shot that would work as a cool way to end the sequence. Rob, the DP, was on board with the idea and we wound up the camera, started the motor and threw it out the window. The grips below caught it perfectly like a bunch of firemen with a net.

When the film came back from the lab, we saw that the shot worked perfectly. It really captured the "feeling" of falling out of a window. Now we just needed to pick up a random shot of the bad guy lying on the ground, which we could do anywhere.

My little improv had put us back on time and on schedule and the producers liked the shot once they saw it cut into the sequence. Another problem solved.

Often, these low-tech solutions can save the day. One afternoon on *Bones*, in a circus tent, I had to have our star David Boreanaz throw knives at Emily Deschanel and pop balloons placed around her head and body. In the story, David and Emily were undercover as a knife-throwing circus act.

The producers had a whole plan in place that would require us to shoot "plates" of Emily *with* the balloons, and *without* the balloons. Then plates *with* the knives and *without* the knives. "Plates" are shots that are "locked off," which means the camera doesn't move *at all*. In a computer, the CGI and visual effects team can combine these "elements" to create convincing scenes … in this case, a knife flying through the air and popping a balloon inches from the lead actress' face. As I was conferring with the visual effects supervisor, I realized this approach would take so long that it would ruin the rest of the afternoon and we would never make our day.

* * *

I remembered a similar situation on my second film *Getting Even*: A Russian guard posted outside a military complex was going to be shot by one of our heroes with a crossbow. The special effects team had come up with a wire rig that would guide the arrow through the air and plant it in the (fake) chest of the guard. The props department had another idea: a "pop-up" arrow, attached to the stuntman, that would spring into place so quickly that the camera wouldn't notice the sleight of hand. Both of these ideas seemed to me like they would take hours to do and lead to a lousy result.

I turned to an old prop guy who must have been in his seventies. He'd been working on films going back decades. In fact, he'd been retired for ages, but couldn't keep away from movie sets. It was all he knew.

I walked over to him, suspecting that he would know what to do. And of course, he did.

"Kid," he said, "put the arrow in the guy's chest plate and then just whip-pan the camera really fast and land on the arrow. Have the guy grab his chest, make a noise and fall. That's it. Should take less than ten minutes."

"And that will work?"

"Sonny," he said, "I've killed more cowboys that way than you can count. A few Indians too."

I explained the new plan to the camera operator and stuntman. We did three or four takes, whip-panning the camera to the actor with the arrow already in place. It all worked like a charm because the eye can't really distinguish what it's seeing at that speed. A proper sound effect does the rest of the work.

* * *

Back on the *Bones* set, I explained to everyone what we were going to do: put the knife through the balloon and stick it into the plywood. We'll

Eight. Too Many Cooks in the Kitchen

whip-pan from thin air to the knife, and Emily will react. We did this with multiple knives and balloons. In a half hour, we had the whole scene.

When the scene was cut together, it was fantastic. I saved the producers money and saved my own ass by making an otherwise un-doable day doable, using a trick from some 1950s cowboy movie.

At the end of the episode, I was able to shoot a really memorable television ending. David and Emily's knife-throwing act had helped solve the crime, and now it was time for them to put their alter egos away and return to their regular jobs. At first, we see David and Emily coming out of their aluminum Airstream-style circus trailer still in their circus act clothes. David had been Boris, a knife-throwing Russian czar, and Emily had been Natasha, a gypsy princess. As they look around at the empty circus camp one more time, a gust of wind comes up and blows an old promotional poster for "Boris and Natasha and the Knives of Death" across the dusty ground until it stops at David's feet. (When we put on the wind machine, the poster actually did this ... *as scripted*.) David picks up the poster and looks wistfully at the advertisement for their spectacular act. Emily joins him and then they watch the trucks with the clowns, animals and gymnasts drive away on their journey to the next town.

You could feel the longing in the hearts of our characters to "run off and join the circus." But they had to stay, be responsible, go back to their real jobs. The longing was also in the hearts of the actors. In all of us, really.

I photographed David and Emily in a two-shot and then pulled back on the crane watching them become smaller and smaller in the frame; and then panned away to the trucks disappearing over the horizon. What a moment! I swear they had tears in their eyes and so did I. There is something timeless about the universal longing for freedom and adventure in all of us.

Besides, if you think about it, the entire film business is a version of "running off to join the circus."

* * *

In his book *Outliers*, Malcom Gladwell popularized the idea that only after 10,000 hours of correct practice could the artist-athlete achieve expert mastery of his or her discipline. Doing the math on this, that would mean 20 hours per week of practice over ten years. By this metric, I figured out that I had by now become a master of directing, and this thought did give me a certain confidence. This theory has been somewhat debunked recently, but I think there is a grain of truth in it. Keep directing long enough, you get pretty good at it.

Chris Carter called me in to do an *X-Files* episode shooting in L.A. The show was now in its 11th season and star David Duchovny had moved on. But Gillian Anderson was still there and had been joined by Robert Patrick and Annabeth Gish.

* * *

Robert Patrick had exploded onto the scene as the "T-1000" in Arnold Schwarzenegger's *Terminator 2: Judgment Day*. After that, he never stopped working, starring or co-starring in movies and TV shows: *Walk the Line, Copland, Flags of Our Fathers*. Annabeth Gish had broken a million hearts, including mine, with her first film, *Mystic Pizza*.

* * *

I was excited to be a part of this landmark series, but I hadn't really watched a lot of it. I tried to catch up, but 11 seasons is a lot of television.

On one of my first days, I had set up a shot where Gillian (Agent Scully) runs up onto a porch and into a farmhouse where a boy is reported to have supernatural powers. I explained the shot to Gillian, and she seemed fine with the approach to the scene. Right before calling *action*, I asked the DP to roll the camera at 60 frames a second because I thought a little slo-motion would really sell the moment and add to the drama.

The DP gave me a funny look.

"What?" I asked.

"There is no slow motion on *The X-Files*," he announced.

Apparently, very early on, a decision had been made not to film any of the *X-Files* scenes in slow motion. I probably should have been briefed on this, or maybe I just should have known it. It's hard to come onto a show that has been going so long and be completely up to speed.

"Okay," I said. "Thanks for telling me."

We put the camera back on 24 frames and did the shot. It wasn't as good, and confirmed what I have longed believed: "Rules" should never apply to directing or filmmaking in general. The *best approach* to the scene should be the rule. But I was a guest in this *X-Files* world and needed to be a team player.

Gillian was a trooper and did her job, but after 11 years you could tell her heart just wasn't in it any more. (After *The X-Files*, she moved to England and did a lot of highly regarded work in television there, culminating with a Golden Globe–winning turn as Margaret Thatcher on *The Crown*.)

Even the most successful shows eventually wind down, and all the people who have become friends and family to each other are scattered to the winds.

John Huston said that directing is the loneliest job in the world because you become so close to so many people on each project. Then,

Eight. Too Many Cooks in the Kitchen

when the movie or series wraps, you most likely will never see them again. That truth really hit home one afternoon on one of my last shooting days on *The X-Files*.

It turned out that after 11 years, it was on *my* episode that the announcement was made: *The X-Files* was being cancelled. Chris Carter gathered the cast and crew into the Fox lot's storied Stage 6 and broke the news just after lunch. This was wrenching news for those who had been with the show for all those years.

At the phones on the back wall of the sound stage, I could hear crew members calling their spouses and telling them to freeze credit cards and stop all unnecessary spending. The gravy train had run out of track.

I had the thankless job of prodding the shocked crew back to work. They were now mostly hugging and crying. I was in an impossible position since I was the one who was pushing to keep going, while they were thinking about how to manage their lives without the steady *X-Files* paycheck.

* * *

Crisis must be averted. Stars must be managed. Writers and producers assuaged. Production problems have to be met and overcome. But in the middle of all this, there still must be time for artistic ambition.

Like my "circus episode" on *Bones*, I have occasionally found myself very moved by television material. When this happens, I have tried to elevate the good writing to the point where I feel I have made a legitimate artistic contribution.

* * *

Millennium was about the real and imagined coming of what was then known and feared as Y2K (the year 2000). In the Christian calendar, the end of the second millennium marks the Judgment Day and the Second Coming of Christ. According to the Bible, Christ was to come back after 2000 years and pass judgment on people both living and dead. Needless to say, there was a lot of real unease about the impending arrival of this symbolic date.

The fulfillment of Christian prophecy lined up with a so-called "computer glitch" which was going to bring down banks, shut down the power grids, disrupt the food supply and cause the general overall collapse of society. Planes were going to fall out of the skies because of the impending programming disaster when 1999 became 2000. Some people would be snatched and taken up to Heaven. Some would be sent to Hell or *left behind*. These events were described in scripture as "The Rapture."

I was shooting a scene with the great Terry O'Quinn (who went on to fame on the TV show *Lost*). Terry's character was sitting in front of a fire and explaining winter solstice, the origins of the Christian calendar, and the Second Coming to Lance and the rest of the *Millennium* cast. This was all part of the story and written as dialogue.

I was very taken with the scene because I thought we were really digging into the emotions and questions that so many people were feeling at that time. I moved the camera very slowly across Terry's face and then moved on to show the rest of the actors absorbed in what Terry was saying. I had the lighting team create a convincing firelight effect so that the movement of the flames would reflect in each actor's eyes. Finally, I pushed in to show a close-up of Lance listening to these words as if his life depended on it. And in the story, it did.

I did several takes to make sure I got it right, then let the first AD know that I was done. He asked what close-ups I would be doing, and I said that for this scene I wouldn't be doing any. I really wanted this scene to play in the shot I had *designed,* and I didn't feel I needed any additional "coverage" (close-up shots).

"Okay, it's your funeral," the AD said ominously.

This scene turned out to be the rare case where I was not reprimanded for skipping the close-ups, because the shot *did* work. I was moved by the actor and the script. I really tried to step up and do a visual treatment of the material that would resonate for the audience. It was not enough just to shoot the script. It was critically important to help *interpret* the script.

* * *

Down by a lake near St. Francisville, Louisiana, I was working with country star Kix Brooks. We were making a TV movie, and our young heroine was trying to make up her mind between the boyfriend who was "right" for her, and the boy she had left behind in her hometown, who she really loved. Kix had written an original song for the scene and we were shooting it around an open fire.

Kix Brooks had enjoyed a huge career in country music as half of the famous duo Brooks and Dunn. Along with Ronnie Dunn, Kix had many #1 hits ("Red Dirt Road," "Neon Moon," "Boot Scootin' Boogie," "My Maria") and had won CMAs, Grammys and Billboard awards. With us, he was just happy to be an actor playing a well-to-do father looking after his daughter's marriage plans.

I asked Kix if he would be comfortable playing the song for the first time without the use of "playback." Playback would mean playing a pre-recorded version of the song on a speaker and then Kix would lip-sync the lyrics. But if he could perform the song "live," I felt the actors would react more organically to the emotion of the song. Kix readily agreed, and

Eight. Too Many Cooks in the Kitchen

I hid a "B" camera behind some trees with a long lens so that I could capture the cast listening to the song for the first time.

We set up for the master shot which would include the whole song and rolled on take one.

I watched the monitor as the camera moved around the fire and caught the moonlight dancing off the water. I heard the song in my headphones, then stopped looking at the monitor. I looked out across the fire to Kix as he played, and I also caught the faces of the other actors as they listened. The song, "Barefoot Days," perfectly captured a yearning for innocence and the freedom of youth. By the time the shot was over, tears were streaming down my face. I tapped the first AD on the shoulder and made the universal "cut" gesture with my hand across my neck. I was so choked up I couldn't say the word "cut."

I don't know what it was about that song, on that night, in that moment, but I was overcome with emotion. I guess I was really feeling time passing by and I, like the other eight billion people on the planet, could do nothing about it. I was glad the camera wasn't on me.

I pretended to make notes in my script until I knew I was fully composed, and then we pressed on. There is a magic in moments like that … movie magic.

I have been equally inspired by other singers and musicians while shooting. Performers like Katherine McFee, Jimmy Cliff, Patti LaBelle and Jackson Brown. Popular music bypasses the brain and goes right to the heart. As Noël Coward said, "Extraordinary how potent cheap music is."

* * *

My original plan was to get into television so that I could make my living close to home. But my plan was short-lived. Instead of the "stay at home job" I thought TV directing would be, it was rapidly becoming another "on the road" job just like movies.

* * *

By the time my work on *The Practice* was finished, the studio financing models had changed substantially, and now TV directors were sent wherever there was a tax deal or government incentive. I found myself for weeks or months at a time in Chicago, Dallas, Calgary, Shreveport, Atlanta, Vancouver, Wilmington, Providence, Albuquerque, Toronto or some other non–Hollywood city.

Actors playing key roles are flown out to location from L.A. while many of the supporting roles are cast with local talent. Key crew members are also flown out when the producers can't find quality gaffers, prop masters or dolly grips. Some crew members sell their homes in L.A. and move to Atlanta. I was trying to raise a family in L.A., but like everyone else, I had to go where the money was.

In Austin, Texas, independent filmmaker Robert Rodriguez had built his own studio with profits from his hit movies *Spy Kids* and *Sin City*. When I drove onto the "Trouble-Maker" Studios lot to direct an episode of *From Dusk Till Dawn*, I was suitably impressed. Not only did Robert have sound stages, prop and wardrobe departments, transportation, etc., he also had state-of-the-art visual effects and post-production facilities. On top of all that, Robert was starting his own TV network, El Rey Network, and *From Dusk Till Dawn* was the flagship production.

The empowering thing about this assignment was that Robert was a director first, and had no interest in micro-managing the episode directors. He hired people he liked, then let them do their thing. I was about the only non–Hispanic director hired for the series, and I felt honored to be there.

I fell easily into the aesthetic of the show. My first episode, called "The Place of Dead Roads," written by Alvaro Rodriguez, was one of my best. Full of powerful Tejano music, colorful characters, mystical forces, vampires and criminals, this fantastical world was compelling.

One day, a small army of motorcycles swarmed around me as I was rehearsing a scene outside the famous Titty Twister, home of the vampire

Robert Patrick, Madison Davenport, Zane Holtz, Dwight Little and DJ Cotrona filming *From Dusk Till Dawn*.

Eight. Too Many Cooks in the Kitchen

bar featured in the *From Dusk Till Dawn* movie. Because of the timing of my episode, I was the director who was going to introduce the exterior and interior of the Titty Twister for the whole series. I felt a lot of pressure to get it right. As I worked out the motorcycle action, I saw the AD coming towards me with a cellphone. I couldn't tell by the expression on his face what the problem might be.

"Robert wants to talk to you," he said, deadpan.

Uh-oh, I thought. This was the boss and he rarely called.

My concern was unwarranted. Robert was cutting one of his own episodes and realized he needed some shots of the exterior where I was shooting. He asked if I could work the shots he wanted into my day. He described each shot as he saw it in his head. They all made complete sense. I was more than happy to do this for the boss. I told him to consider it done. That was as much "hand-holding" as I ever had with Robert. He was a director at heart, and I found the communication with him easy … much easier than with some writers.

On *From Dusk Till Dawn,* I was able to reunite with my *X-Files* pal Robert Patrick. Robert performed a scene with his screen daughter that was so powerful, it made me realize he would be perfect for a small movie I was putting together, called *Last Rampage.* We did end up doing that movie and he was fantastic in it, earning rave reviews.

Robert Rodriguez and Dwight Little filming *From Dusk Till Dawn*.

I also reconnected with the great character actor Danny Trejo, who had been a featured player in *Marked for Death*. In the following years, Danny had become a household name with many roles in independent movies, as well as the starring role in Robert Rodriguez's *Machete* and *Machete Kills*. We were able to point at each other and laugh, "We were nobodies!"

* * *

Danny Trejo had one of the most amazing origin stories of any actor I'd ever worked with. He had been locked up in San Quentin as a young man and used much of his time learning how to box. The boxing led to a chance to train Eric Roberts for the movie *Runaway Train*. The director liked him so much that he gave Danny a small part. After that, Danny was on his way.

Feeling like a traveling salesman, I was sent to Chicago where *Prison Break* was shooting. The first season of the famous Fox show was filmed in the Joliet prison outside the city. The classic period prison (shut down in 2002) had housed notorious criminals since before the Civil War. I'm not much for ghosts and "energy," but it was hard not to feel the collective horror of what had gone on in those buildings over the last century and a half.

I had to complete a scene with Dominic Purcell in one of the original small cells. The camera needed to face the bars and stone hallway to the outside. The only way to get the shot was to have the camera operator, myself and Dominic all locked in the cell. Even though the keys and crew were just outside, the feeling of being trapped in that space, even for a few hours, was very unnerving. Dominic had to play a very difficult dramatic scene as the character learns his stay of execution has been revoked. Dominic did an amazing job, and we were out of there after a few takes. But the fact that John Wayne Gacy, or Richard Speck, or Baby Face Nelson might have done time in that cell was spooky. As William Faulkner said, "The past is never dead. It's not even past."

* * *

In a former plantation house in Louisiana, I was shooting in a nineteenth-century drawing room with portraits of the ancestors hanging on the walls. Just underneath that room was a basement where the owners' slaves had lived. There were small stone kitchens and concrete beds. A walkway led to a massive rock well, hundreds of feet deep, and its water was raised up for master and slave alike. The scene we were shooting was so light and fun. And just below us, the haunting memory of subjugation and injustice that the country just can't seem to recover from.

Churches, prisons, graveyards, mausoleums, Native American ruins,

Eight. Too Many Cooks in the Kitchen 175

Eric Roberts and Dwight Little filming *The Finder*.

casinos ... the traveling TV director sees and shoots it all. And though the fresh locations do add a visual interest to many of the scenes, there is really very little that could not just as easily be filmed in Los Angeles. It's all about chasing the money. This really hit home one day when I was changing the outside of a house in Atlanta to look like it was in Pasadena!

For decades, L.A. has successfully stood in for locations all over the world. With a little careful framing, and a good art department, you can go anywhere. I have shot India, Jamaica, Afghanistan, Canada, Russia, Mexico, the Midwest and Africa, all in Los Angeles.

* * *

Part of the fun of living in L.A. is being able to discover Hollywood history wherever you go. Hiking out in Malibu State Park, you come across a "Connecticut" country house used for movies with Paul Newman and Cary Grant. A little farther into the park, there are the dusty "Korean" hills from the *M*A*S*H* TV series. The "Suicide is Painless" theme song echoes in your head. Or look up at the cliff where Redford and Newman leapt into the roaring river for *Butch Cassidy and the Sundance Kid*. (Okay, maybe their stunt doubles.)

Strolling along a beach near Laguna, you'll come across the house built for *Beaches* with Bette Midler and Barbara Hershey. At Zuma Beach, the voice of Charlton Heston can still be heard cursing man for screwing up the planet. The Statue of Liberty from *Planet of the Apes* is not really there, of course, but it is *in your mind*. Heston's "Damn you all to Hell!" still rings out over the same waves that washed up onto Burt Lancaster and Deborah Kerr in *From Here to Eternity*. And right nearby, John Turturro sits in the sand dreaming of his Hollywood fantasy girl in *Barton Fink*.

James Dean is still moping around the Griffith Observatory in *Rebel Without a Cause*; the Santa Monica Pier carousel from *The Sting* is still spinning. Film history is everywhere in Los Angeles. We don't have medieval castles or renaissance cathedrals, but we have the next best thing: Hollywood.

* * *

Over the years, the authority of the TV director has been slowly eroding. Much of this has to do with the changing technology, and some with the rise of the showrunner as the medium's creative force. The Directors Guild has tried to steer some of the decision-making back to the director, mostly to no avail.

In film or television, one of the greatest contributions a director can make is to supervise the final choices in casting.

In my earlier days, on shows like *The Practice, Prison Break, Bones,*

Chris Manley, Dwight Little and Wentworth Miller filming *Prison Break*.

Eight. Too Many Cooks in the Kitchen

Millennium, etc., we always had "in person" casting sessions for each episode. A casting session would be held during prep, and the director would sit with the writer and producer. The actors would come in for each guest role. There could easily be ten or more "in person" candidates for each part, and these "callbacks" would already have been pre-screened from 20 or more with the casting director the day before. After the actor auditioned, the director could give notes and direction to refine the performance and see if it would be right for the episode.

The casting session was a great way for me to *hear* the script, and really find out where the strengths and weaknesses were in the material. At the end of the session, the producer and director would discuss their top choices. Then two or three actors would have their taped auditions sent to the showrunner, studio and network for approval.

For one critical piece of casting on *Bones*, the producer and I were very much in sync. The part was a young boy who would be taken hostage, and finally rescued by FBI Agent Booth (David Boreanaz) and Dr. Brennen (Emily Deschanel). We sent up two candidates, but there was no doubt who the right choice for the part was.

We received a message back from the studio: "Fox Casting wants to go with choice number two."

The producer and I were shocked. Choice one was so much better. Importantly, Hart Hanson, the showrunner, was on board. So, a producer with 20 years of experience, a director with over 50 episodes of experience, and a showrunner who had written successful television for years, were all wrong?

I decided to push the issue. The producers told me to just leave it alone, but I was pissed. I wanted to know who the "head of casting" was over at Fox. Who exactly was "Fox Casting"? I got the number for her office and called. I explained to the assistant that I was the director of the episode of *Bones* now prepping and I had a question. The assistant quickly told me, "The head of casting is in a meeting and she's not available."

It was very unorthodox for me to be calling the studio. I was seriously outside the chain of command. But I explained that my question was pressing and that for production reasons, I needed to speak with her *now*. My tone was pretty direct. The assistant didn't know what to do, so she put me on hold. And then, to my surprise, the casting executive actually picked up.

"Hi, this is Dwight Little, the episode director on *Bones*. Thanks for taking my call."

I tried to speak with a calm but determined voice. "The producers and I sent up an actor for the guest part on my episode and your office passed. I was curious as to why?"

There was stillness on the other end of the phone until finally: "I'm not really aware of this situation, but go on."

"Well, I'm just calling to see why you guys didn't go with our #1 choice. Hart and the writer are on board, so I was just confused."

There was another pause. I waited and didn't fill in the empty space with more chatter.

"I'm going to look into this and call you back," she finally responded.

I figured that would be the end of that. She would probably back up her people and move on. But a few hours later, she did call me back. She explained that although she had not seen the audition herself, one of her casting assistants had seen the tapes and preferred the other choice.

So, even with the *years* of experience between the producer, showrunner and me ... the decision had been made by a 25-year-old *junior* assistant in the Fox casting office.

The casting executive said that if we all felt so strongly about it, we could go ahead with our first choice. We did get the actor we wanted, but I was reprimanded for not going through proper channels and exceeding my authority. There is always blowback when you stick your neck out ... but it was a good episode. Bad behavior will usually be forgiven with a successful result.

I have always been skeptical of groups or organizations that speak as if they are an actual living, breathing entity. "Fox Casting doesn't agree," "The *Los Angeles Times* hates your movie," "Your healthcare provider has denied your claim," etc. It's not the institution as they'd like you to believe, rather an actual person somewhere in an office. *One guy* at the *L.A. Times* didn't like your movie, *one junior assistant* in the casting office didn't like your choice, *one bureaucrat* at the insurance company denied your claim, etc. It's rarely a well-informed group decision.

* * *

In recent times, and because of the new technology, the casting process has completely changed. Nowadays, actors are generally sent the script pages and told: "Put yourself on tape." This means they get their roommate, or boyfriend, or family member to record them on their iPhone while they read the lines of the scene. Then the audition is uploaded to the Internet. So now, the director receives an email file with the auditions from selected actors. Of course, no one was there to guide the actors, or give them notes, so you get what you get.

The director can look at all these auditions and weigh in with his top picks. The problem is ... everyone else has also received this exact same email. Producers, showrunner, writer, executive producers, casting director, studio executives. By the time the director indicates his choices, the

Eight. Too Many Cooks in the Kitchen

decision has often already been made. The ability of the director to use his experience and instincts has been completely neutralized.

Same story with other crucial decisions. Location photos can be posted to 20 people at the same time, inviting 20 opinions; also true with wardrobe, props and sets. There isn't much point in complaining about it now, since the Internet has made everything virtual, and now *everyone* is a decision-maker. Whatever meetings were left for face-to-face discussions have now also been relegated to "zoom meetings" due to the pandemic.

Another change in directing for network television has been the creation of an additional management position, the director-producer.

The head writers (showrunners) have taken on the bulk of the creative chores and found that educating each new director on the style and tone of the show is too time-consuming. The director-producer is meant to help provide continuity for a particular series. This job is filled by a DGA director member who is contracted to work on the show for the whole season. The director-producer directs as many as three or four episodes during the season (although not the pilot) and then helps guide each new episode director through the process. The idea is sensible and many of the director-producers I have worked with have been great collaborators. But there is a catch.

The cast and department heads naturally go to the director-producer *first* with their questions, since he or she is with the show for the full season. So the individual episode director has even *less* authority over the episode. This is a classic case of "unintended consequences." Instead of empowering the guest director, the actual effect is to diminish the input of the guest director. And so the erosion of the job continues.

* * *

There is no way to tell which series will become a success and which will fail. It's a combination of concept, execution, casting and timing. For the TV director, getting in early on a show that airs for a number of years is a miracle. When it does happen, the best thing to do is count your blessings and do as many episodes as you can. "Make hay while the sun shines," as the old saying goes.

The people who put their heart and soul into the hits are the same people who suffer the flops. Here are some shows that I worked very hard on, that were expeditiously exiled to the graveyard of failed TV shows:

Wolf Lake. The Inside. Dollhouse. Matador. Daytime Divas. The Finder. Daybreak. Vanished. Just Legal. John Doe. Veritas the Quest. Citizen Baines. Strange World. Tower Prep. Body of Proof.

Hey, anybody ever heard of these shows? No Emmys, no SAG awards, no Golden Globes; just dead silence.

At some point, a lot of smart people believed that each one of these series was going to be a hit. They were green-lit and ordered into production at the cost of tens of millions. But somehow, they just didn't catch on with the viewing public. A bad time slot, a competing project, bad casting, unappealing subject. No matter how clever TV executives think they are, the audience decides what it wants to watch at the end of a long day, not them.

The advertisers need "eyeballs" to justify the huge amount of dollars that network TV demands. The Nielsen numbers that are so important to them are in the "18–49" demographic, since these consumers spend the most money on cars, detergents, iPhones, beer, beach vacations, frozen foods and all the rest. The older demographic attracts endless ad money from pharmaceutical companies, health care plans and cruise ships. If you don't get eyeballs … you get the axe.

* * *

Here's how Hart Hanson turned an okay police procedural into a hit and got renewed. Hart had developed the previously mentioned show with a female forensic pathologist as the lead, based on a successful book series called *Bones*. In Season One, a very serious crime tone was taken as Temperance Brennan and her FBI partner solve nasty crimes. It was going okay, but it didn't seem to be really flying. Just another cop show.

But then Hart noticed that after each scene was over, and the written words had been spoken, David and Emily just continued on after *cut*. For their own amusement, they ad-libbed funny irreverent lines while still in character. Noticing all this, Hart started asking the directors not to call *cut* after the written scene was over.

"Just keep rolling," Hart said. "Let's see what they do."

Hart had of course noticed that David and Emily had such a natural chemistry that the lines they made up were often better than what had been written. Hart started writing the shows using this new tone that David and Emily were taking on their own. Hart told me, "One night I was writing and started to realize … this isn't really just a crime show. It's a crime show with comedy. It's a *crimedy!*"

And with that inspiration, Hart reinvented a genre. *Hart to Hart* and *Moonlighting* had succeeded in this space years before, but *Bones* did it with a contemporary edge. *Bones* was copied many times in the next few years by shows like *Castle* and *Bull*. For 12 seasons, David and Emily solved crimes and improvised humor to great effect.

When a show does work, millions are able to see it. And if it runs for years, then there is a real chance to make a contribution to the contemporary culture and influence the public conversation. *The Practice, 24,*

Eight. Too Many Cooks in the Kitchen

Emily Deschanel, Dwight Little and David Boreanaz filming *Bones*.

The X-Files, Prison Break, Sleepy Hollow, Millennium, Bones, these became "zeitgeist" shows.

I have always been pleased when I hear a member of the public say to me, "I loved that TV show" or "My son/daughter never misses that TV show," and these are episodes I directed. Viewers get excited because they remember it's a particular night and their favorite show is on. They can come home, have something to eat, then sit back, relax and enjoy the evening. I do feel like this is a useful service, to give people something to look forward to in the middle of a long work week.

* * *

What used to be called "appointment TV," however, has now been replaced with binge viewing. In 2013, when Netflix decided to drop an entire season of *House of Cards* all at once, there was a paradigm shift in the television business. Instead of waiting a week to see the next installment of your favorite story, the viewer could watch two or three (or more) episodes in a single night. This would have been a disaster for a network who counted on ad revenue to keep their business model running. But a streaming subscription service just needed to sell consumers on their platform, $15 at a time.

Without the tyranny of commercial interruptions or broadcast "standards and practices," cable television was liberated to tell more sophisticated adult stories. This new freedom, along with the collapse of the mid-size studio feature, meant that talented high-end writers and directors now were clamoring to do "premium television."

The medium that was once called "The Boob Tube," that was looked down upon by serious filmmakers for decades, was now the belle of the ball. And everyone wanted in. *Breaking Bad, Game of Thrones, The Handmaid's Tale, Mindhunter, Goliath, True Detective, Ozark, The Crown, Black Mirror, Normal People, Fleabag*: The list of series that have changed TV in the last ten years is long and impressive.

The networks still have weekly shows such as *Law and Order, Chicago Fire, Young Sheldon*, etc., but I'm not sure how long the broadcast model can last. The cost of doing a one-hour drama, especially with action and special effects, is huge and the audience just isn't there. Game shows, reality shows, musical competitions and talk shows can all be done at a fraction of the cost and draw the same-size audience.

Before premium television, there was a wildly successful television genre that tackled many social issues and entertained millions. It was a good medium for directors, and I hope and pray it will one day make a comeback to the networks. It was called the TV movie.

NINE

It's Always Personal

Ten years after the death of my father, I was faced with another personal crisis. M.J., my wife of 12 years, was dying of ovarian cancer. She had been fighting and recovering from her illness since her first diagnosis around the time of *Rapid Fire*, many years earlier. When people say "courageous battle," it doesn't really do justice to the kind of love and strength M.J. showed. Throughout her treatments, and despite the hardships, she always managed a smile and found a quality of life that was very much worth living.

I was with her, holding her hand, as she took her last breath; and in that moment, along with the wrenching loss of her, I felt the extraordinary miracle of life and our capacity for love. M.J. was pushed out of this world in a cruel way, but she also made every minute of her life matter, which was her own victory over death. All the books and movies and plays about the arrival of death cannot really convey the experience itself, because death can only be *felt*, it is impossible to *understand*. Each of us has to find our own way forward after the loss of a loved one, parent or spouse or friend. There is no right way to mourn and there is certainly no such thing as closure. But we have to somehow press on, and for me, this meant there were more movies to be made.

Just a few months after M.J.'s passing, my agents sent me a script called *Papa's Angels*. It was from Marian Rees and Anne Hopkins, two highly respected television movie producers. They had impeccable taste and great reputations. Together they had produced the movies *Foxfire*, *The Shell Seekers*, *Miss Rose White*, *The Orphan Train* and many others. *Papa's Angels* was a passion project of TV star Scott Bakula. They wanted to know: Would I be interested in directing it? The script was about a poor Appalachian man in the 1930s, trying to keep his boisterous family together while his wife was dying of tuberculosis.

What?! How was this possible? Out of the blue, I get a script for a movie about a man with a dying wife? There were no odds for this. I read the script, and scene after scene evoked emotions that I had not only just lived through but was barely recovering from. There was no way I could say yes to this. Too soon, too raw, too close to home. How was I even being considered for this? (Turned out it was the Emmy-winning work I had done on *The Practice*.)

I was about to pass on the project, to save myself from reliving the trauma, when my therapist stepped in. "Dwight," she said, "what if you were sent this script as an opportunity to not only face your own demons, but also to bring something real and fresh to a standard network TV movie?"

I gave some serious thought to this, and what she said slowly changed my point of view. Wasn't this the whole point of art? To express ideas and feelings that are extremely personal and difficult? The more I thought about this, the more I realized I would be a coward to shy away from this script just because it might be painful for me. So I called the agent and said I would be willing to speak with Marian, Anne and Scott.

The producers, Scott and I hit it off right away, and I was relieved to be associated with these highly literate, thoughtful people after some of the sideshow barkers I had worked with in the past.

Scott had come out of New York theater and by this time he was a legit TV star from his Emmy- and Golden Globe–winning show *Quantum Leap*. I was impressed by his supporting role in *American Beauty*, one of the all-time great American movies.

After some intensive creative meetings, we all got on the same page about the script, the look and the tone of the movie. And so, up to Canada I went.

I found locations outside of Calgary that would work for 1930s North Carolina, then set about casting the movie. We were over the moon when Cynthia Nixon agreed to play the ailing mother; then thrilled again when Eva Marie Saint came on board to play the grandmother.

* * *

Cynthia Nixon had enjoyed a distinguished career in the theater and had made a memorable appearance as Mozart's housekeeper in *Amadeus*. She had Emmys and Tonys, but to most she would be forever known as Miranda from *Sex and the City*.

* * *

One morning I was working with Cynthia in a small cabin–movie set that we had rebuilt for our production an hour outside of Calgary. Cynthia's character had been brought home from a sanatorium by her husband (Scott), who had built her a glass porch attached to the main house. The glass would protect the children from her tuberculosis. This way Scott's character could have his wife at home while she recovered. (Being a TV movie, though, of course she dies eventually.)

As I was exploring the scenes with Cynthia, I realized I was really talking to M.J. I was asking Cynthia for emotions and behaviors that were right out of my own recent experience. Cynthia was such a good actor that she was able to interpret the feelings I was trying to communicate and make them her own. This story for me had become very personal.

* * *

A director makes hundreds of decisions a day. About camera, locations, performances, wardrobe, production design, etc. Each of these decisions is filtered through *who you are* as an individual and an artist. Your childhood, your experiences, your gender, your social class, your spiritual beliefs … they all contribute to how your intuitive mind works. In post-production, every edit, every sound effect, every music choice are all personal creative choices. So when people tell a director, "It's not personal," it is a real slap in the face.

This is why it is so ridiculous to try and compare yourself to others. Their careers, their successes or failures. They are not you and you are not them. Never spend a moment on envy or jealousy, it's a complete waste of time.

* * *

Between shots, I looked out the cabin window and saw our first AD leading an elderly woman, dressed in a parka, up the stone pathway to the cabin. I had lost track of time and then suddenly realized that the lady was Eva Marie Saint. Holy shit!

Eva Marie Saint had won an Oscar for *On the Waterfront*. She had gone toe to toe with Cary Grant in *North by Northwest*. Eva was a Golden Age *movie star*. We were hurried into production because CBS wanted *Papa's Angels* for Christmas. Consequently, I hadn't even had a chance to meet her until she arrived on set. I introduced her to Cynthia and Scott, and the three of us welcomed her to the movie.

I asked Eva to read the scene we were scheduled to shoot. She did, and soon she was ready to go. Eva's years of set experience were obvious to all of us. Her blocking, timing, and line readings all hit home. And, of course, she knew her lines cold. Eva had complete confidence in herself but no apparent ego. Believe me, that is a very difficult balance for a famous actor to achieve.

Later that evening, it got very cold. We were far up in the woods and there was no insulation in the cabin, which was really just a movie set. I could see that Eva had become quite chilled and was shivering. I offered her the option of going back to base camp where she could warm up.

She pulled her parka up a little higher around her shoulders and said, "Don't worry about me, dear. We have a job to do. Let's get on with it."

I wish I could bottle the commitment and grit of this veteran star and pass it around to some of the young actors coming up, who are used to every indulgence.

One morning at 4 a.m., I got a call from the AD department. I was not happy to be awakened after only five hours of sleep.

He blurted out, "There is snow falling and we're going to have to move everything inside or else we won't be able to shoot at all today. Do you want to go into the barn or the house first?"

It took me a minute to wake myself up and focus on what I was being asked. It was only October and *snow* was falling? Oh, that's right, I had been warned about this strange Alberta weather by the local crew.

One of the main conceits of the film was that the story took place over four seasons. I had been told in pre-production that we wouldn't be able to afford fake snow for the winter Christmas scene. I'd have to figure it out in postproduction with visual effects. But I also remembered being told about Alberta's famous Chinook winds that could cause extreme changes in temperature in just a few hours.

"Hold on!" I said. "Don't move a thing. Get a camera and small crew up to the hill behind the cabin as soon as they arrive this morning. Don't put any equipment or vehicles anywhere near the set and tell the effects department to get some smoke working in the chimney. I'm leaving right now."

My idea was to shoot the snow as soon as the light was up. This way we could get a magical Christmas shot for the opening of the movie ... and for free!

By ten in the morning, the snow had melted and we then made some shots for spring. By noon, we had a blue sky, it was 30 degrees warmer, and I shot the cabin for summer. By "locking off" the camera, I was able to dissolve from one shot to the other and show the seasonal passing of time in a very organic way. This freak weather, that was a potential disaster for us, turned into a great opportunity. Snow in October. Four seasons in a day. Preside over the accidents.

Even though we had a very tight 22-day schedule, the shooting of this TV movie was a huge emotional boost for me. Creatively, it was like shooting a film, and my producing partners were real collaborators. This had been much more satisfying than working on a TV series.

I was able to edit the movie, work with the composer and supervise the mix. If this was what it was like to make a TV movie, then I was

Nine. It's Always Personal

all-in. In the end, we scored great Nielsen ratings, and enjoyed strong reviews.

In the early morning, on the last day of the shoot, I was having coffee near the set before most of the crew had arrived. I looked out over the valley as the sun came up. It was a spectacular autumn morning in the wilds of Canada. I absorbed this beauty and at the same time felt the weight of M.J.'s death still hanging onto me. The world was both beautiful and awful *at the same time*. This may be the hardest part of living a full life: knowing that joy and suffering, hope and despair, luck and disappointment happen right alongside each other. It's the reality of nature. Light and shadow, good and evil, Yin and Yang. It's not just you, it's everyone who's ever lived.

* * *

Mulberry Street is in the heart of Manhattan's Little Italy. It has a long and colorful history going back to the American Revolution. It is more commonly known as the home turf of the Italian Mafia. There are many shops, restaurants, bars and "social clubs" with established mob histories baked in over the years.

I was walking down Mulberry Street with Chazz Palminteri and Lou DiGiaimo, who were noticed by all the locals and treated with great affection and respect. Chazz had asked me to direct his TNT movie *Boss of Bosses*, based on the life of Paul Castellano, former head of the Gambino crime family. I was a Gentile from the Midwest and an unlikely choice, but Chazz had seen *Murder at 1600* and thought it was very well-directed. Now I was getting an education in all things Mafia and taking in the lay of the land.

* * *

Chazz had made a huge name for himself with an Oscar-nominated turn in Woody Allen's *Bullets Over Broadway*. He had written both the play and film version of *A Bronx Tale* about his colorful upbringing in the Bronx. I was very flattered to have been invited into his world.

Lou DiGiaimo was a legendary New York casting director with credits like *Gladiator*, *Donnie Brasco*, *Thelma and Louise*, *Rain Man* and *The Godfather*. Lou brought in all kinds of actors who had themselves been "made men" once upon a time. Despite our different backgrounds, I felt like Lou and I had the same reactions to most of the auditions.

He was another man who seemed very serious until I started to crack some jokes, mostly on myself. Once I got him laughing, the intimidating credits with all the huge directors just sort of melted away, and we were just a couple guys having a good time casting a movie.

* * *

Angela Alvarado, Dwight Little and Chazz Palminteri filming *Boss of Bosses*.

The movie was based on the well-known book *Boss of Bosses* by Joseph F. O'Brien and Andris Kurins, the FBI agents who had helped bring down Mafia godfather Castellano. As I was studying the life of "Big Paulie" (Castellano), I found myself relating to his story in the most unlikely ways.

Castellano had been born one year before my father in 1915, and lived through the Depression, World War II, Korea, Vietnam and the American cultural earthquake of the 1960s. These years mirrored precisely my own father's life. Castellano fancied himself a businessman more than a mob boss. If you looked at his business life *without* the contract hits, extortion, racketeering, loan sharking, etc., it bore a resemblance to my father's business efforts building drafting machines in Cleveland in the 1950s and '60s.

As I dove into this script and learned about Castellano's life, I found that it was becoming another personal story to me, just as *Papa's Angels* had become. I didn't want to glorify Castellano's violent life of crime, but I did want to show how he had struggled to keep his family and marriage together while fighting off competitors and hanging onto his business interests. The fear of aging, the longing for love, and the effort to stay on top were universal human themes—not just relevant to a Mafia Godfather.

One night we recreated the famous hit on Castellano in front of Spark's Steak House on 46th Street. *Our* Sparks Steak House was in Toronto, in front of a restaurant that was a dead ringer for the real thing. The way Chazz stepped out of his 1980s town car and was gunned down by

John Gotti's hit men was uncanny. Even the way Chazz slumped down to the street matched exactly how Castellano had fallen while Gotti watched from less than a block away.

One of our "Mafia" technical advisors pulled me aside as Chazz was lying on the street and said, "You fuckin' guys are good. It feels like it's 1985 and I'm there all over again."

Okay, so I'll take the compliment. I never was able to get anyone to tell me if it had been snowing that night, but since no one seemed sure, I added the snow myself. It made the whole scene feel mythic and operatic. In the story, as Castellano is dying like a dog in the street, he reflects back on his life, both the good and the bad. It was an old storytelling device commonly called a "bookend"; for the right story, this device can be very effective.

* * *

Lawrence of Arabia begins with Lawrence racing his motorcycle along a country road in England. The way David Lean builds tension with the editing and sound is simple but very effective. The motorcycle suddenly crashes and, instead of seeing a broken body, we see Lawrence's goggles hanging from a tree branch.

At Lawrence's memorial, much of the English ruling class shows up and we get snippets of what he was like as a man from a few who knew him. Then the film flashes back to when Lawrence (Peter O'Toole) started as a clerk in a remote office of the far-flung British Empire. Three and a half hours of adventure, spectacle and drama later, Lawrence rides in a Jeep heading home. A motorcycle speeds past the Jeep and we get a foreshadowing of the fate that awaits him. It's all very poetic and "very David Lean." Bookend.

* * *

The opening titles of Fred Zinnemann's *Julia* show an old woman in a rowboat drifting poetically in a lake. In voiceover, she describes how painters have a word, *Pentimento,* which describes the process of removing paint from the surface of a canvas, to reveal the painting which often lies underneath, having been painted over. *Pentimento* is about the peeling back of layers.

Julia is about the famous twentieth-century playwright Lillian Hellman, played by Jane Fonda. The old woman in the boat is *actually* Lillian Hellman, and she takes us back to a time in her life during the war when she had to smuggle money through Nazi checkpoints to get it to her resistance leader friend Lilly (Vanessa Redgrave). After the drama of the movie is over, we return to the old lady in the boat and she reflects on her daring, youthful adventures and the loneliness she feels with the passing of time. Another excellent example of a bookend.

* * *

For *Boss of Bosses,* I was required to recreate a truly famous New York crime: the assassination of Paul Castellano. I knew that a lot of people from that world of 1985, cops, mobsters and politicians, were still alive and I didn't want to screw it up. I thought a lot about what I could bring to this sequence as a director to make it memorable.

Boss of Bosses was a biopic based on Paul Castellano's life, and though it was not a documentary, I thought we should get as many of the details right as we could. Who else had recreated a famous American assassination? The obvious answer was Oliver Stone with *JFK*.

Stone was a master of "mixed mediums" and had been using this technique in multiple films from *The Doors* to *Natural Born Killers*. He would create images on 16mm, Super 8, 35mm and even video, and cut them all together in a kind of crazy stew that became very compelling. I took inspiration from *JFK* and decided to add the ragged black and white look of gritty 16mm to give the assassination sequence a documentary-feel.

I asked our DP to get me two 16mm cameras and some black and white film. We would recruit two camera assistants to operate these cameras (they were thrilled) and I just told them to shoot whatever they saw that was interesting and under our lights. We kept going with our main unit cameras, and the 16mm film of the same sequence was shot as an "experiment." I didn't have the nerve to tell the network what I was doing, so I just did it. "Easier to ask forgiveness'than permission," as the saying goes.

We cut the sequence together using both the 35mm film and the 16mm film. The editor would cut back and forth between the two mediums without much rhyme or reason, but the effect played out just as I'd hoped. The sequence was scary and unpredictable, and also felt like it was from another time (1985).

When we showed the sequence to the network execs, they were quite enthusiastic, and didn't ask how we did it. The line producer buried the cost of the extra cameras and film into some line item in the budget, and the whole scheme ended up a huge success. If you have an idea, just go for it! Odds are, it will probably be good.

As I worked with Chazz through his character's problems with his sons, his girlfriends, his business associates and his wife, I realized why Chazz wanted to play Paul Castellano. Paul was a Mafia kingpin; but more than anything, he was Everyman. Chazz clearly saw himself in Castellano the same as I saw my father in him. Hard-working, patriotic, loving and loyal ... but of course, in Castellano's case, also a ruthless mobster and killer. Hey, nobody's perfect!

* * *

Another network TV movie I enjoyed was a light Hallmark feature called *Home by Spring*. Hallmark had raised its profile from the "ghetto" of treacly family movies, to a kind of counter-programming staple for the middle of the country. When every network's ratings were in decline, Hallmark ratings actually went up.

One day I was trying to get the perfect shot to show the rekindling romance between the hometown boy (Steven R. McQueen) and the "one that got away" girl (Poppy Drayton). I was standing in a verdant green cow pasture directing the DP to line up a shot looking back into the late afternoon light. There was a perfect, cloud-dotted sky framing stately Magnolia trees and we had a cherry vintage Chevrolet pick-up truck. We also had a better than average country song playing under the scene. Hallmark magic.

* * *

Steven R. McQueen was the grandson of Steve McQueen, one of the biggest film stars of the 1970s. Steven had made a strong impression on a CW TV show and was making his way up the ladder. Poppy Drayton, a striking and talented British actress, had made an impression on *Downton Abbey* and was also on her way up. It's fun to work with actors in their twenties. It's great to have their energy and enthusiasm rub off on everyone involved ... especially me.

* * *

As the pick-up truck approached our cameras, I felt that we had created a perfect movie moment. But film only sees and hears ... it doesn't *smell*. It turned out, the pasture was so full of cow manure that when the wind picked up, the smell of fertilizer was overpowering. Once the pick-up truck shot was done, and we moved the cameras in for the close-ups, the stench was so bad that the actors were practically choking. How romantic! In the end, everyone powered through and we got the scene; but talk about the difference between fantasy and reality! In the movie, you would never know we were all breathing through our shirts. I think this is one of the things we like most about movies ... they clean life up a bit.

* * *

Since my experience with television so far had been good, I decided that instead of developing more features that would most likely never be made, maybe I should try my hand at developing material for television.

* * *

The television network model demands a concept that can allow for *repeatable* stories, week after week, for 22 weeks. A cop show can have its main characters solve a different crime every week, and there is inherent drama as the criminal is brought to justice. "Chalk outline to handcuffs" in one hour is the general idea. Every *Bones* episode started with a body. Then, through careful forensic work, the culprit was nabbed.

Hospital shows have a solid repeatable story engine. Every time a new patient comes through the Emergency Room doors, another story comes in too. A gunshot, a beating, a rare disease … good for 42 minutes. Toss in the commercials and you've got an hour show. Lawyer shows have a wide variety of new cases and dramatic trials every week.

Dick Wolf put this all together with his *Law and Order* series. Show the crime first and then the punishment. *In one hour.* Then he took it a step further with *Chicago PD, Chicago Fire* and *Chicago Hospital.* There's a guy who knows he doesn't have to reinvent the wheel. Just *give* them the fucking wheel.

I had several meetings with my writer friend Jeff Rothberg (*Getting Even*). We teamed up with an LA homicide detective as a consultant to find ideas. But even though this guy was the real deal, we were never able to come up with anything fresh enough to go out and pitch. Cop shows are a hard genre to crack because it's been done for so long and often so well: *Hill Street Blues, NYPD Blue, The Shield.*

With my old writing partner Alan McElroy, I almost made it work. We came up with a different take on the cop story. *Shark Island* told the story of a Philadelphia cop who fakes his own death because both the cops and the mob want him dead. He retreats to a Caribbean island, but the magistrate figures out who he is and blackmails him. Our hero has to solve crimes for the magistrate, or get exposed to his old enemies back in Philadelphia. This was a repeatable idea since there were so many crimes happening on this tranquil paradise called Shark Island. Drugs, money laundering, real estate and tax fraud, missing persons, crimes of passion, etc. We had a cop with skills, lots of fresh characters, an interesting setting, and each story could be told in 42 minutes!

We set up the pitch at 20th Century-Fox (where they knew me) and went out to "the town" to sell it, hitting all of the likely studio and network buyers. (A network would have to pay for development.)

There were two problems.

First, I was just a director and had no real value to the buyers as a developer of material. Second, Alan—mostly a writer of features—didn't have a successful network show on his résumé. In TV, the executives are buying the *writer* and his or her track record as much as they are buying the concept. The network needs to know that this writer can deliver 22 hours of drama per season, deliver material week after week … and keep it going for five or more years if it is a hit. David E. Kelley, John Wells, Chris Carter, Vince Gilligan, Ryan Murphy, Shonda Rhimes … the studios are happy to buy from these creators since their track records are so solid. They are stars in this universe. In movies, Spielberg, Nolan, Scorsese, Cameron, Scott, Fincher … these are the stars.

We also struggled because there was suddenly a glut of projects that were then referred to as "blue sky" projects. Series that took place in locations where there was blue sky, like Florida. *Burn Notice*, *Hawaii Five-0*, *Lost*. These shows were doing well, so more were in the works. So many more that we didn't seem all that fresh.

Alan and I tried again with a supernatural thriller called *Division 44*. It combined the work of a clinical psychologist and a fallen psychic priest. Buried in the basement of the NYPD, *Division 44* was kind of an urban *X-Files*. We had many important meetings with this pitch, but we were never able to sell it. Each meeting with executives who can develop your pitch requires more than half a day of your life. Preparing, dressing properly, driving across town, parking, waiting, the pitch meeting itself, lunch.

A few years later, CBS made a series called *Evil* which was exactly the same concept. I hope it was a coincidence.

* * *

I wasn't really "winning" in TV development, so I decided to double down on my directing career: *Sleepy Hollow, Scorpion, Agents of S.H.I.E.L.D., Arrow, Nikita, Dollhouse,* etc.

But while I was paying the mortgage and raising a family, I was also beginning to secretly plot my comeback to movies, which is the main thing I really cared about anyway.

It's a tired cliché now to quote Joe Campbell who wrote *Follow Your Bliss*. But like most clichés, it's also kind of true. You do better at things if your heart it is in it.

Ten

The Long and Winding Road

As luck and hustle would have it, I was going to get another bite at the studio-feature apple, and I was available because I had been fired from TNT's *Monte Walsh*.

Sony/Columbia had been trying for years to figure out how to do a sequel to their sleeper hit *Anaconda*. They had commissioned many drafts and hired multiple directors, but the project had never come together.

My manager Todd Smith (formerly at CAA) had a relationship with Verna Harrah, the producer of *Anaconda*, and he helped me get a meeting with Doug Belgrade from Columbia, Clint Culpepper from Screen Gems, and Verna.

I don't know what the other director candidates had said, but I thought about what movie I might want to make, and I pitched them John Boorman's *The Emerald Forest*. Yes, we would need to have snakes, and yes there was something inherently cheesy about a snake movie. But what if you went *away* from the cheese and *toward* a real adventure movie? The executives I was presenting to, and their VPs, all gave me a kind of blank stare. I'm sure they thought I was going to say, "Let's make *Tremors*" or "Let's make *Jurassic Park* with snakes," not "Let's do a dramatic action-adventure movie."

The first *Anaconda* had been extremely campy with Jon Voight famously chewing up the scenery, so I thought, "Why not go the other way? Tell a compelling dramatic story."

I went to seven or eight different meetings pitching myself for this movie before I got the assignment. Many directors were in the mix, including the talented George Cosmatos (*Tombstone*). I don't know what the deciding factor was, but I must have said something that got their attention. Was I cheaper? Faster? The executives actually liked the fact that I had been directing television. A television director is used to tough schedules and putting a lot on the screen for very little.

Ten. The Long and Winding Road

But once you get attached to a project at a studio, you are still a *long way* from actually making the movie. Trying to get a "green light" on this (or any) studio project is nearly impossible. New writers, new drafts, more meetings. Meetings with the marketing people, the distribution people and, most importantly, the physical production executives. Amy Pascal, the head of the studio, had decided she would not spend a dime more than $30 million on a sequel to an eight-year-old snake movie. So $30 mil was the number we would have to hit. But there was already $5 million "against" the movie; that $5 million covered overhead, producer, director and writers' fees spent over the last six years. All of this money had to be recouped by the studio from our budget. So we really had just $25 million to make the movie.

We did multiple budgets, cut down the number of snakes, and cut out whole sequences. The studio started chasing down tax and rebate incentives from all over the world to try and bridge the gap between our script and the budget.

Australia had incentives, but that faraway continent was too dangerous for this kind of movie, because of all the *actual* predators that lived in and around its jungles: spiders, crocs, scorpions and of course real, live, aggressive, venomous snakes. Expensive actors could not be put in that kind of situation.

Brazil had a good exchange rate, but Verna had been there already on the first *Anaconda*. Suffering from food poisoning, bad weather, local crew problems and an unhappy cast, that production eventually left Brazil; it was finished at the Los Angeles Arboretum. Jennifer Lopez, Ice Cube and Owen Wilson may have been early in their careers, but they could only take so much hardship.

South Africa and Mexico were too unstable politically, and Hawaii was way too expensive. Puerto Rico was a possibility, but they had no money to offer. After all the studio politics, work on the script, storyboarding and VFX work, it seemed like we were going to be dead in the water.

Then out of the blue, an angel appeared.

Gary Martin was the head of physical production at Columbia and, for another project, he had been approached by the government of Fiji. The Fijians wanted to bring filming (and hard currency) to their country. They were offering generous cash rebates and incentives; and we could get equipment and a good crew from Australia. Suddenly Fiji looked like the secret weapon we might be able to use to make this movie work.

I was instructed to fly down to Fiji to check out the locations. The question the studio wanted answered: Could these locations work creatively for the movie?

One day, I'm at a Chucky Cheese in the San Fernando Valley for my son's sixth birthday party, and less than 24 hours later I'm upriver on a wooden skiff watching locals free-dive for crabs using plastic buckets and clothesline. It had taken a jet, a prop plane, a Jeep and a boat to get there. And now I'm tossed back into the mists of time, watching people live completely off the grid. From sprawling urban Los Angeles to indigenous village life, just like that. Talk about culture shock!

Because Fiji had been cut off from most of the world for so long, the river waters were much safer than places like Australia or Brazil. There were no crocs, snakes, piranha or other poisonous critters. They did have wild boars, but like Hawaii, Fiji protected its habitat and borders. The wild boars were shooed out of the way by government wildlife rangers so we didn't have to worry about them.

The locations that I visited were all appropriate for the script, but there was no practical way to bring a studio army of 200+ people, and their trucks full of gear, to any of these places. Finally, with the help of a local guide, I found a small town with a decent tourist hotel and a good road next to an accessible river. I took lots of pictures for the studio and planted our flag.

If we used the Fijian government's rebate money *and* did all the post-production in tax-haven Australia (including the music score), we were going to be able to hit the $25 million number.

So now we had an approved script, an approved budget, a workable location. All we needed was the blessings of Amy Pascal.

Back in L.A., I was invited to a big meeting. I joined five or six studio types and boarded an elevator to the third floor of the Thalberg Building, to have our audience with Amy and her lieutenants.

Even though it read **Columbia Pictures** over the entrance of the famous art-deco building on the Culver City lot, this was not the original home of Columbia. The Thalberg Building was built in 1936 and dedicated to Irving Thalberg, the former head of production at MGM. Thalberg was the young president of production at MGM for many critical years (1926–1936) and was a legendary genius as a producer and studio executive (*Ben-Hur*, *Mutiny on the Bounty*, *Strange Interlude* and scores more). The building was dedicated to him several years after his early death at age 39. F. Scott Fitzgerald memorialized Thalberg in popular culture with his novel *The Last Tycoon*.

Louis B. Mayer's office had been on the third floor of the Thalberg Building during MGM's heyday and that's where we were headed. Some wild deal-making over the years had seen the original MGM lot become the Columbia Pictures lot (with more elaborate maneuvering by the Coca-Cola Company), and then the whole enterprise was sold to the Sony Corporation of Japan. Now the former MGM studio lot with the roaring

Ten. The Long and Winding Road

Dwight Little filming *Anacondas*.

lion logo was owned by the Japanese.

Yet no matter who the new corporate owner is, these Culver City movie stages will always be remembered as the home of MGM where Atlanta burned in *Gone with the Wind,* and Gene Kelly went *Singing in the Rain.*

Today, other big corporations have moved in to buy the entertainment companies built by the original moguls. AT&T owns Warner Brothers, Disney Corporation owns Fox, Comcast owns Universal, CBS/Viacom owns Paramount, Sony owns Columbia, and on down the line. Just wait and see: Soon Netflix and Amazon will own it all.

A different kind of person runs a corporation from the kind of person who likes betting on movies. *Industry, product, content.* Not the most romantic or artistic words. Sequels, remakes and pre-sold titles will now, more than ever, be the coin of the realm.

* * *

All the executives and department heads gathered around a large oak table in Amy Pascal's perfectly appointed office. Water and fruit were served, and we waited for Amy to enter. Each attendee had an untouched legal pad in front of him or her, and the room was unusually quiet. You could feel the ghosts in the air.

Deals had been made in this room with Clark Gable, Joan Crawford, Greta Garbo, Edward G. Robinson, Elizabeth Taylor, Judy Garland; plus, a long list of Hollywood royalty now largely forgotten by the new corporate Hollywood, by the tech giants of Silicon Valley.

* * *

Amy finally breezed in and was pleasant and thanked us all for being there. She asked Doug Belgrade if the script was ready. He said, "We're still tweaking the dialogue but it's in good shape."

She asked Clint Culpepper if he thought this film could fit into the model of what his division (the genre division) was tasked to make. He said, "It's a great Screen Gems movie and fits our brand perfectly." (Amy didn't want the movie released as a Columbia movie because it might be too "B" for the great old lady with the torch.)

Amy asked the marketing people about the worldwide prospects for *Anacondas*. Their #1 guy announced, "Based on the first movie, the interest is very high from the foreign distributors."

She asked Gary Martin about the budget. He said, "With the involvement of Fiji and Australia, the numbers are now down under 30 million. And Columbia will get their five million bucks worth of development money back."

Finally, Amy looked around the room and said matter-of-factly, "I don't understand the snake, what's it supposed to look like? Do we see it a lot? I hate snakes, but is it scary?"

Up until then, I had been completely invisible in the room. But now, all eyes turned to me. No one else was going to take this question.

Doug Belgrade, the most senior man there, turned to me. "Dwight, why don't you take this one? Amy, this is Dwight Little, our director."

After months of work and round-the-clock meetings, it was only *at this moment* that the head of the studio had any idea who was directing her $30 million movie? Yikes! That's where I fit in the food chain!

I felt the eyes of the whole table swivel to me. Because of my years-earlier meetings with Steven Seagal, Wesley Snipes, Arnold Kopelson and Lauren Donner, I suspected this exact moment might happen. I had come prepared with three "concept" drawings of the snake that illustrated scenes right from the script.

"Amy, I have a few images here that I'd like to show you that might be useful." I felt quite comfortable and confident in this moment. I think it was because I had prepared so thoroughly.

Amy leaned forward, perking up at the thought of seeing something visual. I slid the artist's concept renderings down to her end of the table. In one drawing, she could see the snake in a spectacular jungle setting, wrapping around an unfortunate victim. There was a computer-created image of the snake lunging out of the river to strike another unsuspecting character. In the final picture, the creature was curled up on the back of a riverboat ready to strike.

I explained what was happening story-wise for each image. I also explained how we were going to use real anacondas shot against blue screen, state-of-the-art-CGI anacondas and animatronic anacondas, blending them all together to create a realistic but frightening monster. I was taking a page right out of my *Free Willy 2* playbook from ten years earlier; I knew it had worked well with the orca whales.

Amy studied the images and listened closely. She didn't give much away and asked a few simple questions.

"This is all in the budget, Gary?" she asked the production executive.

"Yes," he said. "We have VFX companies in Brisbane and Sydney."

Then she turned to each one of her people around the table and asked point blank.

"Do *you* want to make this movie?" (marketing-distribution).

"Do *you* want to make this movie?" (creative development).

"Do *you* want to make this movie?" (physical production).

"Do *you* want to make this movie?" (Screen Gems partner).

Amy strategically wanted everyone in the room to go on record, so if this whole thing blew up, there'd be no place for anyone to hide. This is how someone like Amy Pascal becomes the head of a studio: by being smart. She had just built a firewall around herself that would protect her from angry stockholders in case of a bomb. If *Anacondas* was a hit, then it was all to her credit.

After each corporate division went on the record, Amy slowly stood up and said, "Okay, let's make the movie."

And that was that. She was off to her next meeting and wouldn't think about us again until there was a Director's Cut to show her many months from now. I had never before been witness to the actual decision to green-light a studio movie. This was the inside of the sausage factory and I found it fascinating. It is a business decision, a political decision and a gut decision about the director.

I realized later that I was in that room because she *wanted* me to be in that room. Amy needed to get a *feeling* about whether or not I knew what I was doing. Could I be trusted with $25 million? (It would cost another $25 mil to market it.) Did I have a vision for the movie? She didn't really want to know about the snake. She wanted to know about me. I was naïve assuming she didn't know who I was. When dealing with high IQ people, assume that they are always one step ahead … because they are.

While leaving Louis B. Mayor's office with a green lit movie, I was reminded of a famous observation the mogul had made about movies and audiences. "They don't like to be challenged or instructed, rather comforted and entertained." Our little river adventure was going to *entertain*!

* * *

In the last few years, I had been blessed with a beautiful wife, Sandy, and a beautiful baby boy, Jackson. Sandy had courageously taken on the caring and mothering of my first son, Graeme, with my first wife. We were now a blended family and going on this adventure together. How Sandy had the strength to take all this on and travel for months to Fiji and Australia, I will never really know, but off we went with high hopes for both the movie and our new family.

* * *

We were in the Southern hemisphere, one full day ahead of California, and somewhat on our own. I knew that the studio would either get behind us or shut us down, based on the first few days' dailies. (They would take a few days since the lab was in Sydney.)

I had been getting daily calls from Gary Martin reminding me that if our budget kept creeping up, he was going stop the production and bring everyone home. I had a noose around my neck and the trap door under my feet was ready to open.

I planned my first days carefully. Day One would involve one Australian guest actor in a patrol boat going up the river. He'd be attacked by an anaconda and the boat would veer off course, crashing into the rocks on the shore. By using a guest actor, I knew I wouldn't have to fight any "star behavior" and could focus on the suspense of the scene. The studio would get to see the wild river and the boat (a real introduction to the beautiful location) and see a snake attack, even though there was no snake.

As I expected, there were lots of complications with transportation and logistics on Day One. We didn't get out on the water until ten o'clock with a seven o'clock call. *Three hours lost!* We finally got the first shot and the bad luck spell was broken. The crew fell into customary habits and we all started to work together (Americans, Australians, New Zealanders, Fijians, Indians). My Australian actor was a real trouper, as I knew he would be. When I pulled him up by wires to be eaten by the snake, he just sucked it up and did it.

In the afternoon, I was even able to get some shots of the replica snake gliding through the water. By the end of the day, I had the boat wildly swerving toward the shore with the engine on fire.

I knew the studio was going to want to see their cast in the first batch of dailies, so on Day Two, I picked a scene where *all* the "first team" was together trying to cut through the jungle. Since this scene happened two-thirds of the way through the movie, the continuity for each actor would have to be worked out well in advance.

Each bruise, cut, wardrobe tear or hair change that may have happened to the character during the story would have to be accounted for now. Was the actor cut in the fistfight? Where and how badly? Banged up going over the waterfall? How much damage? Wounded in the crocodile fight? Across the neck or arms? All these decisions, times seven, had to be made and locked down.

I could have made this easier on myself by shooting a simple dialogue scene, but I knew Gary, Doug and Clint would make up their mind about the movie based on these early impressions. It's human nature.

Morris Chestnut led our ensemble cast as the head of a U.S. pharmaceutical company searching for a rare plant purported to be the fountain of youth. Morris, along with all the lead actors, had to report to set camera-ready for a scene that was taking place on page 70 of the script. Continuity is another not-very-glamorous job of the director, but it is essential.

Amy Pascal had made it clear that she didn't want the faces of her actors *too* marked up no matter what the "reality" of the scene. "I'm spending a lot of money to see those fucking faces!"

* * *

Morris Chestnut was a rising star who had broken through with John Singleton's first movie, *Boyz n the Hood*. He kept busy with the studio and independent movies *Ladder 49*, *Half Past Dead*, *G.I. Jane* and *The Best Man*. We were lucky to have him. Morris was calm and focused and set a good example for all of the cast. His character ended up being eaten by the snake, so we often joked about him traveling all the way to Fiji "just to be an anaconda's dinner." Morris ended up being my neighbor some years later and our sons grew up together.

* * *

To achieve Day Two's first scene, I would have to complete the dialogue and then march the cast off into the swampy bog. Once they were all ankle- or knee-deep, I would be able to move to a "bog set" that we were building on a field near the production office. The set was like an above-ground swimming pool where we could have fresh water, movie-ready plants and easy camera and crew access.

Since it was the first day for each actor, there were a million questions for me to answer about their character and his or her tone and motivations. They were all nervous. I had set aside a fair amount of time for this scene since I knew this actor anxiety was bound to be at Defcon 1.

The location was about 40 minutes of rough road from the production office. It was visually perfect for the scene but was hauntingly primal and remote. I stood on the edge of the bog and looked into marshy waters that seemed as if they had been untouched since the beginning of time. This swamp looked like the primal ooze from which life had first appeared a few billion years earlier. Frankly, it gave me the creeps.

When I encouraged the cast to walk into the muck, I knew I had to go in too. I put on rubber boots and a game face; but, when the shot was over, I was just as happy to get out of there as the actors were.

What really made the scene work was the eighth character in our movie, a trained spider monkey we named Kong. The mascot "rally monkey" for the L.A. Angels, he had been brought in with trainers from Los Angeles. Whenever we filmed Kong, he could be counted on for a scene-stealing performance. No matter what the actors did or didn't do, I would always be able to *cut to the monkey!*

A few evenings later, we all gathered to watch dailies at a village community center near the town where we were staying. It was a cement-style building with a tin roof. When we arrived after another full day of shooting, it was pouring rain. Pouring rain on a tin roof is thunderous! The sound from the makeshift speakers would be completely drowned out by the noise, but we'd be able to see the pictures!

The dailies had come back from Australia and the projector was ready to go. Cold beers were passed out. I had not heard anything from the studio, so I didn't know if they loved the footage or hated it.

The rain, the remoteness, the mix of people, all reminded me of the Joan Crawford movie *Rain,* based on the Somerset Maugham short story. Foreigners in the tropics going slowly mad.

The fluorescent lights were turned off and the projector rattled to life. We watched the famous countdown leader and waited for the "2 pop" familiar to all moviegoers. Then the magic happened.

Up on the screen, in a wide anamorphic frame, the patrol boat chugged up the Fijian river. Dense green jungle cascaded down to the water from both banks; birds circled in the air. This *looked* like an adventure movie from the first frame.

I stopped thinking about studio politics and put on my director hat. What did I have? How would it cut? I had *a lot* and I was thrilled. It did look like *The Emerald Forest*. This was a magical moment for me. I felt the same feeling I'd felt in eighth grade when one of my Super 8 films was projected onto a screen. I loved movies then and still did on this night 30 years later.

By the time we got to the bog footage, the mood was even better. Each department was able to see their work shining up on the big screen. Wardrobe, props, camera, art department, sound, everyone.

I was sure that these dailies would be enough to keep the studio happy. I was right. The next day, I got a terse message from Gary through the production office: "Good stuff, keep going and don't spend too much money."

That was the warmest embrace I was likely to get. Now that we had the studio fully on board, we had one more task: We needed to shore up our relationship with the Fijian government.

In Fiji, there is a very real political and racial tension going back generations between the indigenous Fijians and the Ethnic Indian population. Tensions boiled over in 2000 when a coup attempt was made against the first Ethnic Indian prime minister by a rebel group of Fijian nationalists.

Since we were receiving money from the government and we represented a big Hollywood movie company, there was a lot of discussion about whether we were colonialist exploiters or intrepid foreign investors creating jobs.

A large presentation for business and government reps was set up by the American ambassador from the U.S. consulate. Grievances would be heard, questions answered. We would also be able to make our case that we were the good guys. We needed all the help we could get from the local businesses for building materials, boats, land access, drivers, transportation equipment, etc.

Many VIPs were gathered in a hot ballroom with actual ceiling fans which made the whole setting seem like a scene from David Lean's *A Passage to India*. Dignitaries were invited to speak and there was even a Kava ceremony.

* * *

The Kava root grows abundantly in Fiji and over the generations it has become the centerpiece for the welcoming Kava ceremony. The root is ground up, mixed with water and poured into a large Kava bowl. The bowl is then placed in the center of a selected group and everyone drinks the brownish liquid while music is played. The Kava has a slightly narcotic effect and can instill a feeling of calm among those who partake. The Kava ceremony has also been used as a traditional way to calm tensions between villages where there may be arguments over land or livestock.

* * *

I was seated with my wife Sandy behind Fiji's prime minister. I was getting a bit nervous since I had been asked to speak to the whole room about the nature and purpose of the movie. I have never really liked public speaking, and this was a crowd of heavy hitters.

A few minutes before my speech, a man from the film office

Dwight Little and Johnny Messner filming *Anacondas*.

approached Sandy and me. He asked if we would mind vacating our seats and be seated closer to the podium, but off to the side. Of course, we agreed. We later learned that there had been threats against the prime minister's life. Sandy and I were moved because we were seated directly behind him. If bullets started flying, I guess they thought that an American movie director and his wife being shot would be bad publicity, and not great for tourism.

In my speech, I avoided politics. I just tried to express the creative thrill we were all feeling about shooting in their spectacularly beautiful country. I told the audience that a big studio adventure movie would be a great visual introduction to Fiji for people all over the world. The speech was a pretty obvious "butter up" job, yet it seemed to do the trick. I think we got everyone on board and now we could go run around the island and shoot whatever we wanted. The director really does wear many hats. Just try not to get shot!

The production itself was an up-and-down rollercoaster ride. Some days went smoothly, others were disastrous. The Australian crew would get off work at five in the morning (night shooting), then go right to the hotel bar where they insisted the establishment be open. The Australians would drink, sometimes fight, and make noise until noon (disturbing everyone), crash until four or five in the afternoon, then set off for work. A lot of these men were on a distant location away from their wives and children, and the unleashed rowdy behavior mixed with cheap beer created no end of troubles for the producers.

The cast started fighting and breaking up hotel rooms, as if they were jaded rock stars. There was little or nothing to do on the days off except drink and sit on the sandy beach. A few of the locals were tempted to steal the expensive equipment that was often lying around. Cellphones, laptops, walkie-talkies and cameras started to disappear. Soon there was massive theft and the finger-pointing created stress everywhere. People were fired, threats were made. Yep, just another week in paradise.

I worked very closely with my Australian first AD. His job was to manage the crew and my job was to manage the cast and producers. If he and I remained joined at the hip, then the whole crazy juggernaut could keep moving forward. We had our own disagreements, but we worked them out privately and showed only a united front to the world.

Near the end of the long shoot, I came down with some kind of local virus. One night I was filming at 4 a.m. in the jungle near a crumbling old temple. I felt myself growing weaker and becoming a little nauseous. I had been going nonstop for many weeks and may have just been wearing down. I stood up to make an adjustment to the animatronic snake and toppled right over. Out cold.

The first aid team and some crew members got me onto a cot in a clean tent. A doctor was called and I was revived. The doctor surmised that I had acute dehydration and started filling me full of liquids. The last time I had been "down" was in Thailand many years earlier.

This news from Fiji travelled to Australia quickly, and with a twist: "The director of *Anacondas* has had a heart attack and is in the hospital!"

Within hours, directors' résumés flooded into the Sydney production office offering to take over the movie. The director is down, *everybody moves up one*, is the old expression. (I was reminded of *Rosemary's Baby* where John Cassavetes' character gets his big Broadway break when the lead actor goes blind.)

I'm sure my recovery was a disappointment to many, but Sandy was relieved. She had been extremely resourceful this whole time. She was teacher, creative consultant, driver, chef, nurse, events planner, accountant and security guard, all in a country foreign to her, with no friends or extended family. And then, having done months of duty in Fiji, we packed up and took the whole circus to Australia for three more months of post.

New housing, new schools, new nannies, new shopping, and learning to drive on the left! Every day I drove in to work (at the beautiful Fox studios in Sydney), I would have to concentrate hard on keeping to the left-hand side of the road to avoid getting myself or anybody else killed.

* * *

Being a film director and keeping a marriage together while raising children is a very complicated proposition. Impossible choices have to be made all the time. There really is no winning formula for bringing the two worlds together. It's a very tricky dance, but in the end, raising a family creates a feeling of usefulness and importance in this world that just being a movie director never can. At least for me.

* * *

My Australian editors were first-class. We were ensconced in fancy post-production suites right next to Baz Luhrmann. (After Peter Weir, Baz is probably Australia's most famous director. *Moulin Rouge, Strictly Ballroom, Romeo and Juliet*.) I found a terrific Australian composer and the time passed rather quickly.

Sandy and I managed to keep our Saturday "date night" intact, and we did touristy things on the weekends: the opera house, the blue mountains, the zoo, wine country. The children had an Australian Christmas and New Year. When there was a Director's Cut of the movie, it was time to go home. I hope to never see Australia's nasty black flies again!

* * *

Back on the Sony lot, the time had come to show *Anacondas: The Hunt for the Blood Orchid* to Amy Pascal and her executive team. I found myself in a basement screening room of the Thalberg Building, the same building where I had screened *Halloween 4* for the first time! I felt like a different person than the one who had wandered off into the jungle to make a movie all those months ago.

At first screenings, the director customarily has to stand up and introduce the movie to the assembled brass. Ugh! More public speaking!

The common approach is to lower people's expectations for what they are about to see so that the final emotion will be "pleasantly surprised" instead of "slightly disappointed." I spoke briefly about the "roughness" of the cut they were about to see (unfinished visual effects) but expressed our belief that the film was going to be exciting for an audience when it was finally finished and thanked my producer and editor. I took my seat next to Verna Harrah and the lights dimmed.

The movie started to play and the room was quiet. There were small laughs at some of the early jokes, and I was pleased that the picture and sound were reasonably good. About 15 minutes into the movie, there was a "snake event" and somebody in the room screamed out at the top of their lungs. I turned to Verna.

"Who was that?" I whispered.

Ten. The Long and Winding Road

"That was Amy," she said.

Amy Pascal, the head of the studio, had just screamed at a scene in our unfinished *Anacondas* movie! I felt home free. The rest of the screening was amazing. We had laughs and scares. *It played.*

There was polite "industry applause" when the lights came up. Amy walked to the front of the room. She thanked everybody for working so hard on the movie, and asked Verna and me to stay for some questions.

When we were alone, Amy asked me, "If you had more money, what would you do with it?"

"Amy, I need more money for the visual effects. The snake shots are harder and more complex than I imagined, and I need to finish them properly. I could also use more money for the waterfall, the collapse of the sinkhole, and some digital rain to help continuity. I need more time for the mix and more instruments for the Australian orchestra. Plus, I need a better title sequence."

Amy turned, indicated her assistant and instructed me, "Call Evan in the morning with a list of everything you say you need and how much it will cost." And then she left.

The next day, Verna called to tell me we had been approved for another *million* dollars in post and the marketing people had decided to put our trailer on the front of *Spider-Man*, which would give us huge exposure setting up our August release. The cherry on top was that Amy had decided to attach the Columbia Pictures logo (the lady with the torch) to the front of the movie! I was thrilled. This was now a *Columbia Pictures* release!

Even though there was still an enormous amount of work to do, I had a feeling that good things were happening. Some scripts began drifting into my agent's office, so there must have been some early buzz coming out of the screening. Insiders talk all the time about what they've heard from different industry events.

Verna invited Sandy and me to a private dinner at her house in Bel-Air.

* * *

Verna was born and raised in Idaho. Through her early work as a real estate agent, she met the casino entrepreneur Bill Harrah and became his third wife. Harrah's was a name that became nearly synonymous with Reno and Las Vegas casinos. When Bill Harrah died unexpectedly, Verna inherited most of his fortune. Verna then pursued her interest in movies.

* * *

Verna's home was expansive and beautiful. The grounds were immaculate and the inside stunning. I had been in many elegant L.A. houses, but this one was different. There were original pieces by seventeenth- and eighteenth-century masters; I recognized more than one painting from my college art history books! The carpets, drapes, antiques and furniture were all perfectly selected. This elegance was not the outcome of mere movie money. This was Harrah's *casino* money. A whole other level of wealth.

At dinner, the great movie star Sidney Poitier sat to my right. The music wizard Quincy Jones was next to Sandy. I spoke with Mr. Poitier about, of course, movies. Along with his classic starring roles (*In the Heat of the Night, Guess Who's Coming to Dinner, To Sir with Love*), Poitier also had a substantial career as a director. He talked about the stamina and endurance that was required of the director, and said, "It was particularly challenging when I had to direct myself." He mentioned films like *Buck and the Preacher, Uptown Saturday Night* and *Stir Crazy*.

"Directing is a young man's game," Poitier concluded. He had that special quality of great men: He was interested in *other* people. In this case, me. Some stars are narcissists, of course, but others are gentlemen.

There was a sharply dressed woman sitting on my left and I engaged her in a short conversation as well. She said she was a writer. Her name was Jackie, and I asked, "Might I have read one of your books?" I was somewhat embarrassed to find out she was Jackie Collins, who had written many steamy bestsellers: *Hollywood Wives, The Bitch, The Stud* and more. I had not *heard* of any of these titles, let alone read them. In her own world, though, she was a huge deal (and the sister of actress Joan Collins). I'm quite sure *she* hadn't heard of *Marked for Death, Rapid Fire* or *Murder at 1600*.

* * *

I had to commute back and forth to Sydney several times to finish the mix and the score, but finally it was time to have our Westwood premiere.

We had a great turn-out of industry people and stars of various levels, including Sidney Poitier. After the screening, the invited guests headed to Trader Vic's for a glamorous after-party. This was *fun*. The audience seemed to love the movie and I had always loved any excuse to go to Trader Vic's.

* * *

Trader Vic's was one of the last of the great Tiki bar chains. The one in Beverly Hills was a celebrity crossroads for years, and the list of stars that hung out there is miles long. I'd had several meetings there over the years, and always had the original Mai Tai, which was their signature drink.

There are many destination restaurants in L.A. that cater to Hollywood meetings and lunches. The trendy ones come and go, but there

Ten. The Long and Winding Road

are some stalwarts that are always a pleasure. Geoffrey's, the Ivy, Chateau Marmont, the Polo Lounge, Spago, the Grill, the Palm, Musso and Franks, Le Dome and Maestros, to name a few. Enjoy them while they still exist. And enjoy them even more when somebody else is picking up the tab!

* * *

As our release date approached, there was a flurry of activity. Our late August date was still looking good for a non-star-driven sequel, and the hopes of us opening at #1 at about $20 million were holding. Release prints were checked, press releases finalized. The actors started going on talk shows to "talk up the movie."

And then, out of the blue, three weeks out from release, Harvey Weinstein announced that he was going to release a Jet Li movie called *Hero* on our weekend.

Weinstein had picked up the domestic rights to this two-year-old Chinese hit, which had already been released internationally. Quentin Tarantino, a huge fan of Eastern martial arts movies, championed the film to Miramax and agreed to lend his name to the marketing campaign, and consequently signed on as an executive producer.

Weinstein cut new trailers, new TV spots, created English subtitles and threw lots of money behind an opening. The filmgoing public thought there was a new Tarantino movie coming out! The poster shouted: "Quentin Tarantino presents Jet Li in *Hero*!"

* * *

It was inconceivable at that time that a man like Harvey Weinstein, with almost unlimited Hollywood power, would end up in prison for various sex crimes. When people read about him now, it's hard to remember how giant a figure he was.

* * *

I went to an early evening screening of *Anacondas* at the AMC in Woodland Hills and found a line of eager ticket buyers queued up. Could this be *Halloween 4* happening all over again?

I went up to a few people standing in line and asked them what they had come out to see. Four people said *Hero*, and one couple said *Anacondas*. And even though the reviews were surprisingly good for a snake sequel, I knew it was game over.

We came in second at $13 million for the weekend, a far cry from the projections of $18 to $20 million. The problem was that the Jet Li movie was direct competition to our genre and demographic. And Tarantino was practically bulletproof on opening weekend whether he directed the movie or not. As Yogi Berra famously said, "It was *déjà vu* all over again."

By Monday, my agents at CAA had called my manager (not me) to say they thought I'd be better off going forward with a more "boutique" agency. In other words, they were dumping my ass. The few meetings on new scripts I had booked were suddenly "rescheduled." It had been a good 15-year run since *Marked for Death*, but the hopes of Friday night had turned to despair by Monday morning. Nobody can make anybody buy a ticket to a movie. They have to *want* to. Picking a movie, driving to the theater, parking, paying $50 bucks (or more with concessions) and driving home is a very different behavior than clicking a button on your unlimited Netflix queue.

No time to cry in my soup, though. I had a family and a mortgage. On Wednesday, I called every single TV contact I ever had and said, "I want back in." In moments like this, you don't just call your agent to do the work for you; you get on the phone yourself!

Barry Berg picked up the phone in New York. He had worked with me on *Rapid Fire* and was now the line producer on *Law and Order: Trial by Jury*, the umpteenth *Law and Order* spin-off. As luck would have it, Barry had an opening and, miracle of miracles, I was heading off to New York within a week to direct an episode.

After that good fortune, I took as many TV shows as I could get and hoped I could live to fight another day. I worked on many series that only lasted one season and then got the axe: *Just Legal*, *The Inside*, *Vanished*, *Tower Prep*, *Dollhouse*. Nothing seemed to stick though I was making good money. But then, a good one landed in my lap.

I was in Chicago scouting the famous Ambassador Hotel for the series *Prison Break*. My agent called on my cell to say that there was a new Fox TV show that was having difficulty. "Would you be able to leave *Prison Break* a day early and come right back to L.A. to start prep on *Bones*?" The idea sounded a little exhausting, but I had resolved not to turn down work for *any* reason and I responded, "Just say when and where." (This is how I became involved in *Bones* in the first place.)

* * *

Ever since *Millennium*, I had enjoyed support at Fox TV. *The X-Files*, *John Doe*, *Prison Break*. I had always delivered for them and that relationship was a rare gift.

* * *

My first episode of *Bones* was difficult because the writers and actors were still trying to figure out the tone of the show. A lot of questions the

Ten. The Long and Winding Road

actors had for me about their characters, I just couldn't answer because the show was still evolving. But I got along great with the showrunner, Hart Hanson, and both stars, David Boreanaz and Emily Deschanel.

* * *

I stayed with *Bones* for 12 seasons! *Bones* provided me with an income to raise my family and have a real home in Los Angeles. I got to know everyone on the cast and crew like a family. I went to the holiday parties, wrap parties, birthday parties and baby parties and generally enjoyed the kind of stability one rarely finds in Hollywood.

Each *Bones* episode took us into a different world, and we had a blast discovering each new "culture." We filmed with Civil War re-enactors, BMX enthusiasts, circus performers, art collectors, religious cults, gay football leagues and a myriad of others. All full of incredibly interesting people.

When *Bones* came to an end, I went on to do some other shows, but I could tell that things were slowing down for me in television. Many of the writers and producers I had worked with were retiring. There was a natural generational shift in the air.

There was also a cultural change happening. Gender and diversity considerations were increasingly important in television, especially in visible jobs like director.

I needed some wind back in my sails … but how?

Epilogue

One winter, back in high school, I was continuing my "outward bound" training program on a wilderness camping trip. On this particular challenge trip, my group of ten peers and a group leader were deep in "the bush" somewhere near the Monongahela River in West Virginia.

One kid, David, had been moaning all night from some kind of stomach pain. Assuming he had eaten something contaminated, we just gave him water and tried to help him sleep. The strange thing was, no one else was sick. By morning, his fever had spiked and he was really hurting on the right side of his lower abdomen.

The group leader, Mr. Warner, was also our math teacher and football coach. In the light of day, Mr. Warner quickly surmised that David had appendicitis, and the question was, had it already burst? A burst appendix causes sepsis (infection) and can easily lead to death if not treated with surgery and antibiotics. This was an emergency.

Mr. Warner consulted our "topo" (topographic) map and figured there might be a way to get some help if we moved quickly. He turned to me: "Little, grab some extra dry socks, gear up, and be ready to leave in five minutes."

"What?" My eyes went wide. Leave for where, and why me?

Mr. Warner had a plan. He and I would head out cross-country, traveling due west. Mr. Warner had seen a fire service road on the map about seven miles away. Without a trail, and with lots of drifting snow, we would probably travel at about two miles an hour tops. Once we hit the fire road, we would then go north for another six miles until we hit a state highway. On the service road, we could probably top three miles an hour. If we didn't stop, Mr. Warner estimated we could be at the highway in six to eight hours, depending on conditions. It was 7:30 in the morning.

"We're not stopping, Dwight," he said. "So get your mind right."

I was oddly flattered that of all the guys, he had picked me for this rescue mission. But I knew this day was going to be a burn.

Epilogue

The first few hours were manageable, but then things got pretty rough. Hills, ravines, ice and snowbanks kept our progress slow. But he was right, we finally got to the fire road just as the map had indicated, and then our pace picked up a bit.

We had water and power bars which were enough to sustain us to the state road by about 4:30 in the afternoon. It was nearly dark already. Numbness and blisters didn't really factor in since a kid's life was at stake. When we reached the state road, we dropped down in a snow drift, completely spent.

Within minutes, a car's headlights appeared. We jumped to our feet and started waving our hands like crazy people. The car that stopped was, of all things, a state trooper's car!

Mr. Warner told him the story while we warmed up in the back of the cop car. The trooper called in our emergency to the fire department one town away. The fire guys called a regional hospital that had a Medevac helicopter, and Mr. Warner was able to provide exact coordinates for where our party was camped by the river. Longitude and latitude, with a lot of ruler and compass work, was the key to navigation in those days … no GPS.

Thirty minutes later, the Medevac chopper touched down in a field less than a hundred yards from the campsite. I heard about this all later from the other guys: They told me how they had heard the helicopter and started waiving at it, not realizing that it was coming for David anyway. Once David was loaded onto the Medevac, it took him right to the regional hospital. By 6:30 p.m., he was under the knife and on an antibiotic infusion. The appendix had indeed burst, but they got it out; and in a few days, the infection was under control. (Not long after the helicopter, a group of park rangers brought in snowmobiles to get the rest of our gang out of the forest.)

Mr. Warner and I had been incredibly lucky to have that state trooper come by just at the moment we needed him. But the question is … was it really luck? Or was it the decision by Mr. Warner to just walk out of there on the *chance* that we could get help? The answer is that luck only happens (or doesn't happen) once you've done everything *you* can to change your own fate and circumstances.

After 20 years of directing for TV, I was not getting any younger and I felt like I needed to change my fate and circumstances in show business.

* * *

The first rule of filmmaking is, *never* put your own money into a movie. Always risk someone else's money. I took this rule seriously for years, and then broke it.

* * *

Years earlier, my stepson Jason Richter (from the *Free Willy* films) gave me a book by James B. Clarke called *Last Rampage—The Escape of Gary Tison*. He thought I might like it, and there was a part that could be right for him.

The book was a non-fiction account of a 1978 Arizona state prison break that had gone terribly wrong. Tison, a career criminal and convicted killer, managed to convince his three teenage sons to break him out of prison. An accomplice named Randy Greenwalt was also part of the plan. The five of them drove around the west for several weeks trying to make their escape into Mexico. Along the way, Gary and Randy killed several innocent travelers, and the subsequent manhunt finally led to a bloody shootout. The story was so wild that I would have passed on it had it not been true. I optioned the book.

* * *

A book option is a common way that producers make a deal with authors to acquire the rights to their story for a reasonable period of time, so that it can be turned into a screenplay. Most options are for a year or two and cost a fraction of what the outright purchase of the book rights would be. If the movie or TV show is made, then the author gets paid the full amount for the worldwide rights to his or her book. If the author is famous and has leverage, he or she may get a percentage of the gross receipts and/or be able to collaborate on the script.

* * *

I enlisted my *From Dusk Till Dawn* writer, Alvaro Rodriguez, to work on the screenplay. I became even more excited about the project when I read his first 20 pages. Alvaro's writing really captured the flavor of 1978 rural Arizona. The book was so well researched that we had a perfect road map to follow, plus a wild *true* story to tell.

How do "the sins of the father" visit each of us before we are even born? Are our lives predetermined by accident of birth? Or do we choose our destiny? What is the nature of evil? How do you deal with it when you encounter it? Can it be reasoned with? Understood? Contained? Why do boys spend their lives looking for their father's approval? Does everyone deserve to be understood? Even a stone-cold killer? As a neighbor in Ohio once said, "If you have a rabid dog, you can either chain it up or put it down. That's it."

Once I had the finished script, I needed a lead actor to play Gary Tison. And I knew just where to turn.

I called Robert Patrick and said, "I don't really know how I'm going to make this movie, but could you just read the script and tell me if you might want to play Gary?"

It usually takes many weeks to get an answer back from a star actor, but Robert called me the next day.

"I'm in," he exclaimed. Robert loved the part and said he would do whatever he could to help get *Last Rampage* made. But it was already April, and he would have to be back on his CBS-TV series *Scorpion* by July.

That gave me *one* slim window, the month of June, to film his part in the movie. June was also the hottest time of year in Santa Clarita-Palmdale-Newhall, where we hoped to shoot the movie. But we'd just have to deal with that.

My agents suggested a few buyers who might be interested in a low-budget package like *Last Rampage*; but production companies would have to like it, commit to it, make development notes, do further drafts, consult with financiers and distributors, create budgets and approve more casting. This would all take a year at least before we would even know if we had a "go" movie. And *Last Rampage* was a difficult, bleak subject with a star who was seen as more of a "character actor."

The whole process just sounded exhausting and I would probably lose Robert. I was sure I would hear, "We'll make it if you get Woody Harrelson or Kevin Costner." I was excited about the script and too restless to wait another year, so I just decided to do it myself.

I had a very resourceful business manager, Bruce Lagnese, who had been working with me for years. I was sure he'd make every effort to talk me out of this reckless move. Much to my surprise, he said, "Give me a few days to see what I can do."

Bruce was able to use my various home and retirement assets to create enough collateral that we were able to get a bank loan to cover the production part of the movie. I wasn't sure how I would get the funds to finish the movie, but I figured I'd deal with that when the time came.

With the help of independent producer Eric Breiman, we put together a non-union crew and signed up for a SAG low-budget agreement. We opened an office, set a start date in early June, and dove in.

Something quite amazing happens when word gets out that you are actually making a movie, no matter how small. The agents see the cast listings in "breakdown services" (a weekly list of movies with parts for actors) and suddenly the phone starts ringing.

We had to move quickly because of Robert's schedule, so we started searching for locations. I had to meet with new DPs since I didn't know any non-union directors of photography. It was surprising how many people were interested in working for very low wages. They were young! Opportunity matters more than money in your twenties.

Epilogue

Within weeks, we had added Heather Graham (*Boogie Nights*), Bruce Davison (*X-Men*), John Heard (*Home Alone*), Chris Browning (*Ray Donovan*), Alex MacNicol (*13 Reasons Why*), Jason Richter (*The Little Things*) and a few other first-class actors. Our crew was also coming together, and before we knew it, we were on our final week of pre-production. This whole experience was invigorating, but also terrifying since it was *my* financial ass on the line. On the other hand, I had no one to answer to. I could only bitch, moan and complain to myself!

The first day of shooting was at a prison in Lancaster, and it was 115 degrees by 11 in the morning! Chris Browning didn't have the signature glasses he needed to play Randy, and the picture car would barely run. But somehow, we figured out how to solve each problem and survive the heat. When I did my first shot with Robert Patrick as Gary Tison, I knew we had a *movie*. We had no time and no money, but we had a terrific script and a great cast.

The whole film was "in the can" in 18 days and we finished with Robert *one day* before he reported back for work in Manhattan Beach on *Scorpion*.

Dwight Little filming *Last Rampage*.

Epilogue

I started editing the movie on the third floor of my editor's house in Burbank where he had his own equipment. I knew I had to have something to show, and as I cut it together, I felt more and more sure that we had really captured something special.

From this point forward, I had to pay for everything with personal credit cards. I was really putting myself out on a limb! But all the effort and risk led us to a big night in Santa Monica at the Royal Theater. We decided to screen an early version of the movie for some indie distributors and other industry types who might be willing to help us.

The movie played great, and the audience seemed impressed. It was nerve-wracking beyond belief, because not only was I being judged as a director, but I was also hoping for a financial lifeline from some distributor to dig me out of the money pit I was in.

By Monday morning we had a call from Epic Pictures, a small distributor mostly known as a weigh station for sci-fi and horror projects. They expressed real enthusiasm about our film. We heard from a few other small companies, but Epic was the most proactive and aggressive.

Epic offered to give us a minimum guarantee for the domestic rights against a revenue-sharing plan for future sales. Epic made deals with Netflix, Redbox, Vudu, iTunes and Amazon. They also guaranteed a 20-screen theatrical release in five of the major markets, Los Angeles, New York, Chicago, Dallas and Phoenix. Given that I had made this movie basically out of my garage with credit cards, it seemed like a pretty good offer and I took it.

An old friend from way back in Sandy Howard days picked up the movie for foreign sales. His name was Robbie Little (no relation) and he had a long and well-established track record as a foreign sales agent. He made some profitable sales in Germany, the U.K., the Netherlands, the Middle East, South Africa, Japan, China, etc. But as misfortune would have it, Robbie had a heart attack in his hotel room on the way to Cannes to sell our remaining territories. As well as losing a friend, there was some real money left on the table, and it was my personal money. That was a blow, and a situation that I could never have seen coming. I found out later that Robbie had been suffering with a weak heart for years, but I had no idea.

One day I was having lunch with Robbie at his favorite place in Studio City, laughing about old times and making plans for *Last Rampage* (the film had just been accepted into the Sitges film festival in Barcelona); and the next thing I know, he's gone.

As you get older, the losses do start to pile up. How each of us learns to cope with illness and death is the most personal part of who we are. No one is right or wrong about matters of life and death or spiritual-religious beliefs. It's not politics. There are no "sides" and there are no winners and losers. *Every* person's story leads to the same ending, and in that sense, life is very fair. The Prince and the Pauper are both treated the same by the end credits.

At the end of *Barry Lyndon*, there is a powerful voiceover that kind of cements the film into greatness, which is a quote straight from William Thackery's novel: "It was in the reign of George II that the above-named personages lived and quarreled.

Good or bad, handsome or ugly, rich or poor, they are all equal now."

You can't really top that for an ending.

* * *

When all was accounted for, I did lose some money on the *Last Rampage* enterprise, but I was able to take most of the loss as a tax break, so I kind of broke even in the end.

But here was the upside: *Deadline Hollywood* ran an article about *Last Rampage,* and the assigned reporter was a huge Robert Patrick fan. The *Deadline* article was the first press release that made people in town aware of my indie project, and it was very upbeat and positive. Then, the reviews started to come in.

> "The staunch resolve of two-fisted director Dwight Little to tell the truth about a family of celebrated monsters, scars and all, deserves respect, and the cast is awesome."—Rex Reed, *New York Observer*

> "Dwight Little's sturdily constructed true-crime drama showcases a potent performance by Robert Patrick as a mood-swinging sociopath."—Joe Leydon, *Variety*

> "It is ultimately the hardened intensity of Patrick's commanding portrayal that gives *Last Rampage* its take-no-prisoners tautness."—Michael Rechtshaffen, *Los Angeles Times*

There were many more and we were all "over the moon." There were also a few doubters, of course, but not enough to spoil the fun.

Several projects started to find their way to my door. (Somebody was reading these reviews!) There was a horror thriller called *Natty Knocks* that was coming together, and a new interest in Dwight Little seemed to be stirring with the release of *Last Rampage*. I had managed to walk out of the woods and somehow find a state trooper.

After five studio movies, six independent features, three TV movies and 90 episodes of network television, I was now re-branded as the indie *Last Rampage* guy. That was fine with me. I was very proud of the film.

Each project is fragile. The cast comes together. The cast falls out.

Epilogue

The money comes together. The money falls out. You just have to tirelessly push each project up the hill hoping that one of them will hit paydirt. Then you can say "Action" again.

Since I began, the movie and TV business has changed multiple times, and it is wildly changing now. This cycle will not be the last time. The theatrical business collapsed in the wake of a global pandemic and the streaming services exploded with fresh content, some of it very good. Disney buys Fox, CAA buys ICM, and who can say where it's all headed. But...

Whether it's movies or television or theater, people will always want to hear stories and the director's job is to tell those stories in the most interesting way possible. The director must protect a singular vision of the story from beginning to end.

It's not the Writer's Cut, not the Producer's Cut, not the Studio's Cut ... the most important telling of the story is the Director's Cut. It's always worth fighting for.

* * *

Index

ABC Afterschool Special 9
Abdul, Paula 92
Above the Law 48
Absolute Power 137
The Accused 46
ADR 133
AIP 5
Akkad, Moustapha 38
Albert, Edward 27
Alda, Alan 120
Ally McBeal 148
Alvarado, Angela 188
Amadeus 43
Americano 5, 15, 17
The Amityville Horror 31
Amritraj, Ashok 33
Anaconda 194, 197
Anderson, Gillian 168
Anderson, Wes 122
Ansara, Michael 21
Appointment TV 181
Arkoff, Louis 31
Arkoff, Sam 5, 31
ARRI 123
The Art of Dramatic Writing 135
Atlantic 10
Ayutthaya 77

Babe 112
Bacall, Lauren 24
The Bad and the Beautiful 60
Baker, Joe Don 27
Bakula, Scott 183
The Band 101
"Barefoot Days" 171
Barry, Marion 124
Barry, Raymond 78
Barry Lyndon 153
Baruchel, Jay 161
Basic Instinct 60
Bauer, Jack 154
Baxley, Paul 29
Bay, Michael 122
Beck, Michael 6–7
Beethoven 53

Belgrade, Doug 194
Belkin, Al 26
Benzali, Daniel 130
Berg, Barry 210
Berlin Wall 50
Berra, Yogi 210
Besson, Luc 17
Billington, Michael 19
binge viewing 181
Birnbaum, Roger 58
The Black Stallion 96
Bloodstone 34
Bogdanovich, Peter 55
Bonaventura, Lorenzo Di 115
Bones 166
Boothe, Powers 78
Boreanaz, David 161
Boss of Bosses 187
Boston Public 148
Boyle, Danny 17, 122
Brat Pack 131
Breech, Robert 145
Breiman, Eric 215
Brennan, Temperance 180
Bridges, James 106
Broccoli, Barbara 19, 22
Broccoli, Cubby 19, 22
Broken Arrow 86
A Bronx Tale 187
Brooks, Kix 170
Brooks and Dunn 170
Brown, Garrett 9
Brown, Jackson 171
Brown, O. Nicholas 62
Brown, Robert 107
Browning, Chris 25
Budapest 49
Butterflies Are Free 27

CAA 32, 60, 113
Caan, James 46
Cabaret 12
Campbell, Joe 193
Cannon 10
Cannon Films 49

Can't Stop the Music 9, 123
Cape Fear 42
Carolco 10
Carpenter, John 16, 39, 41
Carr, Allan 9
Carradine, Keith 158
Carruthers, Rachael 42
Carter, Chris 140
Cassavetes, John 106
Castellano, Paul 188
Cavallo, Bob 95
Chayefsky, Paddy 68
Cheney, Lon 53
Chernin, Peter 83
Chicago Film Festival 15, 106
Chinese Mafia 85
Chinook winds 186
Christian prophecy 169
Cinergi 10
Citizen Baines 158
Citizen Kane 30
Clarke, James B. 214
The Cleveland Plain Dealer 16
Cliff, Jimmy 67
Clueless 112
Collins, Jackie 208
Collister, Peter 6–7
Columbia Pictures 196
Connery, Sean 40
Conti, Walt 99
Coolidge, Rita 6
Corman, Roger 5, 8
Cornell, Ellie 42
Cosmatos, Goerge 194
Cotrona, DJ 172
Cousteau, Jean-Michel 100
Coward, Noel 171
Crash 57
crimedy 180
Criminal Minds Suspect Behavior 152
Cromwell, James 159
The Crow 84
Cuarón, Alfonso 17
Culpepper, Clint 194

Daily Variety 30, 31
Daley, Bob 108
Dalton, Timothy 19
Davenport, Madison 172
David, Keith 68
Davison, Bruce 216
Day, Christine 51
Deadline Hollywood 218
Deadly Force 5
De Felitta, Frank 58
Del Toro, Guillermo 17
DeNiro, Robert 129
Denis, Stuart 77
DePalma, Brian 43
Deschanel, Emily 152
Desmond, Norma 10, 27

Destination Films 56
DGA 41, 134
Di Giaimo, Lou 187
Digital Pictures 87
The Director's Cut 219
Donavan, Tate 131
Donen, Josh 16
Donner, Lauren Shuler 88, 91
Donner, Richard 88, 91
Dragon: The Bruce Lee Story 86
Drayton, Poppy 191
Duvall, Robert 158
Dylan, Bob 48

Eastwood, Clint 137
Eat My Dust 25
Eichler, David 100
Ellison, David 56
Ellison, Megan 56
The Emerald Forest 202
Emmerich, Roland 17
Englund, Robert 49
Epic Pictures 217
Estevez, Emillio 92, 131
Eszterhas, Joe 60
Etheridge, Melissa 84
Executive Decision 139
Executive Privilege 115
Eyemo camera 165

The Fan 129
Farrakhan, Louis 126
Farrell, Joe 29
The Fast and the Furious 31
Faulkner, William 174
Faust 51
50 Shades of Grey 16
Fiji 195
Fincher, David 57
The Finder 175
Fitzgerald, F. Scott 196
Fitzgerald, Wayne 83
Focus Film Festival 15
Foley, James 16
Fonda, Jane 189
Ford, John 31
Foster, Jodie 46
FOT Studios 50
Franchise Films 56
Free Willy 2, 89, 90, 91, 100, 107, 108, 109, 159, 214
Free Willy 2 90, 91, 95–98, 100, 103, 104, 106, 107, 109, 110, 112, 113, 115–118, 138–139, 199, 214
French Connection 60, 120
Friday Harbor 98
From Dusk Till Dawn 172

Gambino crime family 187
Game of Thrones 56
Getting Even 26

Index

Gibb, Andy 22
Gibson, Mel 134
Gish, Annabeth 168
Gladwell, Malcom 167
Globus, Yoram 49
The Godfather 149
Golan, Menahem 49
Goldman, William 114
Gone Girl 16
Gone with the Wind 5
Goodfellas 72
The Goonies 91
Gotti, John 189
Graham, Heather 216
Grais, Michael 58
Grease 9
The Greek Tycoon 33
Greengrass, Paul 122
Ground Zero Texas 87
Guinness, Alec 76
Gunsmoke 156

Haddonfield, Illinois 41
Haida culture 98
Halloween 4, 38
Hanson, Hart 177
Happy Days 9
Hard to Kill 47, 58
The Harder They Come 65
Harrah, Bill 207
Harris, Danielle 42
Harris, Richard 5, 8
heat stroke 77
Henderson, Lance 143
Herald Examiner 31
"He's Coming Back" 6
"Higher and Higher" 6
Hiller, Arthur 68
Hitchcock, Alfred 10, 44
Holden, William 10
The Hollywood Reporter 6, 15, 107
Holtz, Zane 172
Home Alone 58
Home by Spring 191
Hopkins, Anne 183
The Hospital 68
House of Cards 181
Howard, James Newton 69
Howard, Ron 25
Howard, Sandy 5–10, 12
Huston, John 54, 168

Icon Films 134
Imada, Jeff 75
Iñárritu, Alejandro G. 17
India 34
The Island of Dr. Moreau 5

Jackson, Michael 109
Jagged Edge 60
Jaws 99

Jenner, Bruce 9
Jeremiah Johnson 140
Johnson, Don 160
Johnson, Nunnally 23
Joliet prison 174
Jones, Jim 79
Jones, Leslie 136
Jones, Quincy 208
Jones, Sarah 82
Jones, Tommy Lee 135
Julia 189
Just Legal 160

Keiko 99
Kellerman, Sally 21
Kelley, David E. 145
KGB: The Secret War 18
Kilmer, Val 139
King, Stephen 86
Kingston, Jamaica 68
Kleiser, Randal 16
Kong 202
Kopelson, Arnold 117
Kovacs, Laszlo 101
Kristofferson, Kris 6
Krueger, Freddy 49
Kurins, Andris 188

L.A. riots 111
LaBelle, Patty 171
The Lady from Shanghai 99
Lambert, Christopher
Lane, Diane 116
Lassie 97
The Last Picture Show 55
Last Rampage 25, 173, 214
The Last Tycoon 196
Law and Order 210
Lawrence of Arabia 189
Lean, David 75, 189
Lee, Brandon 73
Leydon, Joe 218
Li, Jet 209
Lion of the Desert 38
Liotta, Ray 72
Little, Dwight **12**
Little, Mark 71
Little, Robbie 217
Little, Sandy 200
Lloyd, Jamie 42
Logan's Run 12
Lonesome Dove 158
Longo, Tony 74
look books 58
Lopez Island 97
Louma Crane 123
Love Story 57
Lowe, Rob 131
Lucas, George 16
Luhrmann, Baz 17, 206
Lumet, Sidney 7
Lundgren, Dolph 74

Index

Ma, Thai 77
Machete 174
Mack the Knife 49
MacNicol, Alex 216
Madsen, Michael 91
The Magnificent Ambersons 30
Magnoli, Albert 16
Malibu State Park 175
Malpaso 137
A Man Called Horse 5
Man in the Wilderness 5
Mancuso, Nick 74
Manhattan Beach Studios 111
El Mariachi 17, 25
Marked for Death 64
Martin, Dean 10
Martin, Gary 195
Mastorakis, Nico 32
Maugham, Sumerset 202
Mayor, Louis B. 199
McDermott, Dylan 147
McDonnell, M.J. 119
McElroy, Alan 39
McFee, Katherine 171
McGavin, Darren 143
McLaughlin, Robert 144
McMurtry, Larry 158
McQueen, Steven R. 191
Messner, Johnny 204
Metero 5
Midnight of the Century 143
Milius, John 16
Millennium 140
Miller, Dennis 128
Miller, Wentworth 176
Minnelli, Vincent 60
Moab, Utah 31
Monte Walsh 155
Monument Valley 31
Morgan, Glen 140
Morrow, Vic 81
Mulberry Street 187
Murder at 1600{en{29, 116
Myers, Michael 38

Nation of Islam 126
Natty Knocks 218
The Neptune Factor 5
Netflix 133
New Line 10
New Regency 91
New World 5, 10
Newport, Oregon 108
The Night Stalker 143
Nightcrawler 31, 32
Nighy, Bill 53
Nikita 149
9/11 111
Nixon, Cynthia 184
Nolan, Christopher 17
Norris Cinema Theatre 105

O'Brien, Joseph F. 188
Oklahoma City 111
Olson, Gerry 85
On the Waterfront 185
O'Neal, Ryan 152
O'Quinn, Terry 169
Orca whales 96–97
Outliers 167
Ovitz, Michael 47

Palmintiri, Chazz 187
Palmisano, Conrad 62
Papa's Angels 183
Paper Moon 153
Pascal, Amy 195
Patrick, Robert 168
The Patriot 134
Penn, Arthur 57
Petty, Tom 119
The Phantom of the Opera 49
Pitt, Brad 55
Pleasence, Donald 39
Poitier, Sidney 208
Poledouris, Basil 111
"Political World" 48
Pollack, Sydney 67
Poltergeist 58
The Practice 111, 146
premium television 182
Price, Vincent 50
Prison Break 174
Purcell, Dominick 174
Purple Rain 16

Q, Maggie 149
Quantum Leap 184

Radio Flyer 101
Ragalyi, Elemer 52
Raj polo club 37
Rajinikanth 33
Rapid Fire 29, 77
Reed, Carol 50
Reed, Rex 218
Rees, Marion 183
Return of a Man Called Horse 5
Revere, Paul 135
Rice, Peter 72
Richter, Jason James 91
Rin Tin Tin 109
Ritchie, Guy 17
River Kwai 75
RKO 30
Roberts, Eric 174
Robocop 154
Rodriguez, Alvaro 172
Rodriguez, Robert 17, 25, 172
Rosemary's Baby 204
Roth, Joe 58
Rothberg, Jeff 26
Roven, Chuck 92

Index

Rowlands, Gena 106
Russell, Kurt 139

SAG 34
Saint, Eva Marie 184
St. Jerome 62
St. Peter 62
Salieri 43
Salt Lake City 41
Sam Goldwyn studios 5
San Juan Islands 96
Sandefur, Duke 51
Sandler, Adam 139
Santeria 62
Savage Harvest 10
Save the Cat 135
Savoy Pictures 92
Schellenberg, August 105
Schellhardt, Mary Kate 106
Schoelen, Jill 51
Schwarzenegger, Arnold 168
Scorpion 215
Scorsese, Martin 42
Scott, Peter McGregor 61
Screwface 63
script supervisor 151
Seagal, Steven 47
Sega CD 87
Segal, Misha 52
Selleck, Tom 155
Semel, Terry 136
Sex and the City 184
Shannon, Molly 51
Shepherd, Cybill 55
showrunner 146
Silver, Joel 135
Simon, Mel 56
Singleton, John 43, 201
Sitges Film Festival 217
Sling Blade 25
Smith, Todd 194
Snipes, Wesley 115
Snyder, Blake 135
Snyder, Tom 18
Sony-Columbia 158
Sparks Steak House 188
Speedman, Scott 150
Spiderman 207
Spielberg, Steven 43, 44
Sri Lanka 75
Stallone, Sylvester 48
Star Trek 70
Steadicam 9, 21
Steel, Dawn 92
The Stepfather 51
Stone, Oliver 190
Sunset Blvd. 10, 27
Sutherland, Donald 155
Sutherland, Kiefer 153
Swiss Family Robinson 71
Sylbert, Paul 96

T-1000 168
Talbot, Bob 100
Tamil rebels 37
Tarantino, Quentin 17, 209
Tejano music 172
Thackery, William 218
Thailand 77
Thalberg, Irving 196
Thalberg Building 45, 196
Thelma and Louise 18
The Third Man 50
Thorton, Billy Bob 25
Three Days of the Condor 22
Tison, Gary 214
Titty Twister 172
TNT 157
Tombstone 139
The Tomorrow Show 18
Tone Meeting 146
Touch of Evil 57
Tower Records 10
Towers, Harry Alan 55
Trader Vic's 208
Trejo, Danny 174
Trimark 10
Triumphs of a Man Called Horse 5, 6
Trump, Donald 17
Tugend, Jenny Lew 88
12 Bar Blues 92
20th Century–Fox 112
21st Century Films 50
Tyson, Mike 124

UCLA film school 39
Unforgiven 5
The Untouchables 40
USA Today 71
USC film school 107

VanDamme, Jean Claude 72
Van Wyck, Jimmy 101
The Verdict 7
vertigo 44
Vestron 10
Vice Squad 5, 10
Victor, Mark 58
video village 20
The Village People 123
Villeneuve, Denis 17
Von Sydow, Max 120

Waite, Ric 61
Walking Tall 27
Wallace, Basil 63
Ward, Kelly 18
Warner, Jack 109
Warner Bros. 48
Warner Hollywood Studios 134
The Way We Were 65
Wayons, Marlon 150
Webber, Andrew Lloyd 49

Index

Webber, Billy 136
Weinstein, Harvey 209
Weller, Peter 154
Welles, Orson 25, 106
West, Shane 149
Wexler, Haskell 93
"Whammy Meter" 135
The Wheelman 150
Whitaker, Forrest 150
Who Needs Sleep? 93
The Wild Bunch 65
William Morris 71
Wincer, Simon 156
Winkler, Henry 9–10
Wolf, Dick 192
Wolper, David 89
Wong, Jim 140
Woo, John 17, 113

workplace hours 93
World Trade Center 111
Wright, Tom 68

X-Files 157

Y2K 169
Yeager, Kevin 53
York, Michael 12
Yost, Graham 112
Young, Christopher 29
Youth Conservation Core 98

Zemeckis, Robert 16
Ziesmer, Jerry 62
Zsigmond, Vilmos 101
Zuma Beach 175

www.ingramcontent.com/pod-product-compliance
Ingram Content Group UK Ltd.
Pitfield, Milton Keynes, MK11 3LW, UK
UKHW041949140426
5217IPUK00014B/713